国际商务函电
（双语教材）

International Business Correspondence

关 兵 张秋平 马慧莲 主 编

中国财经出版传媒集团
经济科学出版社
Economic Science Press

图书在版编目（CIP）数据

国际商务函电＝International Business Correspondence：双语教材/
关兵，张秋平，马慧莲主编 . —北京：经济科学出版社，2018.12
ISBN 978－7－5141－9797－6

Ⅰ.①国… Ⅱ.①关…②张…③马… Ⅲ.①国际商务－英语－
电报信函－写作－教材 Ⅳ.①F740

中国版本图书馆 CIP 数据核字（2018）第 226430 号

责任编辑：何 宁 赵 岩
责任校对：杨晓莹
版式设计：齐 杰
责任印制：王世伟

国际商务函电（双语教材）
关 兵 张秋平 马慧莲 主 编
经济科学出版社出版、发行 新华书店经销
社址：北京市海淀区阜成路甲 28 号 邮编：100142
总编部电话：010－88191217 发行部电话：010－88191522
网址：www.esp.com.cn
电子邮件：esp@esp.com.cn
天猫网店：经济科学出版社旗舰店
网址：http：//jjkxcbs.tmall.com
北京季蜂印刷有限公司印装
787×1092 16 开 16.75 印张 530000 字
2019 年 5 月第 1 版 2019 年 5 月第 1 次印刷
ISBN 978－7－5141－9797－6 定价：46.00 元
（图书出现印装问题，本社负责调换。电话：010－88191510）
（版权所有 侵权必究 打击盗版 举报热线：010－88191661
QQ：2242791300 营销中心电话：010－88191537
电子邮箱：dbts@esp.com.cn）

Preface 前　言

　　国际商务函电作为国际贸易中对外联系和交往的一种主要手段和商务信息交换的载体，以英语语言形式反映世界各国之间的经济贸易往来和商务活动，其作用是不可替代的。本教材从国际商务函电课程的基本定位及教学要求出发，语言规范、纯正，内容适应实际，采用双语对照的体例，有助于学生有效地理解和掌握专业知识，具有系统性、指导性和可读性的特点。

　　本书从实用角度出发，重点介绍外贸企业在现代国际商务活动中与国外企业进行业务沟通时撰写各类英文商务信函的方法与技巧。书中内容涉及客户关系建立、商务活动中的各类业务沟通、对外贸易业务中各环节的信函往来等内容，特别是在外贸业务方面，本书包含了客户联络、交易磋商、报价还盘、签订合同、包装、运输、保险、国际结算、索赔理赔等各个环节里的大量实用性信函范例。此外，本书在编写形式上也多有创新，采取双语形式介绍相关背景、写作策略要点；列出经典信件进行解读分析；根据章节主题提供外贸实战技巧，配有词汇、常用语句及练习等栏目；每章还附上5~7封业务书信供进一步学习，使读者对需要掌握的内容一目了然，更能学以致用，增强动手能力。背景简介部分简明介绍外贸各个环节的背景、业务知识；写作要点部分概述本章信函写作注意事项和写作方法。经典信件分析是本书的重点，每章重点分析5~6篇信函，讲解如何遣词造句，可达到举一反三的功效。外贸实战技巧结合当前跨境电子商务迅速发展的特点，使学生了解外贸实战应注意的问题和函电写作技巧，具有较强的实用性。此外，本书每章配有大量的练习供选择使用。本书选用的资料大多来源于外贸实际业务中真实发生的函电，同时也有以往教材中经典的函电内容。本书的特色在于：①采用双语体例，便于教学和自学；②针对教学的课时要求，内容较为紧凑、实用；③选用外贸最新业务函电，与贸易实践接轨；④将外贸环节分解、细化，并配以相应函电，适用性较强；⑤所有练习都附有答案，便于读者自学时参考。

　　本书适用于高校国际贸易、商务英语、国际金融、市场营销等专业研究生、本科生、辅修生教学，同时也适用于企业相关人员的业务技能培训。

　　本书由关兵担任主编，张秋平、马慧莲担任副主编。全书共11章，具体的编写分工如下：第1章~第5章由关兵撰写；第6章~第10章由张秋平撰写；第11章及附录部分由马慧莲撰写。总体编写框架的拟定和全书的统筹定稿由关兵完成。同时，本书的编写和出版得到了黑龙江省教育科学"十三五"规划2017年度备案课题（GBD1317036）和哈尔滨商业大学教学改革项目（HSDJY2017026）的资助，在此表示感谢。

编者

2019年5月

Contents 目 录

第1章 商务信函写作基础 1
Chapter 1 Fundamentals of Business Letter Writing 1

1.1 商务信函写作介绍 /1
Introduction of Business Letter Writing /1

1.2 商务信函写作原则 /2
Writing Principles of Business Letters /2

1.3 商务信函的结构 /6
Structure of Business Letters /6

1.4 商务信函格式 /13
Format of Business Letters /13

1.5 信封的写法 /16
Envelope Addressing /16

1.6 外贸实战技巧 /17
Techniques in Foreign Trade Practice /17

1.7 有用的句子 /17
Useful Sentences /17

1.8 练习 /19
Exercises /19

第2章 建立业务关系 20
Chapter 2 Establishing Business Relations 20

2.1 背景知识 /20
Background Information /20

2.2 信例 /22
Specimen Letters /22

2.3 外贸实战技巧 /28
Techniques in Foreign Trade Practice /28

2.4 有用的句子 /29
Useful Sentences /29

2.5 补充商务信函 /30
Letters for Further Reading /30

2.6 练习 /32
Exercises /32

第3章 询盘与回复 35
Chapter 3 Inquiries and Replies 35

3.1 背景知识 /35
Background Information /35

3.2 信例 /37
Specimen Letters /37

3.3 外贸实战技巧 /47
Techniques in Foreign Trade Practice /47

3.4 有用的句子 /48
Useful Sentences /48

3.5 补充商务信函 /49
Letters for Further Reading /49

3.6 练习 /52
Exercises /52

第4章 报盘与还盘 55
Chapter 4 Offers and Counter-offers 55

4.1 背景知识 /55
Background Information /55

4.2 信例 /57
Specimen Letters /57

4.3 外贸实战技巧 /65
Techniques in Foreign Trade Practice /65

4.4 有用的句子 /66
Useful Sentences /66

4.5 补充商务信函 /67
Letters for Further Reading /67

4.6 练习 /70
Exercises /70

第 5 章 订单与确认 74
Chapter 5　Orders and Acknowledgements　74

5.1 背景知识 /74
Background Information /74

5.2 信例 /76
Specimen Letters /76

5.3 外贸实战技巧 /83
Techniques in Foreign Trade Practice /83

5.4 有用的句子 /84
Useful Sentences /84

5.5 补充商务信函 /85
Letters for Further Reading /85

5.6 练习 /87
Exercises /87

第 6 章 支付方式 90
Chapter 6　Terms of Payment　90

6.1 背景知识 /90
Background Information /90

6.2 信例 /92
Specimen Letters /92

6.3 外贸实战技巧 /108
Techniques in Foreign Trade Practice /108

6.4 有用的句子 /109
Useful Sentences /109

6.5 补充商务信函 /113
Letters for Further Reading /113

6.6 练习 /113
Exercises /113

第7章　包装　118
Chapter 7　Packing　118

7.1　背景知识　/118
Background Information　/118

7.2　信例　/121
Specimen Letters　/121

7.3　外贸实战技巧　/127
Techniques in Foreign Trade Practice　/127

7.4　有用的句子　/128
Useful Sentences　/128

7.5　补充商务信函　/129
Letters for Further Reading　/129

7.6　练习　/132
Exercises　/132

第8章　装运　135
Chapter 8　Shipment　135

8.1　背景知识　/135
Background Information　/135

8.2　信例　/138
Specimen Letters　/138

8.3　外贸实战技巧　/146
Techniques in Foreign Trade Practice　/146

8.4　有用的句子　/147
Useful Sentences　/147

8.5　补充商务信函　/148
Letters for Further Reading　/148

8.6　练习　/151
Exercises　/151

第9章　保险　154
Chapter 9　Insurance　154

9.1　背景知识　/154
Background Information　/154

9.2 信例 /157
Specimen Letters /157

9.3 外贸实战技巧 /163
Techniques in Foreign Trade Practice /163

9.4 有用的句子 /165
Useful Sentences /165

9.5 补充商务信函 /166
Letters for Further Reading /166

9.6 练习 /169
Exercises /169

第 10 章　索赔　173
Chapter 10　Claims　173

10.1 背景知识 /173
Background Information /173

10.2 信例 /175
Specimen Letters /175

10.3 外贸实战技巧 /184
Techniques in Foreign Trade Practice /184

10.4 有用的句子 /185
Useful Sentences /185

10.5 补充商务信函 /187
Letters for Further Reading /187

10.6 练习 /190
Exercises /190

第 11 章　国际商务合同　193
Chapter 11　International Business Contract　193

11.1 背景知识 /193
Background Information /193

11.2 合同及信例 /197
Specimen Contracts and Letters /197

11.3 外贸实战技巧 /210
Techniques in Foreign Trade Practice /210

11.4 有用的句子 /211
Useful Sentences /211

11.5 补充商务信函 /212
Letters for Further Reading /212

11.6 练习 /214
Exercises /214

附录 I 有用的短语 218
Appendix I Useful Expressions 218

附录 II 练习答案 237
Appendix II Key to Exercises 237

参考文献 255
References 255

Chapter 1
第 1 章

商务信函写作基础
Fundamentals of Business Letter Writing

Learning Objectives

Enable the students to know the importance of business letter writing; to master the principles of effective bussiness letter writing; to be familiar with the structure and format of business letters.

使学生了解商务信函的重要性；掌握撰写有效商务信函的原则；熟悉商务信函的结构及格式。

1.1 商务信函写作介绍
Introduction of Business Letter Writing

在如今的商界，优秀的沟通技巧比以往更重要，因为商务人员必须能够使用不断发展的信息技术清晰、准确并且有效地沟通。商务信函是企业交换信息从而实现买卖商品以及提供服务目标的主要途径。商务信函可以用于询价、订购、洽商、销售、营销、投诉等业务活动。在国际贸易中，商务信函不仅起到契约的作用，同时也可以作为永久性的记录。商务信函从形式到内容都非常重要，这也是对于商务沟通的学习者而言，熟练掌握书写商务信函技能至关重要的原因。

In the business community today, the importance of good communication skills is even more stressed, as it is essential that employees can use the tools of the evolving information technology to communicate clearly, accurately and effectively. A business letter is the principal means used by a business firm to exchange messages that support the goal of buying and selling goods or providing other services. Business letters can be used in inquiring, ordering, negotiating, selling, marketing, complaining, and so on. In international trade, a business letter not only serves as a contract, but also provides a permanent record. It is very important from the form to the content. This is why it is important for learners of business communications to master the skills of writing a good business letter.

1.2 商务信函写作原则
Writing Principles of Business Letters

在书写英文商务信函时，应遵守七个原则，由于这七个原则都以英文字母 C 开头，因此可称为"7C"原则，即谦恭、体谅、完整、清晰、简洁、具体及正确。

There are seven principles which must be observed in writing English business letters. Since all these seven principles begin with the letter "C", they can be summed up as 7Cs, i.e. Courtesy, Consideration, Completeness, Clarity, Conciseness, Concreteness and Correctness.

1.2.1 谦恭
Courtesy

当给客户写信时，不仅要礼貌，而且要体现出真诚、得体、关切以及感激。对于商人而言，快速回复信函以及客户的询问也是一种礼貌，在处理业务时的任何延迟都是不礼貌的。

When writing to your correspondents, it is necessary for you not only to be polite, but also to be sincere and tactful, thoughtful and appreciative. It is also a kind of courtesy for the tradesmen to answer the letters and the enquiries promptly. And delay in dealing with the matters is discourteous.

比较以下两个句子，A 要比 B 更有礼貌并且更有效。

Compare the following two sentences. Sentence A is more courteous and effective than sentence B.

A：我们很抱歉没能清楚地表达我方的意思。

B：我们很遗憾你误解了我方的意思。

A：We are sorry that we did not make ourselves clear.

B：We are sorry that you misunderstood us.

1.2.2 体谅
Consideration

体谅是写出完美商务信函所必须遵循的重要原则。体谅强调"以对方为主"，而不是"以我方为主"的态度。写信时要谨记对方的要求、需要、愿望以及感受，采用最好的方式向对方传达信息。此外，还应以肯定而不是否定的方式来讨论问题。

Consideration is an important rule of good business writing. It stresses "You-attitude" rather than "We-attitude". When writing a letter, keep the reader's request, needs, desires, as well as his feelings in mind. Plan the best way to present the message for the reader to receive. In addition, we should try to discuss problems in a positive approach rather than in a negative approach.

（1）以对方为主。比较以下几组句子：

（1）You-attitude. Make a comparison between the following groups of sentences：

以我方为主 We-attitude	以对方为主 You-attitude
我们对现金付款有3%的折扣。 We allow 3 percent discount for cash payment. 这周我们无法将目录发给您。 We won't be able to send you the catalog this week.	如果贵方采用现金方式付款可以获得3%的折扣。 You earn 3 percent discount when you pay cash. 我们将在下周把目录发给您。 We will send you the catalog next week.

（2）采用肯定的表达方式。比较以下两个句子：

(2) Focus on the positive approach. Compare the following two sentences：

肯定 Positive	否定 Negative
或许下次我们可以发送你需要的货物。 Perhaps next time we can send you what you require.	我们很遗憾这次无法向你提供服务。 We regret our inability to serve you at this time.

1.2.3 完整
Completeness

商务信函只有包含收信人所需的全部必要信息，才是成功的信函，才能发挥其应有的作用。因而在商务信函发出前，一定要认真核对信息，以确保所有的事项都已谈及，所有的问题都有回复。不完整的商务信函是不礼貌的，会给收信人留下不好的印象。

A business letter is very successful and functions well only when it contains all the necessary information to the readers. It is essential to check the message carefully before it is sent out to make sure that all the matters are discussed, and all questions are answered. Incompleteness is impolite and it will lead to the recipient's unfavorable impression toward your firm.

1.2.4 清晰
Clarity

写信人不仅应该使用清楚且易理解的词语清晰地表达写信目的、想法以及要求，还应使用正确的词语、时态以及句子结构以避免被误解或曲解。针对同一问题多次交换信件会错失商机。请看下例：

从上海到旧金山，我们双月有一次/一个月有两次直达船。

在这个句子中，"bimonthly"这个单词有两个含义："一个月两次""两个月一次"，因此对于收

The writer should express his aims, ideas and requirements clearly not only by distinct and understandable wordings, but also by correct phrases, tenses and sentence structures in order not to be misunderstood or misinterpreted. Writing letters to and fro for enquiring about the same thing will enable you to miss business opportunities. Look at the following example：

As to the steamer sailing from Shanghai to San Francisco, we have bimonthly direct services.

In this sentence, the word "bimonthly" has two meanings, one of which is "twice a month" and the other of which is "once every two month", thus it is difficult for

信人来说很难判断其真正的意思。为了更清楚地表达，应采用如下能够明确表达意思的语句：

（1）我们每两个月有一班直达船从上海发往旧金山。

（2）我们每月有两班直达船从上海发往旧金山。

the reader to understand the real meaning. To make it clear, the writer should use the words that can express his/her idea clearly as follows：

（1）We have a direct sailing from Shanghai to San Francisco every two months.

（2）We have two direct sailings every month from Shanghai to San Francisco.

1.2.5 简洁
Conciseness

简洁意味着写信时用尽可能少的词语表达自己的想法，同时不偏离信函完整及谦恭的写作原则。为了实现这个目标，应该避免冗长的陈述以及花哨的语言。以下是撰写简洁商务信函的方法：

（1）避免使用冗长的表达。例如：

Conciseness means to write in the fewest possible words without losing completeness and courtesy. To achieve conciseness, the writer should avoid wordy statement and fancy language. The following are the methods of making a letter concise：

（1）Avoid using wordy expressions. For example：

冗长 Wordy	简洁 Concise
我们希望告知已收到贵方来函…… We wish to acknowledge receipt of your letter… 我们已经开始将我们的电子玩具出口到国外。 We have begun to export our electronic toys to countries abroad.	我们感谢贵方来函…… We appreciate your letter… 我们已经开始出口我们公司的电子玩具。 We have begun to export our electronic toys.

（2）避免使用过时的词汇或专业术语。

（2）Avoid the out-of-date words or jargons.

避免使用 You shouldn't use	最好使用 You'd better use
继……之后　subsequent 每日　per diem 在其他事物之外　inter alia 在……之前　prior to 万一；如果　in the event of 随函附上　Enclosed please find 同一日期的　of even day 关于……问题　on the question of	在……之后　after 每日　daily 除了……之外　among other things 在……之前　before 如果　if 随函附上　We enclose 今天的　of today 关于　concerning

（3）使用有效的句子和段落。

句子是语言的基本单位。在

（3）Use effective sentences and paragraphs.

A sentence is the basic unit of language. In business

撰写商务信函时，应使用完整的句子，避免使用残缺句。通常而言，句子的平均长度应为 10～20 个单词。一个段落通常不应超过 10 行，因为短的段落更易让读者读完全文。

letter writing, use only complete sentences and avoid the use of sentence fragments. General speaking, the average length for sentences should be 10 to 20 words. Usually a paragraph consists of no more that 10 lines because short paragraphs encourage the readers to finish reading over the passage.

1.2.6　具体
Concreteness

商务信函的信息表达应具体、明确和生动。咨询事项的信函以及回函必须尊重现实并体现"具体"的写作原则，使用具体的事实、数字以及时间，从而体现具体性。不应使用任何模糊、含糊的词汇。

Make the message specific, definite and vivid. The enquiries of others about something and your answers to the others' letters must be made with reality and concreteness. You need to use specific facts, figures and time to stress concreteness. Any ambiguous and vague words must not be used.

比较以下句子：

Compare：

含糊 Vague	具体 Concrete
刹车在很短的距离之内就能够把车停住。The brake can stop a car within a short distance. 他们决定在东京创办营业处。A decision has been made to set up an office in Tokyo.	蓝天牌刹车可以在24英尺之内将2吨的车停住。The Blue Sky brake can stop a 2-ton car within 24 feet. 董事会决定在东京创办营业处。The board of directors decided to set up an office in Tokyo.

1.2.7　正确
Correctness

"正确"不仅是指符合语法、标点规则以及没有拼写错误的适当的表达，而且还指有助于实现目的恰当的语气。即使是一封投诉信或是针对投诉信的回复，也有可能以不引起冒犯的方式表达真实意思。商务信函必须包含真实的信息、准确的数字，尤其是精准的措辞，因为其往往涉及双方的权利、义务及利益，这通常是各种契约文件的基础。因此，撰写商务信函时不应过于保守或者过于夸大，过于保守可

Correctness means not only proper expression with correct grammar, punctuation and spelling, but also appropriate tone, which is a help to achieve the purpose. It is likely to convey the real message in a way that will not cause offence even if it is a complaint or an answer to such a letter. Business letter must have factual information, accurate figures and exact terms in particular, for they involve the rights, the duties and the interest of both sides, often as the base of all kinds of documents. Therefore, you should not understate nor overstate as understatement might lead to less confidence and hold up the trade development while overstatement would throw

能会导致对方因缺乏信心而阻碍贸易进程；过于夸大则会使人陷入尴尬的境地。

1.3 商务信函的结构
Structure of Business Letters

商务人士在商务沟通中通常遵循着一种标准化的方式。布局合理的商务信函通常包括以下13个部分：

（1）信头
（2）编号
（3）日期
（4）封内名称及地址
（5）注意项
（6）称呼
（7）事由
（8）正文
（9）结尾敬语
（10）签名
（11）附件
（12）抄送
（13）附言

People in business world usually follow a standardized way in their business communication. Well-arranged business letters usually consist of the following 13 parts.

（1）Letterhead
（2）Reference No.
（3）Date
（4）Inside Name and Address
（5）Attention Line
（6）Salutation
（7）Subject Line
（8）Body
（9）Complimentary Close
（10）Signature
（11）Enclosure
（12）Carbon Copy Notation
（13）Postscript

1.3.1 信头
Letterhead

信头包括寄信人公司名称、通信地址、电话号码、传真号码以及邮箱地址等，有时也包括公司标识及网址信息。通常信头印在信纸上方中间位置、靠左或靠右。参见下例：

长虹食品公司
中国哈尔滨道里区

电话号码：（0451）12345678
传真号码：（0451）12345600
邮箱地址：chfc@changhong.net.cn

Letterhead includes the sender's name, postal address, telephone number, fax number, and E-mail address, etc. Sometimes the company logo and website are also incorporated. Usually letterhead is printed in the up-center or at the left margin or right margin of a letter writing paper. Here is an example：

Changhong Food Company
Daoli District, Harbin
P. R. China
Tel：（0451）12345678
Fax：（0451）12345600
E-mail：chfc@changhong.net.cn

在一些国家,信头还会包含其他详细信息,例如,英国的商务信函的信头会包含公司董事的姓名。

1.3.2 编号
Reference No.

在商务沟通中,公司之间来往的每一封信件都应附有编号。可以将文档号、部门号或签署人名字的首字母加打字人名字的首字母作为编号。为了避免混淆,分为"我方编号""贵方编号"。编号应打在信头之下,如果以名字的首字母作为编号,也可以从签名下方两行的左侧边缘打起。

1.3.3 日期
Date

每封商务信函都应注明日期,日期的位置在信头之下。至于靠左或靠右取决于信函所采用的写作格式。日期应该写全,不能简写(如应以 January 代替 Jan)。"日"之后的"-th, -st, -nd, -rd"可以省略(如以 6 July 代替 6th July)。在书写年份时,不能用 18 代替 2018。

应避免用数字书写日期,例如 7/8/2017,因为这会引起混淆,因为英国按照日/月/年的顺序表示日期,而在美国标注日期的惯例则是月/日/年,因此 7/8/2017 可以被理解为 2017 年 7 月 8 日或 2017 年 8 月 7 日。

1.3.4 封内名称及地址
Inside Name and Address

收信人的名称及地址应打在

In some countries the letterhead contains other details. For example, in the U.K., the directors' names of a company are given.

In business communication, when a firm writes to another, each will give a reference. The reference may include a file number, departmental code or the initials of the signer followed by that of the typist of the letter. These are marked "our ref." "your ref." to avoid confusion. The reference numbers are typed immediately below the Letterhead. If desired, the reference initials can also be placed at the lower left margin two lines below the name of the signer.

Every letter should be dated. The position of the date is below the letterhead. Whether on the right or on the left depends on the form you decide to use. The date should always be typed in full and not abbreviated (e.g. January for Jan.). And the -th, -st, -nd, and -rd that follow the "day" can be omitted (e.g. 6 July for 6th July). Don't write 18 instead of 2018 for the year.

You had better avoid typing dates in figures, e.g. 7/8/2017, since it could cause confusion, this is because English form follows the order of day, month and year while the U.S. practice is to write in the order of month, day and year. So 7/8/2017 could be taken as either July 8, 2017 or August 7, 2017.

The name and address of the recipient is typed at the

日期下方 2~4 行左首的位置，与信封上的名称及地址完全一致。

Mr., Mrs., Miss. 和 Ms. 是通常用来称呼某个人的礼貌头衔。男性用 Mr., 女性用 Mrs.、Miss 或 Ms.。如果不了解女性的婚姻状况，可用 Ms., 用 Ms. 称呼女性现已广为接受。若有职务，可在其名字后面加上职务名称。请参看以下信函中封内名称和地址的范例：

克林顿先生
销售经理
亚洲玻璃有限责任公司
塔街 48 号
英国伦敦

left-hand margin about two to four lines below the date. It appears exactly the same way as on the envelope.

Mr., Mrs., Miss. and Ms. —the ordinary courtesy titles are used to address to one person. Mr. for a man, Mrs., Miss., or Ms. for a woman. If you are not sure whether or not the woman to whom you are writing is married, use Ms., this title is now perfectly accepted. After the name, his or her official position should follow, if there is any. The following is an example to show the way of writing an inside name and address：

Mr. Clinton
Sales Manager
The Asia Glass Co. Ltd.
48 Tower Street
London, England

1.3.5 注意项
Attention Line

当写信人把信件寄给某一公司，并希望将其交给某个具体的人或者公司的某个部门时，通常会使用注意项。注意项位于封内名称和地址之下。例如：请交杰克逊先生；请转交销售经理。

Attention Line is used when the writer of a letter addressed to an organization wishes to direct the letter to a specific individual or section of the firm. It generally follows the inside address. e. g. Attention：Mr. Jackson；Attn：The Sales Manager.

1.3.6 称呼
Salutation

称呼是对收信人礼貌的问候，根据与收信人的关系，称呼也有所不同。商务书信用于称呼一个人时，惯常采用的正式称呼是"Dear Sir"或"Dear Madam"，而用来称呼两个及以上人时，应使用"Dear Sirs""Dear Mesdames"或"Gentlemen"（用复数形式，不能写成"Gentleman"）。如果写信人与收信人相识，则推荐采用更温暖的问候方式"Dear Mr.×××"。

Salutation is the complimentary greeting with which the writer opens his letter. Its form depends on the writer's relationship with the recipient. The customary formal greeting in a business letter is "Dear Sir" or "Dear Madam" used for addressing one person；and "Dear Sirs" "Dear Mesdames" or "Gentlemen" (always should be in plural form and never write "Gentleman") for addressing two or more people. If the recipient is known to the writer personally, a warmer greeting "Dear Mr.×××" is then preferred.

称呼通常位于封内地址或注意项下两行的位置,"Dear Sir"或"Dear Sirs"后接逗号;"Gentlemen"后接冒号。当前,一些公司的所有人或管理者是女性,因此更常用"Dear Madam or Sir"作为称呼语。

Salutation is usually two lines below the inside address or the attention line, and followed by a comma for "Dear Sir" "Dear Sirs" and a colon for "Gentlemen". Nowadays, companies are sometimes owned or managed by women, so it is more customary to use "Dear Madam or Sir".

1.3.7 事由
Subject Line

事由实际上用来说明信函的主要内容,位于称呼与正文之间。如果信件排版采用齐头式,则从左边界开始写;如果采用其他排版格式,则应将其置于正文上方居中位置。事由的作用是使对方注意信的主题。通常可以将事由加下划线或者是用大写字母书写。可以用"Re:"或"Subject"开头,也可以选择不用。如:

  关于:我方 325 号信用证
  缝纫机
  主题:关于 345 号订单短交的索赔

Subject line is actually the general idea of a letter. It is inserted between the salutation and the body of the letter either at the left-hand margin for fully-blocked letter form or centrally over the body for other forms. It calls the recipient's attention to the topic of the letter. A subject line is often underlined or typed in capitals. It can begin with or without "Re:" or "Subject:" e. g.

  Re:Our L/C No. 325
  <u>Sewing Machines</u>
  Subject:Claims for the short delivery of Order No. 345

1.3.8 正文
Body

这是商务信函最重要的组成部分。它表达写信人的意见、观点、目的以及期望等,因此应认真规划、设计。信件的主体通常包括三个必要部分。
  1. 开头段
  开头段介绍信件的背景,表明这封信是针对某相关信件、合同或信用证等所进行的回复。
  2. 中间段
  中间段常用于探讨交易的细节。一些与交易相关的细节也应

This is the most important part of the letter. It expresses the writer's idea, opinions, purposes and wishes, etc., so it should be carefully planned. The body of the letter generally consists of three essential parts.
  1. Opening paragraph
  The opening part is actually the background of this letter. It indicates the referring letter, contract or letter of credit etc. to which response will be made.
  2. Middle paragraph
  In the middle paragraph, the details of the transaction are discussed. Some relative details will be

在这部分加以说明。

3. 结尾段

结尾段进行总结,提出进一步的要求及建议。在这部分,应用简短的语句礼貌地结尾,要注意表明写信方和收信方之间的友好关系,确保不会因失礼的信件结尾而影响双方贸易关系的发展。

在写作信函时,应注意以下几点:

(1) 文字要简单、清楚、礼貌、语法正确且切题;

(2) 正确划分段落,一段一个主题;

(3) 确保信件打印正确,并富于美感,使信件看起来有吸引力并且令人愉悦。左右边界的确定尤其重要,因为它起到为信件设置边框的作用。

商务信函通常在是一页之内完成。对于非常短的信件,除了收信人的名称及地址应始终使用单倍行距外,其他部分可以采用双倍行距。有时无法将信件的全部内容打在一张纸上,如果需要续页,一定要使用和信头页相同质量的空白纸,在续页纸的开头部分标明下列内容:

(1) 页序(居中)

(2) 收信人名称(居左)

(3) 写信日期(居右)
例如:

also illustrated in this part.

3. Closing paragraph

The closing paragraph is to end the letter in a way of summation, further request and suggestion. A short close must be made politely in this part. Attention must be paid to the keeping of friendly relations between the letter writer and the letter recipient. Business development should not be hindered by a discourteous letter close.

When writing, pay attention to the following:

(1) Write simply, clearly, courteously, grammatically, and to the point;

(2) Paragraph correctly, confining each paragraph to one topic;

(3) See that your typing is accurate and the display artistic. Aim at an attractive and pleasing appearance for you letter. Margins especially are important, since they serve to "frame" your letter.

Business letters are usually one page long. For very short letters, you may adopt double line-spacing except for your correspondent's name and address for which single line-spacing should always be used. Sometimes, it is impossible to write the entire letter on one sheet of paper. If continuation sheets are needed, plain paper of the same quality as the letterhead must be used and typed with a heading to show the following:

(1) The number of the sheet (in the center of the page)

(2) The name of your correspondent (on the left-hand side)

(3) The date of the letter (on the right-hand side)
For example:

中国食品公司		2018年8月6日
China Food Corp		August 6, 2018

1.3.9　结尾敬语
Complimentary Close

结尾敬语仅仅是礼貌地结束信件的方式，其正确的位置应在信件正文下方 2~4 行处。结尾敬语要与称呼相匹配，最广泛使用的与结尾敬语搭配的称呼如下：

Complimentary close is merely a polite way of ending a letter. The correct position for it is two to four lines below the body of the letter. It should match the salutation. The most commonly used sets of salutation and complimentary close are:

正规 Formal	半正规 Less formal
Dear Sir(s)→Yours faithfully(Faithfully yours) Gentlemen→Yours truly(Truly yours)	Dear Mr. Smith→Yours sincerely(Sincerely yours)

此外，当希望展现私人关系或者商务关系时，可以使用"Cordially"。如果与收信人非常熟悉，可以使用"Best regards"或"Best wishes"结尾。

Besides, "Cordially" may be used when it is desired to show personal or business relationship. You may also end with "Best regards" or "Best wishes" if you know the person very well.

1.3.10　签名
Signature

所有的信件都必须签署，没有签名的信件不具有效力。通常在结尾敬语下打出写信人所在公司的名称，写信人应该在其下方用钢笔手写签名。手写签名往往难以辨认，因此签字人的姓名应该在手写签名下方处打印出来，还要写明职务或职位。注意不要用图章代替签名。

All letters must be signed. Unsigned letters have no authority. It is common to type the name of the writer's firm or company below complimentary close. Then the person who dictating the letter should sign his name by hand and in ink below it. Since hand-written signatures are illegible, the name of signer is usually typed below the signature, and followed by his job title or position. Never sign a letter with a rubber stamp.

例如：
此致

海外公司
（签字）
约翰·史密斯
总经理

Example:
Yours truly,

The Overseas Corp.
(Signature)
John Smith
General Manager

1.3.11 附件
Enclosure

如果信函中有附件,应在签名之下,信纸的左下角标注出来。可以采用以下任何一种标注附件的形式:

  附件:5 份
  附件:价格表 1 份
  附件:2018 年产品目录

If something is enclosed, note it below the Signature in the lower left-hand corner. The marking may be in any of the following ways:

Enclosures (5)
Encl.: 1 pricelist
Encl.: 2018 Catalogue

1.3.12 抄送
Carbon Copy Notation

当信件的副本被发送给其他人时,可以用分发符号 C.C.、c.c. 或 CC、cc 表示。应将这个标识置于签名下方 1~2 行的左边界处。如:

  抄送:哈尔滨分公司
  抄送:库珀先生
    J. 纽曼先生

因为现在大多数的副本都是影印,因此一些打字员会使用 XC(影印)、PC(静电复制)作为抄送标志。如果不希望主收信人知晓信件的副本被发送给其他人,可以使用 bc(密送)或 uc(密件抄送)标志。注意应将密送标志仅打在抄送副本上,而不能打在原信上。

  例如:密送:霍普金先生
    密送:霍普金先生

When copies of the letter are sent to others, indicate using the distribution notation: C.C., c.c., or CC, cc. Place this notation one to two lines below the signature at the left margin. For example:

c.c. Harbin Branch
CC Mr. Cooper
  Mr. J. Newman

Since most copies are now photo copied, some typists use the notation: XC (xerox copy), PC (photocopy). If you don't want the prime recipient to know that copies of the letter have been distributed, use a "bc" (blind copy) or "uc" (undisclosed copy) notation. Type this notation on the copies only, not on the original.

For example: bc Mr. Hopkins
     uc Mr. Hopkins

1.3.13 附言
Postscript

如果写信人想要加一些在信件中忘记提及或希望强调的事情,可以在抄送下方隔两行的位置加上附言。如:

If the writer wishes to add something he forgot to mention or for emphasis, he may add his postscript two lines below the carbon copy notation:

P. S. 价格单将另函邮寄给您。

P. S. The price list will be mailed to you under separate cover.

尽量避免使用附言,因为这可能使对方认为你在打印这封信之前没有组织好信函。

Try to avoid using P. S. since it may suggest that the writer failed to plan this letter well before he typed it.

下面是一封商务信函的典型样例:

The following is a typical model of a business letter:

China Food Industrial Products Imp. & Exp. Co.

56 Chang'an Street, Beijing, China

Tel: ******** Fax: ********

E-mail: ****** Post Code: ******

9 September, 2016

Your Ref. No.: ******
Our Ref. No.: ******

Mr. John Smith
Sales Manager
Eastern Imp. & Exp. Inc.
28 Empress Ave., Willowdale, Ontario, Canada

Dear Sirs,

<u>Chinese Refrigerators</u>

  Thank you for your inquiry of July 8 about our refrigerators. Here we enclose our price list and catalogues for your reference.

  In case of your requiring further information, please fax us. We look forward to hearing from you soon.

Yours faithfully,

China Food Industrial Products Imp. & Exp. Co.

(Signature)

Wang Lei

1.4 商务信函格式
Format of Business Letters

商务信函通常有几种不同格

Generally speaking, there are several forms of

式,比如齐头式、缩进式、混合式等。其中齐头式以及混合式是目前广泛使用的两种格式。

business letters, for example, full-block form, indented form, modified block form with indented paragraphs, etc. Among them, full-block form and modified block form with indented paragraphs are the two main patterns in use at present.

1.4.1 齐头式
Full-block Form

在齐头式信件中,每部分均从信纸左边界打起。在信头和封内名称和地址部分经常采用开放式标点,即无论是寄信人地址还是收信人地址都避免使用多余的标点符号。商务人员更推崇齐头式,因为其形式简单,使打字速度更快。以下是齐头式信件的样例:

In the full block form, every part of a letter is typed from the left margin. Open punctuation is often adopted in the parts of letterhead and inside name and address, which means that both sender's address and recipients' address must avoid more punctuations. Business people generally prefer the full block form, for it has a simple appearance, and is quicker to type. The following is an example of full block form.

Micko Textile Group M. V.
Ossterstra 15897DS Enschede
The Netherlands

Your ref.: D3206
Our ref.: cece

Date: March 25, 2018

Harbin Textiles Import & Export Corp.
54 Dazhi Street
Harbin, Heilongjiang Province
P. R. China

Dear Sirs,

Thank you for your letter of March 19, 2018. We are a company that is engaged in importing clothing items from your country. We are interested in contacts as mentioned by you. Our Purchasing Manager, who is in the U.S.A., will contact you when he returns.

Yours faithfully,

(Signed)
F. Volskivia, Manager

1.4.2 混合式
Modified Block Form with Indented Paragraphs

在混合式信件中，寄信人地址应打在或印在信纸顶部中间部分，日期靠近右边界，收信人名称和地址从左边边界打起，结尾敬语以及签名从中部略偏右的位置开始打，事由居中，段落缩进。

In this form, the sender's address is typed or printed in the up-middle part. The date is in the right part. The recipient's name and address starts from the left margin. The complimentary close as well as the signature is typed from the middle little towards the right. Subject line is in the middle of the line. The paragraphs are indented.

Shanghai Electronic Products Imp. & Exp. Corporation
22 Nanjing Road, Shanghai, China
Tel：********　Fax：********

October 18, 2017

Mr. John White
Sales Manager
Super Electronics Ltd,
23 Clifford Street
UK.

Dear Mr. White,

Re: Chinese Electronic Products

  Your letter of October 12 enquiring about the possibility of importing Chinese-made electronic goods into the United Kingdom has been passed on to us by Shanghai Chamber of Commerce.

  We are one of the largest exporters of electronic products in our country and have handled with various kinds of the products for about 20 years. We enclose our latest illustrated catalogue together with our price lists and terms and conditions of sales for your reference, and shall be pleased to deal with any specific enquiries you may have concerning any of our products. We look forward to hearing from you soon.

Yours sincerely,

Wang Hongwei
Export Manager

1.5 信封的写法
Envelope Addressing

信封上的地址和信纸上的封内地址应采用同样格式，可以采用缩进式或者齐头式。商务书信信封通常应把寄信人地址安排在左上角，收信人的名字和地址应该打在信封的中间靠下位置。邮戳或者邮票放置在右上角，而左下角可以用来标注诸如"绝密""机密""印刷品"等。为了便于邮件分拣，应确保写明邮政编码。

The address on the envelope and the inside address on the letter should be in the same form. It can be written in the indented form or blocked form. Business envelopes ordinarily have the return address printed in the upper left corner. The recipient's name and address should be typed about half way down the envelope. The postmark or stamps should be placed in the up right-hand corner, while the bottom left-hand corner is for post notations such "Confidential", "Secret", "Printed Matter", etc. It is important to include the postcode (zip code in the U.S.A.) in order to facilitate mechanical mail-sorting.

(1) Blocked Form 齐头式

```
Harbin Textiles Import & Export Corp.
54 Dazhi Street                                           (Stamp)
Harbin, Heilongjiang Province
P. R. China


                        F. Volskivia, Manager
                        Micko Textile Group M. V.
                        Ossterstra 15897DS Enschede
                        The Netherlands

Registered
```

(2) Indented Form 缩进式

```
Harbin Textile Import & Export Corp.
   54 Dazhi Street                                        (Stamp)
      Harbin, Heilongjiang Province
         P. R. China


                     F. Volskivia, Manager
                   Micko Textile Group M. V.
                      Ossterstra 15897DS Enschede
                          The Netherlands

Registered
```

1.6 外贸实战技巧
Techniques in Foreign Trade Practice

外贸信函写作技巧

商务函电是贸易双方传递商务信息，促进贸易关系的重要方式。随着时代的发展，商务函电的形式变得更加灵活，富有现代气息。拟写规范且得体的函电需要充分了解国际商务函电的语言特点。

1. 用词礼貌、谦虚，语气委婉

撰写商务函电时要注意措辞，尽量避免使用不礼貌、会令读信人产生不愉快情绪的词句，应使对方感到既有说服力又不失诚恳，立场坚定而又不失亲切。因此，商务英语函电中经常会出现一些礼貌委婉的表达方式，如"Would you please…"，"We shall appreciate it if…"，"We are grateful that…"等，这类表达的运用会使函电中的意向表达更为礼貌、得体。

2. 表达清楚、简洁

清楚指确保所拟写的信函意思清楚、明了，不产生误解。函电讲究的是实效性，写作的目的是尽量与对方建立互利互惠、友善的关系，因此，所有意思模棱两可、含混不清的词句均应避免使用。简洁指用最少的语言表达最丰富、完整的内容，且不影响信函的正确性，当确定要表达的内容后，就要用清晰、简洁的语句表达出来。

3. 语言简单、朴实

根据西方的语言习惯，商务人员更愿意采用简练而朴实的语言，使用意义明确、易读易懂的常用词，避免浮夸的辞藻、有歧视色彩的词汇、画蛇添足的空话。同时，应注意在同一函电中，不要使用多个相同含义的单词。比如，用了"goods have been sent"，再提到"发送"时就不要用其他单词，如"forward""dispatch"等，因为这样会误导读者。

4. 用词专业、严谨

为了减少纠纷，顺利开展对外贸易活动，买卖双方必须对各自承担的责任、费用、风险等作出明确的规定和划分，这就构成外贸英语函电中的最大特点—精确地运用价格、支付、保险等专业术语，如 FOB、CIF、L/C、FPA 等。

1.7 有用的句子
Useful Sentences

1.7.1 开头句
Opening Sentences

（1）We thank you for your letter of July 20.
感谢贵公司 7 月 20 日来函。

（2）We are interested in your electronic toys and shall be pleased to have a catalog and price list.
我们对贵公司的电子玩具很感兴趣，希望能寄来产品目录和价格表。

(3) We are pleased to inform you that we dispatched the goods yesterday.
货物已于昨天发出，特此通知。

(4) Thank you for your interest in our electric heaters, expressed in your letter dated June 6.
贵方在 6 月 6 日函中提到对我公司电加热器感兴趣，甚表感谢。

(5) We understand that you are exporters of bicycles and should like to know if you can supply us with 100 sets by the end of November.
我们知道贵公司是自行车出口商，不知可否在 11 月底前提供 100 台自行车。

(6) We read with interest your advertisement in the *China Daily* and should be glad to receive some samples of your woolen carpets.
我公司对贵方在《中国日报》上登载的广告很感兴趣，并希望收到一些贵公司羊毛地毯的样品。

(7) We are pleased to inform you that we have just marketed our new product.
我们的新产品已经上市，特告之。

(8) We are obliged to you for your inquiry of September 12.
承蒙贵公司 9 月 12 日来函询问，甚表感谢。

(9) We thank you for your letter of April 1, from which we note that you are desirous of establishing business relations with us.
感谢你方 4 月 1 日的来信，我们从信中注意到你方愿意同我方建立业务关系。

(10) We are in receipt of your letter of Nov. 8, for which we thank you.
贵方 11 月 8 日函收悉，谢谢。

1.7.2 结尾句
Closing Sentences

(1) We look forward to hearing from you soon.
期盼能很快得到你的回音。

(2) We should appreciate the opportunity of showing you how efficiently we can serve you.
我们希望能有为您展示我们的服务效率的机会。

(3) Your prompt attention to this matter would be highly appreciated.
如果你能立即处理此事，我们将非常感激。

(4) We hope that this will meet your immediate attention.
我们希望这将引起贵公司的注意。

(5) We should be pleased if you would respond to our request at your earliest convenience.
如果你方能尽早回复，我们将不胜感激。

(6) We trust you will give this enquiry your prompt and careful attention.
我们相信你方将迅速、认真地办理此询价。

(7) Please let us have all necessary information regarding your products for export.
请告知你方出口产品所有情况。

(8) We shall always be happy to hear from you and will carefully consider any proposals likely to lead to business between us.
我们期待你的回复，也会认真考虑任何可能带来双方交易的建议。

(9) Your information on this respect will be highly appreciated.

如能提供此方面的信息，我们将非常感谢。

(10) We trust that we shall hear favorably from you soon.

我们相信会很快得到好消息。

1.8 练习
Exercises

Ⅰ. Answer the following questions.
  1. What are the principles of writing business letters?
  2. How many forms are there in business letters? What are they?
  3. What is the body part of a business letter composed of?
  4. What is the P. S. ?
  5. What is the position of the recipient's name and address on an envelope?
  6. What is the position of the sender's address on an envelope?

Ⅱ. Write a letter using the items given below, inserting the necessary capitals and punctuations.
  1. The sender's name: Sandy Han Stationery Co., Ltd.
  2. The sender's address: 15 Zhongshan Road, Shanghai, P. R. C.
  3. The sender's telephone number: 86-21-64339808
  4. The sender's e-mail address: shangtex@ sina. com
  5. Date: March 4, 2017
  6. The recipient's name: Vermeer Manufacturing Company
  7. The recipient's address: 675 Maple Street, Lagos, Nigeria
  8. Salutation: Dear Sirs
  9. Subject: Filing cabinets
  10. The message: We thank you for your letter of January 5 inquiring for the captioned goods. The enclosed catalogue contains details of all our filing cabinets and will enable you to make a suitable selection. We look forward to receiving your specific enquiry with keen interest.
  11. Complimentary close: Yours faithfully

Ⅲ. Address an envelope in blocked form using the following names and addresses.
  1. The sender: Mr. Wang Gang, China National Food Corporation, 48 Dongsanhuan Road, Beijing, China
  2. The recipient: Mr. John Smith, Sales Manager, Horizon Food Corporation, 58 Lancastor House, Manchester, U. K.

Chapter 2
第 2 章

建立业务关系
Establishing Business Relations

Learning Objectives

Enable the students to know about the necessity of establishing business relations; to be familiar with the channels to find a business partner in a foreign country; to master the structure and common expressions in this type of letter.

使学生了解建立贸易关系的必要性;熟悉找到国外贸易伙伴的渠道;掌握撰写建立业务关系类函件的结构以及常用的表达方式。

2.1 背景知识
Background Information

无论是对于一个新成立的公司,还是一个希望扩大业务范围和营业额的老公司而言,与预期的客户建立业务关系都是至关重要的环节。建立业务关系是实现国际贸易交易的第一步。获得潜在客户的信息可以通过以下渠道:
(1) 网络;
(2) 海外商会;
(3) 银行;
(4) 企业名录;
(5) 中国驻外经济商务参赞处;

To establish business relations with prospective dealers is one of the vitally important measures either for a newly established firm or an old one that wishes to enlarge its business scope and turnover. Establishing business relations is the first step in a transaction in international trade. The following are the major sources where information about potential customers is available:
(1) Internet;
(2) Overseas Chambers of Commerce;
(3) Banks;
(4) Trade Directory;
(5) Chinese Economic and Commercial Counselor's Office in foreign countries;

（6）同业商会；
（7）广告；
（8）国内外举办的贸易展销会及展览会；
（9）第三方公司或朋友的介绍。

在撰写建交信时，除了向目标公司说明写作意图外，也可以介绍自己的公司和产品。通过适当的媒介，如网站或宣传册等，提供公司相关信息以期达成交易，吸引潜在客户和合作伙伴也非常重要。

当第一次致信一家公司或机构时，应告知对方信息来源，表达进行商务合作的意愿以及说明希望购买或是销售商品。第一封信函对开拓及扩大市场至关重要。

通常这类信函包含以下内容：

（1）信息来源；
（2）写信目的；
（3）公司业务范围以及分公司和联络处（如果有的话）；
（4）提供公司资信证明人；
（5）期望能收到回复。

针对建交函的回复应包括：
（1）简略提及收到信件的日期和内容；
（2）直接回复信中提出的要求及询问；
（3）表达希望建立业务关系的愿望，期待互惠合作。

（6）Business House of the same trade;
（7）Advertisements;
（8）Trade fairs and exhibitions held at home and abroad;
（9）Introduction from other firms or friends.

When writing letters of establishing business relations, besides extending your desire to target companies, you may also introduce your own company and products. It is also important to provide relative information through appropriate media, such as website, brochure, etc., to solicit business and attract potential customers and partners.

When you write to a company or an organization for the first time, you should tell them how you come to know them, your intention to do business with them, and what you hope to buy or sell. The first letter is crucial for opening and enlarging market.

Generally speaking, this type of letter usually includes:

（1）the source of his information;
（2）the purpose of the letter;
（3）the business scope of his firm and also its branches and liaison offices, if any;
（4）the reference as to your firm's financial position and integrity;
（5）the expectation of receiving the response.

The response should include:
（1）a brief mention of the date and contents of the received letter;
（2）responds to the requirements or inquiry directly;
（3）express hopes of establishing business relations and mutual beneficial cooperation.

2.2 信例
Specimen Letters

Letter 2-1　Self introduction by an exporter

Dear Sirs,

　　We owe your name and address to the Commercial Counselor's Office of the Chinese Embassy in London. We also learn from them that you are in the market for silk products.

　　Our company is one of the leading manufacturers of silk products in China and has 20 years of business experience in this field. Its products range from the traditional embroidered silk blouse to the latest fashion. We wish to enter into business relations with you by the commencement of some practical transactions.

　　To give you a general idea of the various kinds of silk products now available for export, we are enclosing our latest brochure and a price list for you reference. And for our financial standing, you can get reliable information from the Bank of China, Shanghai Branch.

　　We are looking forward to receiving from you soon.

　　　　　　　　　　　　　　　　　　　　　　　　　　　　Yours faithfully,

Letter 2-2　A letter written by an exporter to an importer

Gentlemen:

　　We thank you for your letter of April 25, from which we note that you are desirous of establishing business relations with us. As we are always willing to do business on the basis of equality and mutual benefit with those who desire to trade with us, we welcome you too.

　　Under separate cover, we are sending you a range of pamphlets to give you a general idea of our products. Please advise us of your specific requirements and we will make our offer promptly.

　　　　　　　　　　　　　　　　　　　　　　　　　　　　　　Yours truly,

Letter 2-3　A letter for seeking investment

Dear Sirs,

　　We understand from the Swiss Business Guide for China that your organization is helping Swiss firms to seek investment opportunities in China and business cooperation with Chinese partners. We are writing to establish business relations with you and we are willing to attract Swiss companies' investment to Zhejiang Province.

We are seeking foreign investment for capital construction, e. g. highway construction, etc. We invite Swiss companies with most favorable policies to set up their firms in any form in these fields.

Our committee provides advice and assistance to firms seeking to export their services or goods to foreign countries and import goods and services from abroad. We can also provide companies with information on the world market and business opportunities as well as organizing trade missions, seminars and business briefings.

Should you have any questions, please feel free to contact us. For our credit standing, please refer to the Bank of China.

Thank you for your attention and we are looking forward to your prompt reply.

Yours faithfully,

Letter 2-4 A letter written by an importer to a producer

Dear Sirs,

The Bank of China here has recommended your corporation as being interested in establishing business relations with Chinese companies for selling computers of your country.

We are one of the principal importers of computers in China. We invite you to send us details and prices of your products, and shall be glad to study the sales possibilities at our end.

We shall always be happy to hear from you and will carefully consider any proposals likely to lead to business between us.

Yours faithfully,

Letter 2-5 A letter of credit enquiry of a new customer

Dear Sirs,

We have received an order for US$80,000 worth of goods from Pakistan Trading Company. They have given us your bank as a reference. We wish to know if they are good for this amount and in every way trustworthy and reliable. We shall be most grateful for any information you give us.

We should treat as strictly confidential any information you tell us and be only too pleased to perform a similar service for you should the opportunity ever arise. We enclose a stamped and addressed envelope for your reply.

Yours faithfully,

Letter 2-6　A letter written by an importer to an export

Dear Sirs,
　　We have come to know the name of your firm and are now writing you for the establishment of business relations.
　　We are very well connected with all the major dealers here of light industrial products, and feel sure we can sell large quantities of Chinese goods if we get your offers at competitive prices.
　　As to our standing, we are permitted to mention the Bank of England, London as a reference.
　　Please let us have all necessary information regarding your products for export.
　　　　　　　　　　　　　　　　　　　　　　　　　　　　　　　Yours faithfully,

Notes

1. owe

    v. 该把……归功于；认为是靠……的力量（后接介词 to）
    He owes his success to chance.
    他认为自己的成功在于机遇。
    We owe your name and address to…
    承蒙……告知你公司的名称和地址。
    类似的表达法还有：
    to be indebted to…for your name and address
    to come to know the name and address of your firm through…
    through the courtesy of…, we come to know your name and address
    to have obtained your name and address from…
    to be recommended to sb. by…
    on the recommendation of…
    欠（债等）；该向……支付
    owe sb. a large sum = owe a large sum to sb.
    欠某人一大笔钱
    IOU = I Owe You 欠条

2. market

    n. 市场；销路
    auction market　拍卖市场
    bond market　债券市场
    exchange market　外汇市场
    financial market　金融市场
    futures market　期货市场
    securities market　证券市场

service market 劳务市场

in the market for 要买

We are in the market for wool. 我们要买羊毛。

come to（into）the market 上市

We will contact you as soon as the new crop comes to the market.
一俟当年收成上市，我们定将和你方联系。

find a market 找销路

（1）We are trying to find a market for this article. 我们正在努力为此项商品找销路。

（2）We regret we cannot find any market for this article. 我们很抱歉不能为此项商品找到销路。

good（poor, no）market 畅销（滞销，无销路）

There is a good（a poor, no）market for these articles. 这些商品畅销（滞销，无销路）。

3. enter into

开始；建立；达成

To enter into business relations 建立业务关系

This agreement is made and entered into by and between ABC Co. and XYZ Co.
本协议是 ABC 公司和 XYZ 公司所缔结的。

4. enclose

v. 封入

We enclose a copy of our latest price list. 随函寄出我方最新价格表一份。

也可用下列句型：

Enclosed is a copy of our latest price list.

Enclosed please find a copy of…

Attached please find…

5. for you reference

供你方参考

for your information

for your consideration

for your guidance

for your perusal

Regarding stock shirts, we are enclosing a list for your reference.
关于现货衬衫，现附寄一张清单供你方参考。

6. be desirous of doing…

渴望做……

We are desirous of being able to get the business done at a lower price.
我们急切希望能以较低价格成交。

7. establish

v. 建立

to establish business relations 建立业务关系

to establish new business 开拓新业务

to establish a letter of credit 开立信用证

8. trade

   n. 贸易；行业

   In recent days, there has been a slow down in our trade with you.

   最近我方和你方的贸易有所减少。

   v. 从事贸易；做生意；经营（和某人做贸易后接介词 with；经营某项商品后接介词 in）

   (1) We do not trade with them. 我们不和他们进行贸易。

   (2) They trade mainly in cotton piece goods. 他们主要经营棉布。

   有关 trade 的常见短语

   barter trade 易货贸易

   barriers to trade 贸易壁垒

   compensation trade 补偿贸易

   frontier trade 边境贸易

   trade representative 商务代表

   trade terms 贸易条件

9. under separate cover

   另邮；另寄

   We are sending you catalogue under separate cover. 目录将另函寄出。

   如表示"随函"，可用"Enclosed please find…"

10. contact

    v. 联系

    We will contact you as soon as the supply position improves.

    供货情况一好转，我们将立即与你方联系。

11. refer to

    查看；提及；提交

    (1) The matter of difference shall be referred to arbitrators. 有争议的问题须提交仲裁人处理。

    (2) We refer you to our letter of August 25, 2017. 请你方查阅我方 2017 年 8 月 25 日函。

12. look forward to

    盼望（to 为介词）

    look forward to sth./doing sth.

    (1) We look forward to your early reply. 盼早复信。

    (2) We look forward to hearing from you soon. 盼早听到你的回复。

13. be only too pleased to…

    too 前若有 only 修饰时，结构表示肯定，相当于 to be very much pleased to…，十分乐于做某事……

    请注意：若"too"前面没有 only 时，就有反义的含义。

    (1) I would be only too glad to go with you.

        我很乐于与你同行。

(2) We would be only too glad to make offers on RMB basis.
我们十分乐于以人民币为基础向你方报盘。

(3) Your letter of credit arrives here too late for us to ship your order before the end of this month.
你们的信用证到得太迟,我们不能在本月底之前装运你方订货。

Words and Phrases

establish	v. 建立
owe	v. 应把……归功于;感激
market	n. 市场;需求
leading	adj. 主要的;重要的
manufacturer	n. 制造商;制造厂
experience	n. 经验
field	n. 领域
embroidered	adj. 刺绣的
commencement	n. 开始;开端
practical	adj. 实际的;实用的
available	adj. 可用的;可得到的
enclose	v. 把……装入信封;附入
brochure	n. 小册子
price list	n. 价格表
reference	n. 参考;资信证明人
note	v. 注意
desirous	adj. 渴望;希望
pamphlet	n. 小册子
general	adj. 总的;大致的
specific	adj. 具体的;特定的
seek	v. 寻找;探索
opportunity	n. 机会
invest	v. 投资
cooperation	n. 合作
partner	n. 伙伴
attract	v. 吸引
introduce	v. 介绍
committee	n. 委员会
field	n. 领域
favorable	a. 有利的;良好的
advice	n. 忠告;建议
assistance	n. 协助;援助
seminar	n. 研究会

briefing	n. 发布会；介绍会
proposal	n. 建议
amount	n. 金额
trustworthy	adj. 值得信赖的
confidential	adj. 秘密的；机密的
dealer	n. 商人
competitive	adj. 有竞争力的
regarding	prep. 关于；至于
Commercial Counselor's Office	商务参赞处
silk product	丝织产品
equality and mutual benefit	平等互利
under separate cover	在另函中
a range of	各类的
financial standing	财务状况
capital construction	基本建设
highway construction	公路建设
trade mission	贸易代表团
look forward to	盼望；期待
at our end	我们这边
perform a similar service	提供类似服务
a stamped and addressed envelope	回邮封
light industrial product	轻工业产品

2.3 外贸实战技巧
Techniques in Foreign Trade Practice

外贸建交信撰写技巧

对于刚刚入行的外贸新手来说，通过建交信自我介绍来寻求客户是一种最为普遍的方法，几乎不需要什么成本。然而这种方法的成功率很低，很多业务员会陷入一些撰写建交信的误区。要想写一份卓有成效的建交信，需要注意以下几点：

1. 要有明确的主题

客户每天打开邮箱时，里面可能都会有几十封来自陌生人的邮件。不明确的主题会使客户根本没兴趣去点击打开你的信件。

2. 避开垃圾邮件（SPAM）过滤词

每个邮件服务器运营商都预设有 Spam Keyword List。国外邮件服务器运营商拦截垃圾邮件的力度要远远超过国内的邮件服务器运营商。为了防止邮件被反垃圾邮件系统拦截，在撰写建交信正文时需注意信件中的词语，尽量避免使用以下这些 SPAM 高频词：Free、Discount、Opportunity、Cheap、Deal、Loan、Money、Price、Rate、Profit 等。

3. 文字和内容处理得当

如果需要强调某些事项，可以加粗或加下划线，但最好不要改用其他颜色。一般用 Arial 或 Times New Roman 字体，字号为 10～12 磅，如果信件内容较多，字号可以相应改小。在写作正文时应多用被动语态，外商的行文里很少采用 I、We 之类人称。建交信只要告诉客户你是谁，你做什么，你的优势在哪里就足够了。

4. 建交信不能写得过长

外商一般处理每一封邮件的时间是 2～3 秒。有些业务员喜欢在建交信里面加上长篇大论的公司或工厂介绍或者一些炫耀英文水平的文字，这些都是不可取的。开发信的内容要言简意赅，切中要点。

5. 留下联络方式

对业务员来说，同客户的交谈不仅依靠电子邮件，有时还要使用电话，为了使客户及时联系到你，一定要在信函中留下签名、电话、传真、邮箱、地址等信息，确保在一些紧急的情况下不会错过机会。

总之，要想写好建交信，应有意识地模仿外商的行文方式和遣词用句，忘记中国人的行文和思维方式，简洁、目的明确是关键。

2.4 有用的句子
Useful Sentences

1. Your name and address have been given/introduced to/referred to/recommended to us by…
   承蒙……的介绍得知贵公司的名称和地址。
2. Being closely connected with reliable wholesalers here, we shall be able to do considerable import business with you.
   我公司与此地可靠的批发商有密切联系，能与你公司做可观的进口业务。
3. We have obtained your name and address through the Bank of China and understood that you would like to establish business relations with us.
   我们从中国银行得到贵公司的名称和地址，并获悉贵公司愿同我们建立业务关系。
4. We have the pleasure of introducing ourselves to you with the hope that we may have an opportunity of cooperating with you in your business extension.
   我们有幸自荐，盼望能有机会与你们合作，扩大业务。
5. We are willing/express our desire to enter into business relations with your firm.
   我们愿意与贵公司建立业务关系。
6. Our mutual understanding and cooperation will certainly result in important business.
   我们之间的相互了解与合作必将促成今后重要的生意。
7. We are now writing you for the purpose of establishing business relations with you.
   我们特此致函是想与贵方建立业务关系。
8. We specialize in the export of Japanese light industrial products and would like to trade with you in this line.
   鉴于我方专营日本轻工业产品出口业务，我方愿与贵方在这方面开展贸易。
9. We have been in this line of business for more than twenty years.

我们经营这类商品已有二十多年的历史了。
10. Being specialized in the export of Chinese Art and Craft goods, we express our desire to trade with you in this line.

    我们专门出口中国工艺品,愿与贵方开展这方面业务。
11. Your letter of September 2, 2016 has been received. We are glad to inform you that the articles required by you fall within the scope of our business activities.

    你方 2016 年 9 月 2 日来函收到。我们很高兴告诉你,你所要的商品属我公司的经营范围。
12. To give you a general idea of our products, we are sending you under separate cover our latest catalogue together with a range of pamphlets for your reference.

    为了给贵方有关我们产品的总体印象,我们将另函寄给你们一份最新产品目录以及一套小册子,供你们参考。
13. We have excellent connections in the trade and are fully experienced in the import business for this kind of product.

    我方在贸易界有良好的关系,对这类产品的进口富有经验。
14. Referring to your letter of December 2, 2017, we are glad to learn that you wish to enter into trade relations with our corporation in the line of textiles.

    收到贵公司 2017 年 12 月 2 日来函,我方非常高兴地得知贵公司有意和我方在纺织产品方面开展贸易合作。
15. We expect/hope to receive your prompt reply.

    盼望能尽快收到你方回复。

2.5 补充商务信函
Letters for Further Reading

Letter 2-7

> Dear Sirs,
>
> We have noted from Beijing Daily that you are the main importer of electrical appliance, and you want to purchase presently fanners.
>
> Therefore, we are glad to inform you that we produce all kinds of fanners. They are of good quality and function. All of them have been checked up strictly. It is worth introducing LingKong Brand fanner which has been improved a lot recently. We are sure that it can be sold well in your market.
>
> We want to establish business relations with your firm and make efforts together to expand our business.
>
> Thank you for your attention and we are looking forward to your prompt reply.
>
> Yours faithfully,

Letter 2-8

Dear Mr. Black,

Your company has been introduced to us by Messrs. Smith & Co., London, as large buyers of Human Hair. This article comes within the scope of our business activities, and we shall be pleased to enter into business relations with you.

To give you a general idea of the various types that are at present available for export by us, we enclose a specification list and shall be glad to send you samples and quotations upon receipt of your specific enquiry.

We look forward to your early reply.

Sincerely yours,

Letter 2-9

Dear Sirs,

We are in receipt of your letter of March 14, 2016. In reply, we wish to express our welcome to your desire of establishing business relations with us and importing medicinal herbs from this country. Chinese medicinal herbs have a history of thousand years and are extensively used in medicine at this end.

Under separate cover, we are sending you a copy of our catalog. We hope you will let us know your specific requirements, so as to enable us to make sure whether the items you are interested in are available or not.

Yours faithfully,

Letter 2-10

Dear Sirs,

We write to introduce ourselves as one of the largest exporters, from China, of a wide range of Machinery and Equipments.

We enclose a copy of our latest catalog covering the details of all the items available at present, and hope some of them items will be of interest to you.

It will be a great pleasure to receive your inquiries for any of the items against which we will send you our lowest quotations.

> Should, by chance, your corporation does not deal with the import of the goods mentioned above, we would be most grateful if this letter could be forwarded to the correct import corporation.
>
> We are looking forward to your favorable and prompt reply.
>
> Yours faithfully,

Letter 2-11

> Dear Sirs,
>
> We will be obliged if you will kindly give us the information about credit standing of the Harbor Imp & Exp Corp. in your city. We understand that you have regular transactions with the firm, so we take the liberty to ask you to give your views concerning the actual position of the firm in order that we may take steps to avoid getting into trouble.
>
> Any information you give will be highly appreciated and kept in strict confidence. We shall be pleased to reciprocate if you should need our services at this end.
>
> We are awaiting your early reply.
>
> Yours faithfully,

2.6 练习
Exercises

Ⅰ. Translate the following phrases into Chinese.
1. for your reference
2. state-owned enterprise
3. under separate cover
4. price list
5. economic and commercial counselor's office
6. equality and mutual benefit
7. financial standing
8. light industrial product
9. business partner
10. in the market for

Ⅱ. Choose the best answer.
1. We are glad to learn that you are making plans to visit China _____ .
   A. in next month
   B. in the next month
   C. in the following month
   D. next month
2. We find your quotation _____ and, therefore, place an order with you now.
   A. attracting
   B. attract our attention
   C. attractive
   D. to be attractive
3. We learned from ABC Company that you are _____ electric toys.
   A. in the market for
   B. in market for
   C. in market of
   D. in the market of
4. If you are interested, we will send you a sample lot _____ charge.

A. with　　　　　　　　　　　　　　B. for
　　　C. free of　　　　　　　　　　　　　D. within
5. _____ please find a copy of our latest catalogue for your reference.
　　　A. Enclose　　　　　　　　　　　　 B. Enclosing
　　　C. Enclosed　　　　　　　　　　　　D. Exclude
6. We will _____ you as soon as the crop comes to the market.
　　　A. contact with　　　　　　　　　　B. contact
　　　C. get in touch　　　　　　　　　　 D. get contact
7. Your firm has been referred to us by the ABC Co. of Canada, _____ we have done business for many years.
　　　A. which　　　　　　　　　　　　　B. with that
　　　C. whom　　　　　　　　　　　　　D. with whom
8. I'm sure the quality of our new product will _____ you in every respect.
　　　A. satisfy　　　　　　　　　　　　　B. satisfactory
　　　C. satisfied　　　　　　　　　　　　D. satisfaction
9. The goods you offered are _____ line with the business scope of our clients.
　　　A. out of　　　　　　　　　　　　　B. without
　　　C. outside　　　　　　　　　　　　 D. not
10. We have pleasure in enclosing the samples _____ for in your letter dated December 11.
　　　A. asking　　　　　　　　　　　　　B. asked
　　　C. ask　　　　　　　　　　　　　　D. asks

Ⅲ. Fill in the blanks.
1. Please be good enough to provide the necessary information _____ us.
2. If your price is competitive, we shall be glad to place a substantial order _____ you.
3. This article is of particular interest _____ us.
4. Should your price be _____ line, we trust large business can be concluded.
5. We are gearing our production to your requirements and shall soon be _____ a position _____ offer you substantially.
6. There is nothing _____ at present.
7. Enclosed _____ a copy of our price list.
8. Through _____ a Chamber of Commerce. We have learned that you are one of representative importers of electric goods.
9. Your name has been recommended to us _____ ABC Company in your city _____ large exporter of Chinese carpet.
10. We _____ your sending us a special offer for walnut meat.
11. We can supply you _____ all kinds of leather shoes.
12. We _____ that we are unable to effect shipment in this month.
13. They have been _____ the wool trade for quite a number of years.
14. _____ receipt of your detailed requirements, we shall be glad to give you our latest quotations.

15. We take this opportunity to approach you _____ the establishment of the trade relations with you.

Ⅳ. Translate the following sentences into Chinese.
1. We have heard from China Council for the Promotion of International Trade that you are in the market for electric appliances.
2. We have the pleasure to introduce ourselves to you with a view to building up business relations with your firm.
3. Please submit full specifications of your refrigerators together with terms of payment and discount rate.
4. Our bankers are the Hong Kong & Shanghai Banking Corporation in Hong Kong, they can provide you with the information about our business and finances.
5. Your name and address have been passed on to us by your Chamber of Commerce, and we are glad to forward you this letter in the hope that it will be a prelude to prosperous and mutually beneficial relations between us.
6. We shall be obliged if you would send us samples and prices of your products.
7. If there is anything we can do to help you, we shall be more than pleased to do so.
8. This places our dealers in a highly competitive position and also enables them to enjoy maximum profit.
9. If you are interested in dealing with us in other products of our company, please inform us of your requirements as well as your banker's name and address.
10. Because of the rapid development of our business in Asia, we think it's necessary to open a branch at the following address.

Ⅴ. Translate the following sentences into English.
1. 承蒙我国驻伦敦大使馆商务参赞处的介绍，我方获悉贵方是电子产品的主要进口商之一。
2. 我公司经营轻工产品已有 15 年。
3. 如果你认为我方的价格合理，请与我联系。
4. 我们从互联网得知贵公司的名称和地址。
5. 我们是一家专营陶瓷产品的出口商。
6. 我公司现有各种地毯及其他纺织材料的铺地制品可供出口。
7. 我们借此机会告诉你方我们希望把业务扩展到非洲市场。
8. 一俟收到你方的具体询价，我们马上寄送样品并报最优惠的价格。
9. 随函寄上我公司新产品的价目单和商品小册子各一份。
10. 我们在平等互利的基础上和各国商人进行贸易活动。

Ⅵ. Writing task.
Write a reply to ABC Co. with the following particulars.
1. Acknowledge the receipt of their letter of June 27.
2. Agree to their proposal of establishing trade relations with you.
3. Commodity inspection will be handled by the bureau concerned in Shanghai.

Chapter 3
第 3 章

询盘与回复
Inquiries and Replies

Learning Objectives

Enable the students to know the definition and classification of inquiries; to be familiar with the standard format of inquiries and replies, the guidelines for writing this type of letter; to master the basic sentences and common expressions in the letter of inquiries and replies.

使学生了解询盘的定义和分类；熟悉询盘与回复的标准格式、写作此类信件的原则；掌握撰写询盘及回复函件的基本句式以及常用的表达方式。

3.1 背景知识
Background Information

在商务谈判中，询盘由进口商或者出口商发出，目的是获得价格及其他贸易条件信息，询盘对询盘人无约束力。询盘在内容上通常比较简单，仅仅会写明商品名称或商品描述，这种询盘被称为一般询盘。另一类询盘为具体询盘，其中包含商品名称、品质或规格、数量、付款条件等详细信息。

首次询盘首先应告知获悉对方公司名称的渠道。一些关于自己公司的具体情况，比如经营货物的种类、所需货物的数量、惯常的交易条件以及任何有可能使供应商了解你方需求的信息，都

In business negotiation, inquiries are made by the importers or exporters without engagement to get information on price and other trade conditions. Inquiries may usually be simple in content, in which only the name or descriptions of the commodity will be written. Some of the inquiries called general inquiries are like what we mention above. Others called specific inquiries are in great details including the name of commodity, quality or specifications, quantity, terms of payment, etc.

A first inquiry should begin by telling him how you obtained his name. Some details of your own business, such as the kind of goods handled, quantities needed, usual terms to trade and any information likely to enable the supplier to decide what he can do for you, will also help.

会对交易洽商有所帮助。

撰写询盘信时，要做到简短、具体、礼貌、合理并且切题，信中包含必须表达的内容，必须询问的事项就足够了。询盘信意味着潜在的销售机会，因此，对于询盘信的回复一定要诚挚、热情。如果暂时没有可供的现货，也应即时告知对方已收到询盘，并解释目前的状况。如果询盘来自老客户，要表达对询盘的由衷感谢；如果询盘来自新顾客，回信时应写明很高兴收到询盘并且表达希望建立长期、友好的业务关系，以创造友好的氛围，给对方留下良好的印象。简而言之，对于询盘信的回复一定要迅速、礼貌并且有所帮助。

通常来说，询盘信是要求卖方提供关于商品和贸易条件的信息，尤其是商品的价格，并要求卖方作出报价。询盘会因内容、目的、背景而不同。询盘通常由以下六个部分组成：

（1）信息来源；
（2）欲购买的具体货物；
（3）要求对方寄送最新的商品目录、价格表以及样品；
（4）强调对方应作出有竞争性的、合理的报价；
（5）询问销售折扣、最低价格以及最早交货期；
（6）表达订购商品的可能性。

对于询盘的回复包括以下几部分内容：

（1）感谢询盘；
（2）强调商品的优点，详细介绍相关信息；

When making an inquiry, keep it brief, specific, courteous, reasonable and to the point, say what needs to be said, ask what needs to be asked and no more. An inquiry letter means a possible sales opportunity. Therefore, it must be replied earnestly and enthusiastically. If there is no stock available for the time being, you should acknowledge the inquiry at once and explain the situation. If the inquiry is from an old customer, say how much you appreciate it. If it is from a new customer, say you are glad to receive it and express the hope of a lasting friendly business relationship so as to create goodwill and leave good impression. In a word, answers to inquiries should be prompt, courteous and helpful.

Commonly speaking, an inquiry is to request the possible seller to give the information about the goods as well as the information about trade conditions, especially the price of the goods, and ask the seller to make quotation. Inquiries vary with their different contents, different purposes and different backgrounds. An inquiry is generally made up of the following six parts:

(1) The source of the information;
(2) The specific goods which are wanted;
(3) The request of sending the latest catalogue and pricelist, together with samples;
(4) The emphasis of the competitive and reasonable quotation;
(5) Asking the supplied discounts, lowest price and the best delivery date;
(6) Expressing the possibility of ordering the goods.

A reply to the inquiry is composed of the following parts:

(1) Thanks for the inquiry;
(2) The merits of the goods and relating information in details;

(3) 报出有竞争性且合理的价格，告知报盘的截止日期；

(4) 表明可以接受的支付方式以及可能的交货期；

(5) 表示希望收到对方的订单。

(3) Quoting the competitive and reasonable price and stating the deadline of the offer;

(4) Stating the acceptable payment and the possible delivery date;

(5) Expressing the hope of receiving the order.

3.2 信例
Specimen Letters

Letter 3-1 First inquiry

Dear Sirs,
　　We learn from one Indian company of the same trade that you are producing for export hand-made carpets of different sizes in wool and silk. We are interested in them, for there is a steady demand in our market for carpets of good quality. But stock of carpets is running low so that good prices are obtained.
　　We will be appreciative if you send us a copy of your carpet catalogue, with details of your prices and terms of payment. I should find it most helpful if you could also supply some small pieces as samples of the various types.
　　In view of the demand for your products, an immediate reply is appreciated.
　　　　　　　　　　　　　　　　　　　　　　　　　　　　Yours faithfully,

Letter 3-2 Reply to the first inquiry

Dear Sir,
　　We thank you very much for your inquiry of August 24 and are happy to learn that you are interested in our carpets. I am sure you will receive a copy of our illustrated catalogue with samples of carpets in only a few days.
　　Our carpets have long-standing history and are well-known in Asian markets for their supreme quality. We manufactured carpets of various patterns in wool, silk, cotton and fabric, among which the hand-made woolen ones are particularly of great fame. They are made to be able to stand wear and tear.
　　We also manufacture a wide range of hand-made hanging-rug, traveling-rug, hearth-rug in which we think you may be interested. They are fully illustrated in the catalogue and are of the same high quality.

All orders entrusted to us are given our careful and prompt attention. We sincerely desire to have the pleasure of receiving an order from you.

Yours faithfully,

Letter 3-3 Recommending a substitute for the discontinued item

Dear Mr. Smith,

We really appreciate your letter of May 3 and your interest in our machine model PD-21, but we can not supply it any longer since the production has been discontinued. However, we may ensure that the new product PD-22 with more extensive function will be an excellent replacement.

At quite little extra cost, the quality and specification of Model PD-22 are greatly improved. In order to make you know more about our new products, we have separately sent you a sample, a price list and catalogues.

Your request about exclusive sales is somewhat unusual, but we are willing to grant exclusive agency if you can place an initial order exceeding $100,000. We are happy to increase our sales with you, and we are sure that you will find a ready sale for this excellent product.

Yours sincerely,

Letter 3-4 Asking for a quotation

Dear Sir,

We are so pleased to inform you that now we have enlarged our production scale due to fast sales and are planning to import one more new equipment.

Since your type will fit in well and solid, we would like to get a future acquaintance. So would you please send a complete range of catalogues and sample goods? We wish to know the full details of your products, such as price and other terms. We would like to know whether you can supply from stock.

We will look forward to your reply, and we will appreciate a quick reply.

Yours faithfully,

Letter 3-5 Requesting for products similar to the buying sample

Dear Sir,

  Thank you for your letter of May 11 for the supply of 20,000 Wall shoes. And we have sent our buying sample, which will show you the shape, design and quality required.

  According to our buying samples with the best price CIF for Wall shoes, please mail your samples as soon as possible. And after receiving the order, you should supply your goods within five weeks. All your quotations should be as completely detailed as possible to avoid unnecessary further inquiries.

  We will make our payment by paying your sight draft under our irrevocable letter of credit, and we will be obliged if you give us your immediate and careful attention.

Yours faithfully,

Letter 3-6 A reply to a customer, giving details of the terms and conditions

Dear Sirs,

Our Quotation No. 0024

  Thank you for your inquiry about our PD2000 30-foot Sunvoyager. You have asked us to give you our best CIF price for two of these.

  The price for two PD2000 with specifications as in our 2017 catalogue pages 15~18 is USD 188,000 CIF Puerto Limon.

  If you require the special stainless steel anchors and chains (our catalogue numbers 2300 and 2320), the total price will be 188,000 U.S. dollars.

  From the date of your written order, the goods will be ready for shipment in 4 to 5 weeks. We pack each PD2000 for export in a 40-foot open top container. We understand from our freight forwards that Caribbean lines have a scheduled service to Puerto Limon once a month.

  We would appreciate payment by irrevocable letter of credit confirmed by a London bank and valid for 90 days from the date of this fax.

  We look forward to hearing you soon.

  I shall be pleased to help you personally, if you require any further information.

Yours faithfully,

Notes

1. learn from...

  收到……的来信；从……获知

  (1) He learned from his family every month when he studied aboard.

    他在国外留学的时候，每个月都收到家里的来信。

（2）I learned from his roommate that the he had been in hospital for over a week.

我从他的室友那里得知他已经住院一个多星期了。

2. hand-made

adj. 手工制的，相对于 machine-made（机器制造的）而言。

hand-made pottery

手工制作的陶器

machine-made sweaters

机织毛衣

3. in（wool and silk）

以（羊毛和丝）为原料；以……为手段；以……为媒介

（1）We are in the market for your hand-made shoes and gloves in pure leather.

我们要购买贵方手工制造的真皮鞋和手套。

（2）He is writing a composition in English.

他正在写英文作文。

（3）She likes taking notes in pencil.

他喜欢用铅笔记笔记。

a statue in marbles

一座大理石像

4. steady

adj. 持续的；稳定的；固定的

（1）China's foreign trade has been making steady progress.

中国的对外贸易一直在持续发展。

（2）Our sales have remained steady.

我们的销售额一直保持稳定。

（3）Such fine work requires a steady hand and a steady eye.

做这样精细的工作，手要稳，眼要准。

5. stock

n. 库存；现货

（1）These are the only stocks available.

这些是仅有的现货。

（2）Our new stock of cameras will arrive soon.

我们的新照相机很快就到货。

stock 常与一些介词短语搭配使用，例如：

in stock   有现货；在库存中

out of stock   脱销；缺货

from stock   动用库存；现货

for stock   当作库存

a stock of   一批

6. run low

变少

（1）Our stocks are running low.

我们的存货正迅速减少。

（2）We are out of flour and the rice is running low.

我们的面粉已经吃完，而且大米也所剩无几了。

7. appreciative

adj. 感激的，意思与 grateful 相同，用作表语，后接 of。

（1）We are very appreciative of your timely reply of January 1.

收悉贵方 1 月 1 日的及时回复，我们非常感激。

（2）I am most appreciative of your generosity.

我对您的慷慨感激之至。

appreciate 理解并欣赏；高度评价；体恤；体谅

（1）I really appreciate a good cup of tea.

有一杯好茶，我就真的感到很享受了。

（2）It would be appreciated if you would quote us the lowest prices CIF Hong Kong.

如贵方报 CIF 香港最低价，我们将非常感激。

（3）Your immediate attention to it was greatly appreciated.

非常感激贵方对此事的迅速处理。

（4）We hope that you will appreciate our situation and cooperate with us.

希望贵方能体谅我们的处境并予以合作。

8. in view of

鉴于

（1）In view of the fact that all other customers have accepted this price, we can not give consideration to your counter-offer.

鉴于其他客户都已经接受此价格，我们不能考虑你们的还盘。

（2）In view of your departure tomorrow, can you spare me a few moments?

由于你明天要走，你能抽出一点时间和我谈谈吗？

9. sure

adj. 可以作表语，其后接 of 短语，意思为"确信的，有把握的"，主语必须是人；后接不定式，意思为"一定要，必定会"，主语不一定是人；或接 that 从句，意思为"认为……一定会"，主语是人。

（1）Be sure to remember what I told you.

一定要记住我对你讲的话。

（2）He is sure of himself.

他很自信。

（3）You may be sure of best attention to your request.

你方的要求一定会得到最好的处理，请放心。

（4）Please be sure to make delivery as soon as possible.

请一定尽快交货。

（5）Don't air your clothes outside. It is sure to rain tonight.

不要把衣服晾在外边，今晚一定会下雨。

（6）You may be sure that the goods will arrive in perfect condition.
请放心，货物一定会完好到达。
sure 也可以用作定语，意思是"确实的，可靠的"。
something sure to happen
肯定会发生的事情
A sure thing never takes you by surprise.
肯定会发生的事从来不会使人感到惊奇。

10. illustrated

    adj. 附有插图的

    （1）Please find enclosed an illustrated catalogue and a price-list.
    随函附上有插图的目录和价格表各一份。
    illustrate 做动词作"（用事例或图表）解释和说明"解。

    （2）We are enclosing a set of photos which illustrate the sizes, shapes and structures of our copy machines.
    随信附寄一套照片说明我们复印机的尺寸、形状和结构。
    I have done a comparative analysis to illustrate my point.
    为说明我的观点，我作了比较分析。

11. long-standing

    adj. 长久的；长期存在的

    （1）We have solved the difficult and long-standing problem.
    我们解决了这一长期存在的难题。

    （2）We appreciate very much the long-standing friendship between us.
    我们十分珍视我们之间的友谊。

12. supreme

    adj. 最高的；最大的；最重要的

    （1）He thought it a consideration supreme over all others.
    他认为这是一件高于其他一切而需要考虑的事。

    （2）It is the supreme quality that is the most competitive in market.
    优良的产品质量在市场上才最具有竞争力。

13. manufacture

    v. & n. 大量生产；大量制造

    （1）Furniture nowadays is generally manufactured by machinery instead of by hand.
    现在的家具普遍是用机器制造而不是用手工制造。

    （2）We have been the firm engaged in the manufacture of plastics.
    我们公司一直在从事塑料生产。

14. be of great fame

    "be + of + 名词"意思等于"be + 有关形容词"，前者比后者更正式，多见于书面表达。

    （1）The book is of great help. （= The book is very helpful.）
    这本书很有用。

    （2）Your opinions are of significance. （= Your opinions are significant.）

你的意见意义重大。

(3) Desert is a place of silence and beauty. (= Desert is a silent and beautiful place.)
沙漠是一个寂静而美丽的地方。

15. a range of

一系列的；各种各样的

(1) The new model comes in an exciting range of colors.
这种新式样有各种鲜艳的颜色。

(2) We have being exported a wide range of technology and equipment in electronics.
我们一直出口品种繁多的电子技术和设备。

16. entrust

v. 委托；信托

entrust something to somebody/something

entrust somebody with something

(1) Ought I to entrust to them such confidential and important plans?
我应该把如此机密而重要的计划委托给他们吗？

(2) We entrust this large order to your careful attention.
我们将此大订单提交你方，请慎重处理。

(3) Can I entrust you with the task?
我可以将此事交给你办吗？

(4) We entrusted you with the sole agency for our products in Shanghai.
我们委任你方在上海独家代理我公司的产品。

17. desire

v. & n. 愿望；期望；想要

(1) It happens to agree with our desire.
这同我们的愿望恰好一致。

(2) We have no desire to import any advanced equipment at this moment.
现在我们不想进口任何高级设备。

(3) We desire you to make an early reply.
我们要求你们早点答复。

18. discontinue

v. 停止生产

the sale of a discontinued china

停止生产的瓷器的销售

The production of M12 model has been discontinued, and replaced by T12.
M12 型号产品已停止生产，并被 T12 号所替代。

19. replacement

n. 替换（物或人）

(1) In the unlikely event of damage to any item during delivery, please call us immediately and we will arrange for its return or replacement.
在货物运输过程中遇到不可预期事件而对货物造成损失时，请立即给我方打电话，我方将安排货物的返还及替换。
(2) I have your inventory of broken items. We shall make up a consignment of replacements which will reach you soon.

我方有你方的破损货物清单。我们将尽快寄送替代货物。

replace

v. 替换

The defective machine is beyond repair, and it will be replaced immediately.

此残坏机器无法修理，它将会被立即替换。

20. agency

    n. 代理机构；代理

    They signed an agency for Ford cars.

    他们签约成为福特的代理机构。

    exclusive agency 独家代理，也用 sole agency

    The firm has the sole agency for Ford cars.

    该公司已拥有福特汽车的独家代理权。

    general agency   总代理

    news agency   通讯社

    travel agency   旅行社

    advertising agency   广告公司

    forwarding agency   货运代理

    insurance agency   保险代理

21. initial

    adj. 起初的

    an initial order   第一笔订单

    initiate

    v. 开始；开创；开始实施

    It is mutually agreed that all other income from initiation fee and dues shall be used by the First Party.

    兹约定，来自入会费以及应付款的其他收入应由甲方使用。

    initiative

    n. 主动性

    He lacks the initiative for leadership.

    他缺乏当领导的积极性。

22. fit in well

    非常适合

23. sample

    n. 样品

    representative sample   代表性样品

    type sample   标准样品

    keep sample   留样

    duplicate sample   复样

return sample 回样
counter sample 对等样品
buying sample 买方样品；采购样品

24. sight draft
    即期汇票
25. irrevocable letter of credit
    不可撤销信用证
26. specification
    n. 缩写为 spec., 规格；明细单；说明书
    (1) The vendor e-mailed the specs for the new PCs.
        厂商电邮新电脑的规格。
    (2) Please quote us your best CIF price, giving a full specification of your product and shipping date.
        请报 CIF 最低价，详细说明产品和船期。
    (3) A full specification of our requirements is given on the attached sheet.
        附表上已经详细说明了我方的要求。
    specify
    v. 规定
    (1) The contract clearly specifies both parties' rights and obligations.
        合同明确规定双方权利和责任。
    (2) The L/C terms should be in extra accordance with those specified in the contract.
        信用证条款应严格遵照合同相应条款。
    specific
    adj. 具体的；特定的
    Can you be a little more specific about your instructions?
    能否详细说明你方要求？
27. open top container
    开顶式集装箱；顶部可以打开，多用于装运重货
28. freight forwarders
    承运人；运输行
29. Caribbean lines
    n. 加勒比航线

Words and Phrases

intend	v. 有意图；意欲
inquiry	n. 询问；询价
supplier	n. 供应商；供应者
concerning	prep. 关于
earnestly	adv. 认真地；诚恳地

enthusiastically	adv.	热情地
essential	adj.	主要的；重要的
component	n.	成分；组成部分
typical	adj.	典型的；具有代表性的
state	v.	陈述；说明
brief	adj.	简洁的；简单的
purpose	n.	目的
specific	adj.	确切的；具体的
courteous	adj.	礼貌的；客气的
regular	adj.	经常的；定期的
customer	n.	顾客
cover	v.	包括；涉及；使用于
appreciate	v.	高度评价；体谅
routine	adj.	例行的；惯例
catalogue	n.	目录
promotion	n.	提升；促进
prepared	adj.	备妥的；提前制作好的
compliment	n.	赞美；赞成的表示
request	n.	要求；请求
sample	n.	样品
demonstrate	v.	示范；表明；表示
advantage	n.	优点；优势
sincerely	adv.	真诚地
gratefulness	n.	感激；感谢
lasting	adj.	长久的；持久的
relationship	n.	关系
partner	n.	伙伴；同伴
refusal	n.	拒绝
offend	v.	得罪；冒犯
enumerate	v.	罗列出
mention	v.	提及；提到
summarize	v.	总结；概括
carpet	n.	毯子
wool	n.	羊毛
silk	n.	丝绸
in details		详细地
think highly of		高度重视
price list		价目表
due to		由于；因为
make use of		利用

in addition	此外；另外
in the case of	在……情况下；就……来说
no longer	不再
result in	产生……结果
depend on	视某事物而定
special price	优惠价格
terms of payment	支付条件
in view of	鉴于……
office equipment	办公设备

3.3 外贸实战技巧
Techniques in Foreign Trade Practice

有效询盘的判断方法

在对外贸易实践中，对询盘客户进行分类有助于企业进行客户管理以及交易磋商前期及后期工作的开展。如何从众多的询盘中过滤和剔除无效询盘，使工作富有针对性，从而提高业务质量是每个外贸业务员必须掌握的技能。根据询盘有效性进行分类后，对成交概率比较大的，要根据询盘具体要求回复，以免错过时机；对于成交概率十分微小的，应做好筛查，以免浪费时间。

从询盘的有效性来看，询盘一般可以分为以下三种类型：

1. 高质量的有效询盘

此类询盘目标明确，客户诚意度高，在实际业务中，也是最值得关注和跟踪的。这类买家正在寻找我方所提供的产品或者类似产品，往往手里有订单或者正在执行某项采购任务。他们所查询的产品品名具体或单一，有明确的订货数量，所提问题细致、专业，内容简明扼要，交易意愿强烈。

2. 潜在客户型询盘

这类客户有一定的贸易经验，但对我方产品还不够了解，有一定的交易意愿，但交易意向不明确。有的可能是新手业务员想要经营我方产品，因此会有许多具体问题需要我们帮助解决。其特点是公司名称、地址、电话、传真、联系人等一般信息比较全面，而且有诚意。从其问题的专业度评估，可以做出判断，这类客户是你的潜在客户，总体来说，此类询盘可以分为以下四种情况。

一是询价备用型。此类询盘人已经有固定的供应商，但是为防止原供应商出现意外，导致供货不足或者不能供货而给自己造成重大损失，希望预先找到其他供应商备用。询价备用型询盘的特点是产品比较明确，但是价格等其他交易条款模糊，不会立即回复受盘人发出的函电，但每隔一段时间就又会联系受盘人。

二是初入市场型。有的询盘人刚入行，并不清楚市场行情，因此广发询盘收集资料；有的虽然从事贸易时间较久，但是经营的产品种类繁多，并不局限于某一种或者几种产品，而是看到利润就会涉足，因此要发询盘寻找市场机会。

三是寻找替代型。有些询盘人已有贸易伙伴，想再增加几个；或是与原有的贸易伙伴合作并不愉快，想更换，因此发出询盘寻找合适的供应商。

四是漫天撒网型。刚入行的买家，产品信息的来源渠道有限，于是广发询盘收集资料，目的是获得产品的价格、图片等信息。询盘人在 B2B 网站上发布供求消息，大面积询价，通过比较获得对自己最有利的报价。这类询盘大多通过贸易平台转来，如 Alibaba、Made in China、Tradekey 等。询盘人查询品种繁多，目标不明确，一般会直接索要产品价目表。

3. 虚假的无效询盘

此类询盘有一个共同的特点，询盘目的不是谋求建立业务关系，而是发出询盘的一方为单方面获得利益故意发出询盘，引诱对方上钩。大体上可以归纳为以下三种情况：

一是欺骗性询盘。欺骗性询盘往往表示对某种产品感兴趣，表明打算派业务员来中国工厂考察的意愿，要求工厂发出官方邀请，其目的往往不是真的来考察，而是骗取邀请函以获得来中国的签证，然后滞留中国。还有的询盘实则是钓鱼网站伪装的询盘，先通过外贸询盘函吸引受盘人访问某些钓鱼网站，骗取账号，然后再进行诈骗。

二是索要样品的询盘。一些企业网站或贸易平台网站经常会宣传可为客户提供免费样品，这样就为一些贪图小利者以可乘之机。这类询盘特点是询盘一般由一些小国家的客户发出，他们对产品的质量、价格等都不关心，联系几次后就会要求免费寄送样品，如果样品要收费或者是要求运费到付，就不会再有回复。

三是来自竞争对手的询盘，也称为信息收集型询盘。这类询盘者或许是某同行业技术人员正要开发或仿造与我方产品相同或相似的产品，或是同行销售人员想了解市场、了解产品，欲得到更多的行业信息。该类询盘者的特点是询问内容十分专业，数次沟通后他们就会迅速汇款购买样品。

3.4 有用的句子
Useful Sentences

1. Please make us an offer within this month since we have made an inquiry for your products.
已对你们的产品进行询价，请在本月内给予报盘。
2. Please send us your best offer by Internet stating payment terms and time of shipment.
请在互联网向我们报最优惠价，说明支付条件和装运期。
3. We shall appreciate it very much if you will give our bid your favorable consideration.
如承优惠考虑报价，不胜感激。
4. We are always in a position to quote you the most advantageous prices for higher quality merchandise.
我们始终能向贵方提供品质最佳的产品，最优惠的报价。
5. Full information as to prices, quality, quantity available and other relative particulars would be appreciated.
请详告价格、质量、可供数量及其他相关情况，不胜感激。
6. We assure you of our best services at all times.
我们保证向贵方随时提供最佳服务。
7. It would give us a great pleasure to render you a similar service should an opportunity occur.
我方如有机会同样效劳贵方，将不胜欣慰。

8. We ask you kindly deliver us as soon as possible your latest price list of your sports shoes with the lowest quotations, together with an illustrated catalogue.
   请贵公司尽快惠寄运动鞋的最新价目表和带有图片的商品目录，并给予最优惠的报价。
9. We request you to inform us of the price of Chinese dinnerware and the possibly earliest date of delivery.
   请告知中国产餐具的价格和最早的交货日期。
10. We are interested in Acer computers you stated in your letter of January 12, 2014 and shall be obliged if you could care to offer us competitive quotations.
    我们对贵公司2014年1月12日来信中所提到的"宏碁"计算机很感兴趣，如蒙提供具有竞争力的报价，将十分感激。
11. We shall be grateful to you for further discount off your price list you sent last week.
    如贵公司能从上周寄的价目单中再给些折扣优待，将不胜感激。
12. We would appreciate it if you could let us know the ruling prices of the above items at your end so that we may give you quotations accordingly.
    如贵方能告知我们上述商品在贵地的现行价，则甚为感激，并将作为参考酌情报价。
13. We are on the look-out for the following items and should be grateful if you would send samples of the same.
    我们欲求购下列产品，如贵公司能寄送其样品，我们将非常感激。
14. In reply to your inquiry dated November 25, we are sending you our quotation, along with various samples of leather gloves closely resembling to what you want.
    应贵公司11月25日来函询问，现寄上我方的报价和几副式样不同的与贵方要求近似的皮手套样品。
15. We would esteem it a favor if you would reply promptly.
    如蒙迅速回复我们将不胜感激。

3.5 补充商务信函
Letters for Further Reading

Letter 3-7

Dear Sirs,
   We have been informed by the Bank of U.S. Commerce, New York, that you are one of the leading exporters of textiles in China, and that you wish to export pure silk garments to our market.
   You will be pleased to note that our corporation is one of the leading importers of textile products, having over 30 years' history and high reputation.
   We shall be able to give you considerable orders, if the quality of your products is fine and the prices are moderate. We would be obliged if you will send us some samples with the best terms at your earliest convenience.

                                                            Yours faithfully,

Letter 3-8

Dear Sirs,

We take pleasure to acknowledge receipt of your letter of January 20, from which we learn that you are interested in bringing silk garments to the New York market.

We are enclosing our quotation sheet covering different sizes and colors of our pure silk garments that can be supplied from stock. We are also airmailing you two dozen sample garments in different sizes and colors. Delivery will be within 30 days after your placing an order to us. Payment of the purchase is to be effected by an irrevocable L/C at sight in our favor.

This offer is subject to your immediate reply which should reach us not later than the end of next month. The price will probably be changed once this particular offer has lapsed.

Yours faithfully,

Letter 3-9

Gentlemen:

We learn with pleasure from your letter of April 12, 2014 that you are exporters of Chinese Blanket Cover and are willing to establish business relations with us.

At present, we are interested in Blanket Cover and shall be pleased if you will send us by airmail sample books and all necessary information on Blanket Cover, so as to acquaint us with material and workmanship of your supplies. Meanwhile, please quote us the lowest price CIF London, inclusive of our 3% commission, stating the earliest date of shipment.

Should your price be found competitive and delivery time acceptable, we shall place a large order with you.

Yours truly,

Letter 3-10

Dear Sirs,

Thank you very much for your letter of April 28, 2015, we are pleased to send you samples and all the necessary information on Blanket Cover under separate cover.

At your request, we are pleased to make you an offer, subject to your final confirmation, as follows:

Commodity: "Golden Cock" Brand Blanket Cover No. 21
Size: 180cm × 200cm

Color: all kinds of colors

Quantity: 1,000 pieces

Price: GBP20 each piece CIF London inclusive of 3% commission

Shipment: during August/September

Payment: by 100% confirmed, irrevocable L/C in our favor payable by draft at sight to reach the seller one month before shipment, and remain valid for negotiation in China till the 15th day after shipment.

As you will realize from the catalogue we sent you, our Blanket Cover is a perfect combination of warmth, softness and easy care. We are sure that you can get benefit from our products.

We look forward to your prompt reply.

Yours faithfully,

Letter 3-11

Dear Sirs,

We were very glad to receive your order of November 2 for 200 National television sets, but since you make delivery before Christmas a firm condition, deeply regret that we cannot supply you as we have done on so many occasions in the past.

The manufacturers are finding it impossible to meet current demand for this very popular set. We ourselves placed an order for twenty-four sets a month ago, but were informed that all orders are being met in strict rotation and that our own could not be dealt with before the beginning of February.

I gather from our telephone conversation this morning that your customers are unwilling to consider other makes. I hope therefore you will be able to obtain your needs from some other source. May I suggest that you try Television Services Ltd., Dalian? This I am afraid is the only suggestion I can make that is likely to be of some use.

Yours faithfully,

Letter 3-12

Dear Sirs,

We are much honored to receive your repeat order No. 245 for our Bed Sheet. The high quality of our products and the smooth execution of your first order lead to further cooperation between us. We assure you of our full corporation and trust that you will be satisfied with the high quality of our products.

> We are sending you our signed Sales Confirmation No. LY234 in duplicate via courier. Please sign and return one copy for our file. If there is any problem, please do not hesitate to contact us.
>
> As you need this batch of goods urgently, please instruct your bank to open the relevant L/C as soon as possible so that we can arrange shipment in due time.
>
> We are looking forward to your early response.
>
> Yours faithfully,

3.6 练习

Exercises

Ⅰ. Translate the following phrases into Chinese.

1. illustrated catalogue
2. counter sample
3. quantity discount
4. current price
5. in stock
6. inquiry sheet
7. specific inquiry
8. rock-bottom price
9. business capability
10. usual terms

Ⅱ. Choose the best answer.

1. Will you let us know how long _____ will take to deliver the goods?
   A. that
   B. it
   C. this
   D. these

2. We have an inquiry _____ large quantities of chemical fertilizer.
   A. at
   B. for
   C. in
   D. on

3. Your inquiry is having our prompt _____, and we hope to make you an offer in a few days.
   A. attention
   B. settlement
   C. arrangement
   D. notice

4. We trust our offer will be _____ to you and await your order.
   A. accepted
   B. accepting
   C. acceptable
   D. receivable

5. The buyer _____ whom we have discussed the business offers for both rice and wheat.
   A. with
   B. to
   C. of
   D. from

6. It is a pity _____ your offer came at a time when the selling season is coming to a close.
   A. that
   B. which
   C. /
   D. for

7. _____ to your letter enquiring for our TV sets, we have forwarded your inquiry for the attention of the biggest TV company.
   A. Refer
   B. Referring

  C. Referred   D. Relative

8. We shall be pleased to supply you _____ any information you may require on this matter.
   - A. of
   - B. to
   - C. with
   - D. for

9. We shall _____ to your inquiry when our supply position turns better.
   - A. revert
   - B. convert
   - C. reverse
   - D. pay

10. When an importer intends to make purchases of some goods, he sends a letter of _____ to an exporter.
    - A. quotation
    - B. offer
    - C. inquiry
    - D. claims

Ⅲ. Fill in the blanks.

  We were deeply _____ by the wide selection of Jeans _____ on your stand at the Guangzhou Spring Fair in April.

  We are a large garments import corporation in this area and are looking for an exporter who can _____ us with a wide range of Jeans for _____ men and women.

  As we usually place substantial _____, would you please grant a quantity discount of 5%? Meanwhile, our terms of payment are by L/C at _____ . If you are interested _____ the above conditions, and can _____ our orders of over 5,000 Jeans for each selling season, please send us your catalogue and price list.

  We should _____ it very much if you would give us a _____ reply.

Ⅳ. Translate the following sentences into Chinese.

1. We are interested in your Mickey Mouse stationery. Please send us a quotation CIF Dalian, China.
2. We shall be pleased to receive more information on this matter.
3. Under separate cover, we have sent you our samples, our catalogue and price list.
4. We run a retail business of high quality goods for which we obtain high prices.
5. We use the best quality material, and the high standard of workmanship will appeal to the selective customer.
6. We heard that you are able to supply large quantities at more competitive prices so that we prefer to buy from you.
7. At present, supply exceeds demand on building material market at our end.
8. Please inform us how much coal you require annually.
9. We have been in the toy trade for nearly 20 years.
10. Enclosed please find a copy of our latest price list.

Ⅴ. Translate the following sentences into English.

1. 获悉贵公司对我们的产品感兴趣，非常感谢。
2. 我们在当地销售各种塑料制品。
3. 我公司过去从其他公司购买此类商品。
4. 恳请惠寄商品目录、价格和付款方式细则。

5. 我们有各种皮手套，贵方可能会感兴趣。
6. 我们相信，如你方价格有竞争力，我们能向你方经常订购。
7. 请报下列货物的最低价 CIF 上海及最早交货日期。
8. 我们要求的货物应经久耐用、色彩鲜明、富有吸引力。
9. 如蒙告知试用我们产品后的意见，我们将非常感谢。
10. 你方市场另一位供应商以低于类似产品 3% 的价格向我们报盘。

Ⅵ. Writing task.

You are asked to write a letter to a foreign company for a trial order of tablecloths. The letter should cover at least the following points:

（1）The source from which you got the information of the foreign company;

（2）Your desire;

（3）Asking for catalogs, pricelists, etc.

Chapter 4
第 4 章

报盘与还盘
Offers and Counter-offers

Learning Objectives

Enable the students to know the definition of offers and counter-offers; to be familiar with the differences between a firm offer and a non-firm offer, the legal binding effect of a firm offer; to master the structure and common expressions of letters of offers and counter-offers.

使学生了解报盘和还盘的定义；熟悉实盘与虚盘的区别以及实盘的法律约束力；掌握报盘与还盘函件的结构以及常用的表达方式。

4.1 背景知识
Background Information

报盘是销售者为了达成交易而针对买方的询盘报出的贸易条款及条件。在一些特殊情况下，贸易条款和条件是由买方提出的，被称作买方出价。

在商业交易中，报盘分为实盘和虚盘。实盘采用书面形式，在确定的有效期限内不可撤回、取消或修改。如果在报盘有效期内，受盘人接受报盘，则交易达成；否则，报盘失效。

如果是虚盘，报盘条件可以更改或者修正。基于这种原因，虚盘往往有"以我方最后确认为准"的字样，虚盘的作用与报价

An "offer" is the terms and conditions given by the seller in response to an inquiry made by the buyer for acceptance in order to conclude a deal. If, in some special case, the terms and conditions are offered by the buyer, it is called a "bid".

In a business transaction an offer can be a "firm offer" or a "non-firm offer". A firm offer is a written offer that is not to be withdrawn, revoked, or amended during the validity, which is a specified period of time. If the offeree accepts the offer during the period, the transaction is concluded, otherwise, the offer expires.

In a non-firm offer, the terms and conditions can be changed, or amended. For this reason, the phrase "subject to our final confirmation" is always included in a non-firm offer. A non-firm offer often plays the role as a

相同。

虚盘使卖方在选择商业机会及确定成交价格时有更多的时间及灵活性，使卖方在不断变化的市场中处于有利地位。但是，为了有效交易，虚盘最终都会变成实盘。

当受盘人不认可收到的报盘并作出一些更改时，这个更改了的发盘被称为还盘，发盘一经还盘，则原发盘失效。

如果此还盘再一次被修改，就产生了另一个还盘，直到双方都可以接受的还盘出现。这个最终可以接受的报盘是确定的，对双方均具有法律约束力。在商务谈判中，经常会见到达成协议之前经历几轮报盘和还盘。和报盘一样，还盘时，还盘人应非常明确地说明自己的贸易条件，同时用词应非常谨慎以避免产生歧义或误解。

基于对询盘的回复，发出的报盘信通常应包含下列内容：

（1）如果收到对方询盘，应表达对询盘的感谢；

（2）商品名称、品质、数量以及规格；

（3）有关价格、折扣以及支付方式的具体信息；

（4）对于价格构成的明确说明；

（5）包装及交货期；

（6）报盘有效期。

受盘人拒绝报盘的信函应包括以下内容：

（1）感谢报盘；

（2）表达无法接受报盘的遗憾；

quotation.

A non-firm offer allows sellers to have more time and flexibility in choosing business opportunities and making decisions on prices so that they are more favorable to them in a changeable market. However, a non-firm offer will eventually be made into a firm offer in order to be effective in a transaction.

When the offeree disagrees with the offer sent to him or her and makes some changes, the changed one is called a "counter-offer", while the original one, when expired, will be replaced by the counter-offer.

If it is amended again, another counter-offer is made until an acceptable one is worked out. This final and accepted offer is firm and legally binding to both parties. It is not uncommon for a business negotiation to go through several rounds of offers and counter-offers before an agreement is reached. In making a counter-offer, one has to state the terms most explicitly and use words very carefully so as to avoid ambiguity or misunderstanding, the same way as one usually does in making an offer.

In response to an inquiry, an offer may be sent, in which the following are usually covered:

(1) An expression of thanks for the inquiry, if any;

(2) The name of commodities, quality, quantity and specifications;

(3) Details of prices, discounts and terms of payment;

(4) Clear indication of what the prices cover;

(5) Packing and date of delivery;

(6) The period for which the offer is valid.

When an offeree writes a letter to reject an offer, he/she should:

(1) Thanks for the offer;

(2) Express regret at inability to accept;

（3）陈述无法接受的原因；
（4）如果情况适当，作出还盘；
（5）提出其他进行商业合作的机会。

(3) State reasons for non-acceptance;
(4) Make a counter-offer if, in the circumstance, it is appropriate;
(5) Suggest other opportunities to do business together.

4.2 信例
Specimen Letters

Letter 4-1 A non-firm offer of bed sheets

Dear Sirs,

We have received your kind enquiry dated June 20. In compliance with your request, we included in this letter our quotation sheet for bed sheets Art No. 34 and 35.

The respective quantities are quoted on the basis of CFR Port Copenhagen. This offer is subject to our final confirmation. As to the relative samples, we have dispatched them to you by separate airmail.

The Chinese bed sheets are of good quality and have fine workmanship and look good. They are moderately priced, which is known to all. As our stocks are low and the demand is heavy, it is hoped that you will send us your orders as early as possible. If you need any further information about our products, please do not hesitate to let us know by return.

What you mentioned in your letter in connection with the question of agency has been taken into our account. We shall revert to the matter later on.

We will await your esteemed favors and orders.

Yours faithfully,

Letter 4-2 A non-firm offer to a potential customer

Dear Sirs,

Our Commercial Counselor's Office in your country has referred to us your inquiry for cable as it falls within the scope of our business.

We are a big manufacturer of electric goods established in 1995. Our cables and wires enjoy great popularity for the good quality and reasonable prices.

You have many choices in the color and specification. We have sent you this morning our samples and catalogues by EMS.

We present our offer, subject to our final confirmation, as follows:

Specifications	Quantity (meter)	Price (in Euro)
10 amp.	1,000	200
11 amp.	1,000	210
12 amp.	1,000	220
13 amp.	1,000	240
14 amp.	1,000	260
15 amp.	1,000	280

The above prices are on FOB Shanghai basis.

Our term of payment is by letter of credit at sight, and we are able to deliver the cables within one month after receiving your letter of credit.

We are looking forward to receiving your order.

Yours faithfully,

Letter 4-3 A firm offer of printed pure silk fabrics

Dear Sir,

Thank you for your enquiry of October 10, and we take pleasure in quoting the price as shown in the following firm offer delivered today subject to acceptance by 5 p.m., October 20.

Article: No. 8000 Printed Pure Silk Fabrics

Design: No. 46845-2Acm

Specification: 30cm × 36cm

Minimum: 20,000 yards

Packing: in bales or in wooden cases, at the seller's option

Price: US$50 per yard CIF New York

Shipment: to be made in three equal monthly installments, beginning form October, 2017

Payment: by confirmed, irrevocable L/C payable by draft at sight to be opened 30 days before the time of shipment.

We trust you will take advantage of this seasonal opportunity and favor us with an early reply.

Yours faithfully,

Letter 4-4 Declining an offer

Dear Sir,
　　Thank you so much for your offer for Printed Pure Silk Fabrics on October 12.
　　I regret to inform you that our government has just imposed a ban on imports of Printed Pure Silk Fabrics on our market. So we are not in a position to purchase your products at present.
　　However, we have kept your offer in our file and will contact you when the ban is lifted.
　　　　　　　　　　　　　　　　　　　　　　　　　　　　　　　　Yours faithfully,

Letter 4-5 Making a counter-offer of printed pure silk fabrics

Dear Sir,
　　Thank you very much for your reply to our inquiry. We have studied your offer with our clients and we have to say your price is too high to be acceptable.
　　We would have placed a regular order with large quantities with you, but such a high price makes it impossible for us to do so, as it would leave us with little profits. In order to conclude the deal, we suggest you reduce the price by 5%.
　　In view of our long-standing business relationship, we make you such a counter-offer. Cooperation between us will benefit you not only in making exports, but also in expansion of your market.
　　We are obliged for your careful consideration of our suggestion.
　　　　　　　　　　　　　　　　　　　　　　　　　　　　　　　　Yours faithfully,

Letter 4-6 Reply to the counter-offer above

Dear Sir,
　　Thank you for your letter of October 15. Considering the fact that we have done business with each other for over 10 years, we would like to offer you a special discount of 2% in your request for lower prices.
　　The price of US $49 per yard is only valid for the order of this time. Since the silk price is increasingly rising and our own overheads have been going up, absolutely, our price will not remain the old one and probably rise in the near future. Thus, at the end of this October, you will have to go back to the previous price list.
　　Your wholehearted cooperation is very much appreciated.
　　　　　　　　　　　　　　　　　　　　　　　　　　　　　　　　Yours faithfully,

Letter 4-7　Declining a counter-offer

Dear Sir,
　　We thank you for your counter-offer of October 15, in which you asked for a more competitive price.
　　Unfortunately, that is as far as we could go and we have stretched ourselves to the limit. As you know that the silk price is increasingly rising and our own overheads have been going up.
　　Although we are keen to do business with you, we regret that we cannot accept your counter-offer.
　　　　　　　　　　　　　　　　　　　　　　　　　　　　　　　　Yours faithfully,

Notes

1. offer
   n. 发盘；报盘
   firm offer　实盘
   non-firm offer　虚盘
   to extend an offer　延长报盘
   to renew an offer 或 to reinstate an offer　恢复报盘
   to withdraw an offer　撤回报盘
   to decline an offer 或 to turn down an offer　谢绝报盘
   （1）Our offer is valid for 5 days　我们的报盘5天有效。
   （2）We have extended the offer as your request. 我们已按你方要求将报盘延期。
   （3）The offer holds good until 5 o'clock p. m. October 10, 2016, Beijing time.
   　　　报价有效期到2016年10月10日下午5点，北京时间。
   （4）This offer is subject to your reply reaching us before the end of this month.
   　　　该报盘以你方回复在本月底前到达我方为有效。
2. compliance
   n. 依从；恭维；称赞
   in compliance with　依从；依照
   a compliance to　对……的称赞；赞扬……
   （1）Please forward the following articles. Your compliance with our request will be highly appreciated.
   　　　请发送以下商品，如你方照办，则非常感激。
   （2）In compliance with your request, we made readjustment of the date of the shipment.
   　　　按你方的要求，我们对装运日期作了调整。
3. respective
   adj. 各自的；各个的（其后一般接名词复数）

The teas of different grades have their respective prices.

不同等级的茶叶有不同的价格。

4. confirmation

   n. 确认；证实；保兑

   （1）Your immediate confirmation of our offer is appreciated.

   感谢你方迅速确认我方发盘。

   （2）Should you find our offer agreeable, please let us have your acceptance in time for our confirmation.

   如认为我方发盘合理，请及时告知接受，以便我们确认。

5. workmanship

   n. 工艺；手艺；工作质量

   （1）Many people admire her workmanship in knitting.

   很多人都佩服她的编织工艺。

   （2）Our new refrigerator keeps breaking down due to shoddy workmanship.

   我们的新冰箱老坏是因为质量太差。

6. moderately

   adv. 适度地；不过分地

   Though the house is moderately expensive, it is still beyond my reach.

   尽管这套房子价格不是很高，但是我现在还是买不起。

   moderate adj. 中等的；适度的

   The volume of the business we concluded the first half year is moderate.

   我们上半年成交的数额不太大。

7. hesitate

   v. 犹豫不决；迟疑

   We would hesitate before we accept request of price reduction.

   对于是否接受减价的要求，我们要考虑之后才能决定。

8. take into one's account

   考虑；顾及

   （1）She never takes the price into her account when she meets what she really likes.

   当她碰到真正喜欢的东西时，从不考虑它的价钱。

   （2）Their estimate of the cost didn't take inflation into account.

   他们对费用的估算没有把通货膨胀考虑在内。

9. revert to

   回复到；重议

   We would like to revert to your earlier terms and conditions about your export.

   我们想重新谈谈你们原先提出的出口条件。

10. subject to

    以……为条件

    offer subject to our written acceptance　以我方书面接受为准的报盘

    offer subject to sample approval　以样品确定后为准的报盘

offer subject to our final confirmation　以我方最后确认为准的报盘

offer subject to export/import license　以获得出口/进口许可证为准的报盘

offer subject to goods being unsold　以商品未售出为准的报盘

offer subject to your reply reaching here　以你方答复到达我地为准的报盘

11. at sight

 即期

 a draft at sight = a sight draft　即期汇票

 信用证有即期和远期之分，即期信用证可以有如下表示方式：

 a letter of credit available by draft at sight 或 a letter of credit payable against draft at sight；也可以说 a letter of credit payable against sight draft；还可以说 a letter of credit（or an L/C）at sight 或 sight letter of credit（or sight L/C）。

 远期（或迟期）信用证为 usance L/C 或 time L/C 或 term L/C。常见的有见票后 30 天议付的信用证，见票后 60 天议付的信用证及见票后 90 天议付的信用证。见票后多少天议付的信用证的表达法很多，下面以见票后 30 天议付的信用证为例，列举几种比较常见的说法：

 L/C available by draft at 30 days after sight

 （usance/time/term）L/C at 30 days after sight

 （usance/time/term）L/C at 30 days

 30 days（usance/time/term）L/C

 有关信用证的部分常用词组

 confirmed L/C　保兑信用证

 irrevocable L/C　不可撤销信用证

 transferable and divisible L/C　可转让、可分割信用证

 revolving L/C　循环信用证

 back to back L/C　背对背信用证

 reciprocal L/C　对开信用证

12. quote

 v. 报价；引用

 （1）Please quote us your lowest price.

  请向我们报最低价。

 （2）This is the best price we can quote for the goods.

  对于此产品，这是我们能向你方报出的最优惠价格。

13. installment

 分期（付款）；部分

 （1）Payment by installment can be arranged.

  可以安排我们分期付款。

 （2）We'll make shipment in six equal monthly installments beginning from next month.

  我们从下月起分 6 批等量发货，每月一批。

14. take advantage of

 利用

We are regretful that we can not take advantage of your offer of this time.
我们感到很遗憾不能接受你方这次的发盘。

15. position

    n. 状况；处境

    （1）Under the Floating System, the rate of exchange is determined by the demand and supply position on the foreign exchange market.
    按照浮动汇率制度，汇率是由外汇市场上的供求状况所决定的。

    （2）We should like to know if their financial position is sound.
    我们想了解他们的财务状况是否良好。

    （3）We are not in a position to entertain any fresh orders.
    我们无法承接任何新的订单。

16. place

    v. 放置；提交

    （1）When we find your price acceptable, we will place our order with you.
    当我方认为你方价格可接受时，我们会向你方下订单。

    （2）Welcome you to place orders with us for the new grains.
    欢迎订购我们的新产粮食。

17. consider

    v. 认为；考虑

    This credit is to be considered null after October 31, 2014.
    本信用证的有效期到 2014 年 10 月 31 日。

18. do business with

    经营……；与……做生意

    We have done international business with many countries for a long time.
    我们与很多国家做贸易很长时间了。

19. remain

    v. 剩下；保留；仍然是；保持

    Our offer remains valid for 15 days.
    我们的发盘 15 天之内有效。

20. previous

    adj. 之前的；以前的

    I have previous working experience in exporting.
    我先前有做出口贸易的经验。

21. counter-offer

    n. 还盘

    If you cannot accept, please make your best possible counter-offer.
    如你无法接受，请告知最低还盘价。

22. competitive

    adj. 有竞争力的

    competitive price　竞争价格

competitive edge　竞争优势

If your price is competitive, we will place an order with you.

如果你方价格有竞争力，我们将向你方发出订单。

compete　v. 竞争

compete with (or against) sb. in sth. 在……方面与某人竞争

We should compete with other enterprises in the quality of the products.

我们必须在产品质量上与其他企业竞争。

compete with (or against) sb. for sth. 为……事情与某人竞争

We must compete against other countries in trade for obtaining larger international market.

为了获取更大的国际市场，我们必须与其他国家在贸易方面进行竞争。

competition　n. 竞争

To enable us to meet competition, you must quote the lowest possible price.

为了使我们应对竞争，你方必须报尽可能低的价格。

competitor　n. 竞争者；竞争对手

We trust that the superior quality, attractive design and reasonable price of our products will surely enable us to defeat the competitor.

我们相信我方产品的优良质量、诱人设计、合理的价格定能使我方击败竞争对手。

23. stretch ourselves to the limit

让步到最大限度

24. increasing

adj. 日益增多的；增加的

We are expecting increasing cooperation with you.

我们期待与你们的合作越来越多。

Words and Phrases

conclude	v. 得出结论；断定
deal	n. 交易；协议
bid	v. 出价；投标
transaction	n.（一笔）交易
offer	v. 报价；出价　n. 报价
withdraw	v. 撤回；撤销
revoke	v. 撤销；取消；废除
amend	v. 改良；修改；修订
validity	n.（法律上）有效；合法
enforceable	adj. 可强行的；可实施的
expire	v. 期满；（期限）终止
satisfactory	adj. 令人满意的；符合要求的
quality	n. 质量
quantity	n. 数量

specification	n. 说明书；详细的计划书
discount	n. 折扣
indication	n. 指示；表示
packing	n. （货物）包装
delivery	n. 交货；发送的货物
quotation	n. 报价
flexibility	n. 弹性；适应性
negotiation	n. 协商；谈判
reject	n. 拒绝；谢绝
appropriate	adj. 适当的；恰当的
explicitly	adv. 明确地
destination	n. 目的地
dispatch	v. 派遣；发送
esteem	v. 尊重；敬佩；珍重
manufacturer	n. 制造商；制造者
decline	v. 下降；减少
client	n. 顾客
profit	n. 利润
absolutely	adv. 绝对地；完全地；独立地
keen	adj. 热心的；热衷的；热情的
regret	v. 遗憾；惋惜
non-firm offer	虚盘
counter-offer	还盘
response to	回复
subject to	以……为条件
date of delivery	交货日期；发运日期
in compliance with	依从；按照
revert to	回复到；重议
at sight	即期
take advantage of	利用
in view of	鉴于；考虑到

4.3 外贸实战技巧
Techniques in Foreign Trade Practice

收到询盘后应如何报盘？

总体来说，在收到对方询盘后要及时、有礼貌、有针对性地答复对方询问的所有信息及提供对方要求的资料。报盘信要使对方感觉到该产品在交易中有吸引力。信中通常包含主要交易条件、发盘有效期及其他约束条件。在报盘时应注意以下几点：

1. 做好市场调研，掌握市场最新动态

由于现今市场信息透明度高，市场价格变化迅速，因此，必须依据最新的行情报出价格，买卖才有成交的可能。这就要求卖方在关心自己成本和价格的同时，也要关注同行的成本与价格，做到知己知彼。此外，还要了解这个行业的发展和价格变化历史，从而对近期的走势做出合理的分析和预测。

2. 认真分析客户购买偏好、意向及需求

有些客户将价格作为最重要的因素，如果一开始就报出具有吸引力的价格，则赢得订单的可能性就会大很多；而有的客户有还价的习惯，总觉得报价中含有水分，无论多低的价格，总要砍价，这就需要分清客户的购买意愿和意图，然后再决定是报虚盘还是实盘。

3. 主动推荐优势明显、有独特卖点的产品报价

工厂能生产的产品型号、规格都比较有限，客户询价型号太多太杂的时候，切忌面面俱到，尤其是针对无规格、无数量、无要求的询盘，更需要突出优势产品，强化独特卖点。挑选几个优势明显、有独特卖点的产品报价，可附上最低配置款和最高配置款商品的价格，即区间价格，然后再根据客户的回复进行下一步的磋商。

4. 作出完整报价

完整报价非常重要，特别是针对新客户，在报价表中要体现以下几个方面的内容：价格术语、产品尺寸、清晰的产品图片、包装明细、内盒/外箱的尺寸、装柜量、箱柜、品名、货号、颜色、材质、价格有效期、付款条件等。报价最好附图，对于网上来的询盘，可以把产品图片、包装图片、装箱图片、效果图片发给客户，让客户在看到价格的同时能够看到图片。

5. 报价不能太低

根据以往的经验，报价高，成交价高；报价低，成交价低；报价太低，不成交。价格太低会被人认为质量有问题，或者材料廉价，是廉价货。因此，应在市场现行价格区间范围内，视情况选择较高价格作为报价，在此基础上，再进行进一步磋商。报价方法可以采用美式报价（报一个有余地的价格让客户砍价）或日式报价（报一个最低配版本价格，之后根据客户的要求增加价格）。

4.4 有用的句子

Useful Sentences

1. Our prices are highly competitive when you consider quality.

   如果你们考虑质量的话，我们的价格是很有竞争性的。

2. With reference to your enquiry of July 10, we shall be pleased to supply 50 sets of scanner at the price of US $110 each.

   感谢您7月10日的询盘，我方很高兴以每台110美元的报价供应50台扫描仪。

3. Our offer is reasonable and realistic. It comes in line with the prevailing market.

   我方的报价是合理的、现实的，符合当前市场的价格水平。

4. If you insist on your price and refuse to make any concession, there will be not much point in further discussion.

   如果你方坚持自己的价格，不作让步，我们就没有必要再谈下去了。

5. It is absolutely out of the question for us to reduce our price to your level.

我们不可能将价格降到你方所要求的那么低。

6. We quote you our best price for the following goods, and shall be pleased if you can favor with your orders.
   在此就以下商品向贵公司报我方最低价,盼惠顾试购。

7. We thank you for your offer, but we regret that we are not in need of these goods. We will surely bear you in mind for future demand.
   感谢贵方的报价,但遗憾的是,我公司目前不需要这些货物。我们会记住贵公司,并在将来有需要时接洽贵方。

8. In addition, there will be a discount of 2% on total cost of payment within one month form date of invoice.
   此外,如果从发票日期起一个月内付款,还可以享受2%的折扣。

9. I'm sorry. The different between our price and your counter-offer is too wide.
   很遗憾,我们的价格与你方还盘之间的差距太大。

10. The prices quoted will apply only to order received by September 30.
    所报的价格仅适用于9月30日之前收到的定单。

11. The offer made is subject to the acceptance within a week.
    报盘有效期为一周。

12. This offer is for acceptance within 10 days.
    此报盘必须在10天之内接受有效。

13. Our offer will be withdrawn if not accepted within 14 days.
    如果14天之内未被接受,我们将撤回发盘。

14. If the quantity of the goods does not conform to that stipulated in the contract, the importer will refuse to accept the goods.
    如果货物数量与合同规定的不符,进口商将拒收货物。

15. If you can't arrange for the entire quantity, please offer us at least half.
    如果你们全数办不到的话,请至少给我们半数。

4.5 补充商务信函
Letters for Further Reading

Letter 4-8

Dear Sirs,
　　We thank you very much for your letter of June 30, asking for our leather handbags, together with our latest catalogue.
　　Being requested, we enclose our latest price list of this month. A very full range of the handbags have been sent to you by sample post today, and we are confident that, after examining them, you will see that the quality and the prices of the goods we offer you compare favorably with any others, for the same class of goods.

We can assure you that these goods are very popular in western markets, of which we have had much experience. We are continually issuing new designs and we are delighted to submit further samples to you if there are orders from you in succession from now on.

In case of an order for more than 500 pieces, we would grant a special discount of 5% for settlement within 10 days of invoice.

We hope that this will lead to an enduring connection with you.

Yours faithfully,

Letter 4-9

Dear Sirs,

Many thanks for the enquiry of March 12th, 2017. We have pleasure in quoting as follows:

Commodity: White 50/50 polyester/cotton mixture men's shirts as per samples, label No. 203 in assorted sizes between 35-44, individually packed in plastic bags and boxed in 100's, no less than 50 of each size, packed in export crates of 1,000 shirts.

Unit price: US $5 per shirt FOB Dalian

Payment: by a confirmed irrevocable letter of credit opened in our favor with the Commercial Bank of Japan, Industrial Area Branch.

Quantity: minimum order 1,000 shirts, maximum present capacity 10,000 shirts per month.

Delivery: within 3 months of notification of receipt of letter of credit.

Validity: this quotation is firm for orders dispatched before August, 2016.

We hope that this meets with your approval. Please let us know if you require any further information or samples.

Yours faithfully,

Letter 4-10

Dear Sirs,

We confirm your fax of 5th September asking us to make you firm offers for both cotton and tea. We faxed back this morning, offering you 50 metric tons of cotton at US $700 net per metric ton CIF Copenhagen or any other European Main Port for shipment during October/November, 2016. This offer is firm, subject to the receipt of reply by us before September 25.

Please note that we have quoted our most favorable price and are unable to entertain any counter-offer.

As regards tea, we would inform you that the few parcels we have at present are under offer elsewhere. However, if you should make us an acceptable bid, there is a possibility of your obtaining them.

As you are aware that there has been lately a large demand for the above commodities, such growing demand has doubtlessly resulted in increased prices. However, you may avail yourselves of the advantage of this strengthening market if you will send us an immediate reply.

Yours faithfully,

Letter 4-11

Dear Sir,

Thank you for your letter of August 3, 2017 inquiring about our Forever Brand bicycles.

We are exporting bicycles of many makes, among which the Forever Brand is the most famous. Our products are in great demand and enjoy high sales due to their light weight, good quality and reasonable price.

As requested, we are quoting as below:

20" men's style	USD 27/unit
20" women's style	USD 29/unit
26" men's style	USD 30/unit
26" women's style	USD 32/unit

Payment: by confirmed, irrevocable, sight L/C

Shipment: within three weeks after receiving the L/C

The above prices are understood to be on CIF Karachi basis net. Please note that we do not allow any commission, but a discount of 4% will be granted if the quantity for each specification is more than 1,000 units.

The above offer is firm, subject to your reply reaching us by August 15, 2017.

We look forward to receiving your order.

Yours faithfully,

Letter 4-12

Dear Sirs,

We have been very satisfied with your products. However, we feel your price is too high to accept.

We find that we can obtain a price of $5.00 per piece with a local firm. This is much lower than your price of $8.00 per piece. Unless you see your way clear to meeting these figures, we will not place with you an order that will carry us for the rest of this year. That order is probably to be one of the largest that we have ever placed with you.

We shall eagerly wait for your reply before we decide where to place our order.

Yours faithfully,

Letter 4-13

> Dear Sirs,
>   We thank you for your offer by fax of September 3 for 5,000 pieces of the captioned goods at Stg. £ 9.50 per piece CIF Hamburg.
>   We immediately contacted our customers and they showed great interest in the quality and designs of your products. However, they said your price is too much on the high side, i.e., 10% higher than the average. They told us if you can reduce your price to Stg. £ 8.55 per piece, they will increase 1,000 pieces to the quantity. So there is a good chance of concluding a bigger transaction with them if you can meet their requirement. We hope you will take advantage of this opportunity so that you will benefit from the expanding market.
>   We await your favorable reply with great interest.
>   Yours faithfully,

4.6 练习
Exercises

Ⅰ. Translate the following phrases into Chinese.
1. termination of an offer
2. net price
3. firm offer
4. condition of sales
5. similar products
6. non-firm offer
7. after-sales service
8. at the buyer's option
9. minimum quantity for order
10. article number

Ⅱ. Choose the best answer.
1. We have been _____ with that firm for many years.
    A. making business   B. contacting
    C. dealing   D. supplying
2. Please make serious efforts to get goods _____ immediately.
    A. dispatching   B. dispatched
    C. to dispatch   D. being dispatched
3. At your _____, we are making you the following offer subject to your reply reaching here before July 15.
    A. request   B. requirement
    C. need   D. offering
4. To be frank with you, the price we quoted you only allow us a very small _____ of profits.
    A. quotation   B. margin
    C. order   D. price
5. We are not in a _____ to accept your bid at the present state of the market.

        A. way   B. position
        C. state   D. means
    6. We are making you our quotation for shoes _____ .
        A. as follows   B. as following
        C. as follow   D. following
    7. Please let us know _____ the lowest prices at which you can execute this order.
        A. in return   B. by return
        C. on return   D. at return
    8. The market is strengthening, so it is _____ that we will not be able to quote the same price next time.
        A. sure   B. surely
        C. certain   D. certainly
    9. Please _____ us 500 glass vases CIF Qingdao, China.
        A. offer   B. make
        C. supply   D. bid
    10. This is our best price, _____ which we have already concluded several transactions with your competitors.
        A. in   B. of
        C. at   D. on
Ⅲ. Fill in the blanks.
    1. If you _____ _____ to reduce the price _____ 5%, we shall place an order _____ you.
    2. Our offer is _____ for 10 days, _____ _____ your reply reaching us before April 20.
    3. We are unable to reduce the price to the level you _____ .
    4. While we appreciate your intention to do business with us, we regret that we cannot _____ any fresh orders, as we are heavily committed.
    5. There is a heavy demand _____ bicycles now and we are _____ _____ _____ stock.
    6. Please note that a 5% _____ applies to orders for each item exceeding 1,000 instead of 5% commission.
    7. _____ of your offer would make your bicycles uncompetitive with other stores in our region.
    8. In this case, we are willing to make a(n) _____ as an introduction of bicycles on your market.
    9. It will not be possible for us to accommodate your _____ for a price reduction.
    10. Please _____ us your lowest prices for both men's and women's winter jackets.
    11. The offer is to be _____ if not accepted by the end of this month.
    12. If you care to place an order with us any time in the future, you may be assured _____ the same prompt attention which you have had in the past.
    13. We are sorry to say it is not possible _____ us to meet the price you requested.
    14. In reference to your letter, we cannot _____ a better offer than the one we suggested to you.
    15. We hope that upon reconsideration you will be able to _____ our offer.

16. After discussing the matter with our Board of Directors, we have decided we can comply _____ your request for lower prices.
17. We are aware _____ the fact that your goods are among the best on the market.
18. Our offer is a non-firm offer. It is _____ _____ our final confirmation.
19. _____ _____ _____, we found the quality of the shipment is not satisfactory.
20. If you can _____ the price, we might place a large order.

Ⅳ. Translate the following sentences into Chinese.
1. We're prepared to purchase a shipment quantity of this material.
2. The quantity of rice imported this year is approximately the same as that last year.
3. 5,000 square meters of wool carpet is bigger than any order we've ever placed.
4. We would be willing to discuss a volume discount if the quantity of your order is doubled.
5. Enclosed please find our quotations which are open for two weeks only.
6. We are anxious to do what we can to help you to establish your new business and are prepared to allow you a special discount of 3% if payment is made within one month.
7. Thank you for your letter of December 23 asking us to offer you 10,000 metric tons of the wheat in subject for shipment to Singapore in February.
8. There is not any room for our price to go down.
9. The market is firm and tending upward. There is little likelihood of significant change in the foreseeable future.
10. It is regretful that we cannot entertain your counter-offer.

Ⅴ. Translate the following sentences into English.
1. 2009年1月1日以后我国的出口退税率要降低4%，我们的价格也会相应提高。因此我们希望你方尽早接受我们的再还盘。
2. 由于市场价格正在下跌，我们建议你们立即接受。
3. 坦率地说，我们很遗憾地发现你方的价格偏高，所以我们建议你们给我方一个折扣。
4. 很遗憾，我方不能接受贵方报盘，因为贵方市场的其他供应商以比你方价格低3%的条件向我方提供几乎同样的货物。
5. 鉴于我们之间长久以来的贸易关系，特作此报盘。
6. 我方货物优于市场上其他同类产品，其设计独特，款式新颖且价格合理，近年来一直畅销。
7. 我们的报盘有效期至本周末。
8. 现答复贵方的报价，很遗憾地告知贵方我们的客户认为你们的价格偏高而且与市场行情不符。
9. 希望贵公司认真考虑我方的还盘，如接受，请及早告知为盼。
10. 如不能接受我方报价，请尽可能提出最有效的还盘。

Ⅵ. Writing task.
   You receive an enquiry for tablecloths. Enclose your price list and make a firm offer on CIF basis for delivery during September, and allow a discount of 5% if the order is over USD 5,000, which is the best price you can quote. Require payment by irrevocable L/C reaching you one month before the time of shipment.

1. Begin by repeating the enquiry including the date and the product concerned.
2. Make an offer with necessary details.
3. Describe your product to induce an order.
4. End your letter with expectation.

Chapter 5 第 5 章

订单与确认
Orders and Acknowledgements

Learning Objectives

Enable the students to know the definition of orders; to be familiar with the information that should be included in the letters of order, acceptance and rejection; to master the basic sentences and common expressions in these types of letters.

使学生了解订单的含义;熟悉订购、接受及拒绝订单信函应包括的信息;掌握撰写此类信件的基本句式以及常用的表达方式。

5.1 背景知识
Background Information

订单是订购货物的合同或单据,它要求卖方或供货方按照特定的贸易条件提供确定数量的货物。订单通常以信函或印制的格式订单形式发出。老客户经常会使用格式订单,而新客户或者只下一次订单的客户通常采用信函的方式。订单信应包括完整、清晰的基本交易条件,如商品描述、数量、价格、包装、装运以及支付等。

收到订单信后,卖方通常要发送认收函。一旦订单被接受并确认,交易即达成。一般来说,合同或者确认书可由买方或卖方

An order is a contract or document for ordering goods, which is a request for the seller or supplier to supply a particular quantity of goods according to specified terms and conditions. Usually, the order is given by letters or in printed forms. Regular customers will probably use a form while a new customer or one placing a single order often writes a letter. An order letter should include full and clear essential details, such as description of goods, quantity, price, packing, shipment and payment etc.

After receiving a letter, the seller usually send acknowledgement by letter. Once accepted and confirmed, the business is concluded. Generally, a contract or a confirmation is made out by the seller or the buyer and signed by both parties. However, there are

草拟,并且由双方签署。但是,也有卖方由于库存有限、价格变动或者对买方信用存疑而无法接受买方订单的情况,在这种情况下,拒绝订单信件的写作一定要格外小心,并着眼于未来。

撰写订购信时,应注意以下几点:

(1)确认购买并且提出建议的运输方式。在订购信的开头,应使对方立即知晓这是购货确认而不仅是询问信息。直接用订单类语言开头,例如"请发贵方商品目录中的……商品"。

(2)列出关于交易的所有条件。当订购许多商品时,为了使订单清晰,便于理解,可以在信的主体部分采用列举格式(使用数字和符号突出重点)。力求包含尽可能多的具体信息:订单号、数量、完整的商品描述、单价以及总价。订单信中提供的信息越多,出现错误的可能性则越小。

(3)期待货物发运。在订单信的结尾部分,可以要求在某一具体日期前装运,告知对方支付方式,并表示感谢。

接受订单的信函应包括以下内容:

(1)表达很高兴收到订单。

(2)确认交易达成,列出出口商与进口商之间在先前谈判中所达成的所有交易条件:货号、数量、规格、品质、单价、总价、装运期、包装、保险、支付方式。

(3)期盼收到更多订单。

拒绝订单的信函通常包括:

(1)感谢订单;

times when the seller can't accept the buyer's orders because of the limited stock, change of price, or buyer's suspectable credit, etc. In such situations, letters of rejecting orders must be written with the utmost care and with an eye to the future.

In a letter of ordering goods, the following points should be paid attention to:

(1) Authorize purchase and suggest method of shipping. In the opening, let the reader know immediately that this is a purchase authorization and not merely an information inquiry. Begin directly with order language such as "Please send me the following items from your merchandise catalog".

(2) List all the terms concerning the deal. When many items are ordered, to make your order clear and easy to understand, you could use the listing format in the body of your letter (use numerals and symbols to highlight the main points). Include as much specific data as possible: order number, quantity, complete description, unit price and the total amount. The more information you provide, the less likely that a mistake will be made.

(3) Anticipate dispatch of the goods. In the closing part, you may request shipment by a specific date, inform the method of payment, and express appreciation.

A letter of acceptance should include the following contents:

(1) Express pleasure in receiving the order;

(2) Confirm the conclusion of the business and point out the full details of article number, quantity, specification, quality, unit price, total value, shipment, packing, insurance and terms of payment as agreed upon in preliminary negotiations between the exporter and the importer;

(3) Hope for further orders.

A letter of rejecting always includes:

(1) Thanks for the order;

（2）拒绝订单并说明原因；	（2）Reject the order and explain the reasons;
（3）提供其他替代商品；	（3）Offer the substitutes;
（4）期望及早回复。	（4）Hope for early reply.

5.2 信例
Specimen Letters

Letter 5-1　Placing a trial order

Gentlemen:

　　Thank you for your offer of May 4. We have studied your catalogue and price list and have chosen four models for which we enclose our order.

　　We are glad to hand you a small order by way of trial and if we are happy with your shipment, you can expect our regular repeat orders. In order to avoid difficulties, please make sure that our shipping instructions are carefully followed.

　　For our credit standing, we refer you to our banker, Bank of China, Liaoning Branch, Dalian.

Truly yours,

Letter 5-2　Placing a purchasing order

Dear Sirs,

　　We appreciate your letter of October 5 sending us your quotation and samples. We find both quality and prices satisfactory. Enclosed herewith please find our Order No. 111.

　　We would appreciate early delivery since we are starting an employee recognition program on February 12. Enclosed is our bank's draft for USD 2,000.

　　Please send us your Sales Confirmation in duplicate as soon as possible. Thank you for your prompt attention.

Yours faithfully,

Letter 5-3　Acknowledgement of the purchasing order

Dear Sirs,

　　We are pleased to receive your order of July 8, and we welcome you to be one of our customers.

We hope the payment to be made by a confirmed and irrevocable letter of credit payable at sight upon presentation of shipping documens, Please inform us immediately if you agree to our terms. The moment we receive your reply in the affirmative, we will confirm the supply of the goods, and we will arrange for dispatch by the first available steamer upon receipt of your L/C.

We believe that you will be completely satisfied with them at the prices offered when the goods reach you.

As you may not know the wide range of our goods, we are enclosing a copy of catalogue and hope that our handling of this first order of yours will lead to further business between us and mark the beginning of a happy working relationship.

Yours faithfully,

Letter 5-4 Confirming an order

Dear Sirs,

We are very pleased to receive your order No. MT178. We accept your order on the terms and conditions stated in your letter as follows:

Commodity: Maotai Alcohol

Alcohol Content: 50%~53%

Capacity: 500ml/bottle

Quantity: 200 dozen

Price: USD 200 per doz. CIF Antwerp

Packing: in case of 24 bottles

Shipment: in October, 2017

We are working on your order. As we can supply the goods from stock, we can assure you that we shall meet your deadline. Please open the relevant L/C immediately to enable us to make shipment promptly. We are confident that our product will be a success in your market.

We are enclosing our Sales Confirmation No. 8456 in duplicate. Please sign and return one copy for our file.

We are looking forward to a happy working relationship with your company.

Yours faithfully,

Letter 5-5 Rejecting the buyer's delivery terms

Gentlemen:

Thank you for your fax of Order No. 11. Through careful consideration, we decided to decline your order, because we think it will be impossible to meet your required shipment date before November 15, 2016.

> We are really sorry about being unable to take your order, but hope that you will understand our position. Please let us have any other inquiries, as we shall be only too pleased to meet your requirements if it is within our power.
>
> Truly yours,

Letter 5-6 Confirming a repeat Order

> Dear Sirs,
>
> Thank you for your fax duplicating your order of May 12 for 1,000 doz. Rubber Shoes.
>
> The prevailing quotations are somewhat higher, with the view of encouraging business, we will still accept the order on same terms as before.
>
> As requested in your previous letter, we have made out our Sales Confirmation No. 500 in duplicate and shall thank you to send back one copy duly countersigned.
>
> We are glad to know that a letter of credit will be established in our favor immediately. However, we would like to draw your attention to the fact that the stipulations in the relative credit should strictly conform to the terms in our Sales Confirmation to avoid subsequent amendments.
>
> We appreciate your cooperation and trust that the shipment which is to be dispatched after receipt of the relative letter of credit will turn out to your entire satisfaction.
>
> Yours faithfully,

Notes

1. order

    n. 订单;订货;订购的货物

    place an order with sb. for sth. 向某人订购某物

    (1) We are glad to place an order with you for 50 cases Black Tea.
    我们乐于向你方订购红茶 50 箱。
    (2) We'll accept your order if partial shipments are allowed.
    如果允许分批装运,我们可接受订单。
    (3) The balance of your order will be supplied once the fresh supply comes in.
    一旦新货进来,你方所定的其余货物将被马上供应。
    (4) We will ship our order in May.
    我们将在 5 月装运你方所订货物。

    与订单有关的词组:
    fresh order   新订单
    new order   新订单
    initial order   初次订单

trial order　试订单
repeat order　续订单
duplicate order　重复订单
to accept an order　接受订单
to confirm an order　确认订单
to cancel an order　取消订单
v. 订货
If you order immediately, we can make shipment this month.
如你方立即订购，我们可在本月装运。

2. credit standing
   信用状况，类似表达：credit position 或 credit status

3. satisfactory
   adj. 令人满意的
   （1）If the prices are reasonable and qualities satisfactory, we shall be able to place substantial order.
   如果价格合理，质量满意，我们将大量订购。
   （2）We believe such an arrangement will prove satisfactory.
   我们相信那样的安排会令人满意。
   satisfy　v. 使满意；满足
   Our customers will try their best to satisfy your requirement for Christmas Decorations.
   我们的客户将会尽最大努力来满足你们对圣诞饰品的需求。
   satisfaction　n. 满意
   We trust our goods will reach you in good time and turn out to your full satisfaction.
   我们相信我们的货物将如期到达，并使你们完全满意。

4. herewith
   adv. 同此 = with this
   正式书面用语，常用于正式文件、声明等。类似表达方式有：
   hereafter　此后 = after this
   hereby　在此 = in this
   hereafter　在下文 = in a following part of
   hereunder　在下面 = under this
   hereof　关于此 = of this
   hereto　附此 = to this

5. appreciate
   vt. & vi. 感激；感谢
   （1）I appreciate your help. 我感谢你的帮助。
   （2）We appreciate your efforts for the development of the company.
   我们感谢你对公司发展所作的努力。
   （3）We greatly appreciate your timely help.
   我们非常感谢你们的及时帮助。

鉴赏；欣赏；赏识
（1）Do you appreciate good wine? 你会鉴赏好酒吗？
（2）I think that young children often appreciate modern pictures better than anyone else.
我认为小孩对现代图画往往比任何人都更有鉴赏力。

察觉；意识到
（1）We appreciate the danger ahead. 我们意识到危险临头。
（2）We appreciate your difficulty. 我们意识到你们的困难。

（财产等）增值
（1）This land has appreciated in value. 这块土地增值了。
（2）Houses in this area have all appreciated in value since the new highway was built.
由于修建了新公路，这一地区的房屋都涨价了。

6. Sales Confirmation
销售确认书
Sales Contract　销售合同
Purchase Confirmation　购货确认书
Purchase Contract　购货合同

7. duplicate
adj. 复制品；副的；完全相同
（1）The duplicate copy of the Sales Confirmation is to be kept by us.
此销售确认书的副本由我保存。
（2）We intend to place a duplicate order and wonder if you could accept.
我们打算重复订购，不知你们能否接受。
n. 复制品；副本
v. 复写；复制；使加倍
in duplicate　一式两份
in triplicate　一式三份
in quadruplicate　一式四份
一式四份及以上的也常说 in four copies（in four fold），in five copies（in five fold）等。

8. presentation
n. 提示
We trust you will meet the draft on presentation. 我们相信你方将见票即付。
present　v. 提示
We trust you will meet the draft when presented. 我们相信你方将见票即付。

9. in the affirmative
同意的/地，肯定的/地
Your reply in the affirmative = your affirmative reply

10. work on
v. 对……起作用；从事
（1）He comes to visit his aged parents after work on every Friday.
每个星期五下班后，他去看望年迈的父母。

(2) I'd like to take this opportunity to thank everyone for their hard work on the project.
我愿借此机会感谢每一位为这个项目辛勤工作的人。

11. deadline

    最后期限

    meet the deadline 赶上最后期限

    (1) The boss will really give it to you if you miss the deadline for the job.
    要是到期完不成工作，老板就要给你点厉害。

    (2) The deadline is drawing near, we can't delay any more.
    限期快到了，不能再拖延。

12. relevant

    adj. 相关的；切题的；中肯的

    (1) She gobbled up all the relevant information.
    她如饥似渴地收集一切有关的信息。

    (2) This type of university course is no longer relevant to today's problems.
    这类大学课程对当今的问题而言已没有实际价值。

13. prevailing

    adj. 现行的；流行的

    prevailing price 现行价格

    The prevailing opinion is that the stagnation is about over.
    现在普遍流行的观点就是停滞将要结束。

14. with the view of

    以……为目的

    We give you this special accommodation with the view of cementing our relations.
    为了增进我们的关系，我们给予特殊照顾。

15. make out

    填写；开列；制出

    Please make out your Sales Contract in three originals.
    请作出三份正本销售确认书。

16. conform

    v. 使一致；符合

    (1) It is necessary to conform the specifications to the requirements.
    有必要使规格符合要求。

    (2) This does not conform to the contract. 这个不符合合同。

    conformity   n. 符合；一致

    in conformity with（或 in conformity to 和……一致；依照）

    This is not in conformity with our arrangement. 这与我们的安排不一致。

17. subsequent

    adj. 以后的

    This applies to all subsequent transactions. 这适用于以后的所有交易。

    subsequent to   在……以后

The date of this order is subsequent to your Order No. 70.
该订单的日期是在你方第 70 号订单之后。

18. dispatch

    n. 发送

    v. 发送；迅速办理

    (1) Please do your best to hasten the dispatch of our Order No. 65.
    请尽力加速对我方第 65 号货物的发送。

    (2) We are anxious to dispatch the matter in hand.
    我们渴望快速处理手头的事情。

19. turn out

    结果成为；结果是

    We hope everything will turn out (to be) satisfactory in the end.
    我们希望一切事情结果都将会令人满意。

Words and Phrases

trial	n. 试验；测试
appreciate	v. 感激；感谢
quotation	n. 报价；行情
satisfactory	adj. 令人满意的；符合要求的
herewith	adv. 因此；同此
duplicate	n. 完全一样的东西；复制品
affirmative	adj. 肯定的
range	n. 一系列；范围
inquiry	n. 打听；询问
countersign	v. 副署；联署
amendment	n. 修改；改动
irrevocable	adj. 不可改变的；不可撤销的
branch	n. 分支
recognition	n. 识别；承认
prompt	adj. 立刻的；迅速的
confirm	v. 证实；证明
dispatch	v. 调遣；发送
acknowledge	v. 告知已收到；感谢
commodity	n. 商品；货物
deadline	n. 最后期限
with the view of	为了……
credit standing	信誉
satisfy with	对……感到满意

5.3 外贸实战技巧
Techniques in Foreign Trade Practice

格 式 订 单

  订单是订购货物的合同或单据，它是为了要求卖方或供货方供应某一特定数量、型号、款式等货物而提出的一种要求。交易一方将自己的订单寄给对方，以确保对方能够据此履行交货以及交单等义务。根据商法的规定，买方订单只是一种购买意愿的表示，其在信函中所做出的购买安排不具有法律约束力，只用在卖方表示接受后才具有法律约束力。为了方便买方发出简洁、具体、全面的订单，一些公司多采用已经印制好的格式订单作为订单函件的附件寄送给对方，供对方确认接受。典型的附有格式订单的函件如下：

Dear Sirs,

  We thank you for your letter of July 24. Enclosed please find our Order Form No. 345 for three of the items.

  All these items are urgently required by our clients. We therefore hope that you will make delivery at an early date.

Yours faithfully,

Encl.：ORDER FORM

ORDER FORM

ORDER NO.：345
DATE：July 27, 2017

COMPANY：International Trading Co. Ltd.　　　　ORDERED BY：Robert White
TEL：43783783　　　　　　　　　　　　　　　DELIVERED TO：567 Main Street, London
ATTN：Mr. Nelson　POST：Sales Manager
TEL：87367362　FAX：87367346
E-mail：export123@hotmail.com

	DESCRIPTION	QUANTITY	UNIT PRICE (FOB DALIAN)	AMOUNT
1	B375 Portable Radio	20 units	USD 30	USD 600
2	A43 Portable Video	200 units	USD 1,200	USD 240,000
3	C89 Crassest Radio	100 units	USD 100	USD 10,000
TOTAL		USD 250,000		

PACKING：to be packed in wooden cases
SHIPMENT：prompt shipment
PAYMENT：by irrevocable L/C available by draft at sight

5.4　有用的句子
Useful Sentences

1. With reference to the faxes exchanged between us in the last few days, we are pleased to have been able to finalize the following transaction with you.
   参考过去几天我们彼此互发的传真，我们很高兴能够和你方定下以下交易。
2. We are glad to have finalized/put through/closed/concluded this transaction/business with you.
   我们很高兴和你方成交。
3. We thank you for giving us a trial and promise that your order will be dealt with promptly and carefully.
   感谢你们的试用，同时我方承诺你们的订单将被快速、认真的处理。
4. We have received with thanks your quotation of…and are pleased to send you the following order, which we trust will receive your best attention.
   我们感谢你们……的报价，同时我们欣然订货如下，相信该订单将得到你方认真的处理。
5. We have received your letter of…and should be glad if you would accept our order for the following goods.
   我方已收到你方……的来信，同时如果你方将接受以下货物的订购，我方将会很高兴。
6. We thank you for your quotation of…and enclose our order for the following.
   我们感谢你方……的报价，同时随附对下述货物的订单。
7. Although your price is below our level, we accept, as an exception, your order with a view to initiating business with you.
   虽然你方的价格低于我方的水平，为了开始和你方的交易，作为特例，我们接受你方的订货。
8. We trust we may have further orders from you as time goes on.
   我方相信随时间推移你方将会再次订购。
9. We look forward to receiving your further orders.
   我方期望收到你方的续订单。
10. Please forward the goods named below in strict accordance with the following instructions.
    请严格依照以下指示交付以下货物。
11. Please supply the goods in strict conformity with the particulars given, any deviation from which will be at your own risks, unless agreed and authorized by us.
    除非我方同意并授权，否则请严格按照所提供的资料供货，如有偏离，将由贵方自行承担风险。
12. As this is a trial order, we trust you will attend to it with special care.
    因为这是一次试购，我方相信你方将会格外小心处理。
13. We shall be grateful for prompt delivery as the goods are needed urgently.
    由于急需货物，若能即期交货，我们将不胜感激。

14. We look forward to receiving your advice of shipment at an early date.

    我们期待早日收到你方装船通知。

15. Please deal with the order as one of special urgency.

    请作为特别紧急的订单处理。

5.5 补充商务信函
Letters for Further Reading

Letter 5-7

Dear Sirs,

Re: "Good Boy" Toys

We have received the goods under Sales Confirmation No. 8456. We are glad to inform you "Good Boy" Toys are very popular with children here.

We believe we can sell additional quantity. We would like to place a repeat order for 100 more for type I and type II respectively on the same terms as stipulated in the above Sales Confirmation.

As we are in urgent need of the goods, please effect shipment as soon as possible. We are looking forward to receiving the goods.

Yours faithfully,

Letter 5-8

Dear Sirs,

We have received your letter of May 24. We note with pleasure that you have decided to purchase from us 10,000 metric tons of Copper Concentrates on the basis of our offer, to be delivered in one shipment before the end of July.

We thank you for the confidence you place in us. The draft contract is being drawn up and will be submitted to you for approval as soon as ready.

We share your hope that the deal concluded will pave the way for further friendly cooperation between our two concerns and be of mutual benefit.

Yours faithfully,

Letter 5-9

Dear Mr. Dillon,

We are in receipt of your letter of March 8. In reply, we regret that we are not in a position to accept your order No. 324. The price of this item has risen sharply recently due to its strengthening market and its short supply. Under such circumstance, we have no choice but to increase the price. So if you intend to buy, you should increase the price at least by 10%.

It is in view of our long friendly cooperation in business that we offer you at such a favorable price. We recommend you to take advantage of this and accept our price without hesitation.

Best wishes,

Letter 5-10

Dear Sirs,

We're glad that your clients have accepted our prices, which are narrowly calculated. These goods will be packed in boxes of half a dozen each and 10 dozen to a carton, and shipped in December from China port to London with transshipment and partial shipments allowed. Insurance is to be covered by us against All Risks and War Risk for 110% of the invoice value.

Enclosed is our Sales Contract No. 116 signed in Beijing on November 28, 2017 in duplicate, a copy of which please sign and return.

Yours faithfully,

Letter 5-11

Dear Sirs,

We are pleased to have received your letter of August 4 together with your order for a number of items inclued in our quotation JY045.

All the items ordered are in stock except the last item Model 456. Stocks of the items have been sold out since we quoted for them, and will not be available again by the end of this year.

As you state that delivery of all items is a matter of urgency, we would like to recommend Model 458 as a substitute which is identical in design and quality with the item ordered. It is very popular with our other customers, and perhaps more suitable for your purpose. Though the price is US$72, the improvements made on the older model certainly more than offest the difference of US$3 in price.

> Please let us know whether you can accept it. If you give us your consent, we can ship the good in time.
>
> Yours faithfully,

Letter 5-12

> Dears Sirs,
>   We refer to your Order No. 675 and regret to say that we are not able to accept your bid price for Frozen Rabbit Meat.
>   As you may be aware that the prices for foodstuffs have gone up sharply owing to the rough weather, so it is impossible to purchase supplies at economic prices. Moreover, we have improved our packing method, as you may have seen from our samples, which cost us a lot. The price, therefore, is 8% higher than your bid.
>   For the market is firm with an upward tendency, we advise you to accept our price without delay. In view of our long business connection, we will definitely keep supplies available for you if you amend the price in your order within 3 days.
>
> Yours faithfully,

5.6 练习

Exercises

Ⅰ. Translate the following phrases into Chinese.
   1. initial order   6. sales contract
   2. execute a contract   7. repeat order
   3. price gap   8. in duplicate
   4. purchase confirmation   9. pricing method
   5. additional order   10. counter sign

Ⅱ. Choose the best answer.
   1. A Sales Confirmation should be countersigned by _____ .
      A. the seller   B. the buyer
      C. both parties   D. the bank
   2. _____ an order for 100 pieces or more, we allow a special discount of 5% for payment by L/C.
      A. At   B. In
      C. On   D. From
   3. If business had been carried out to our satisfaction, we _____ to renew the Agency Agreement.
      A. had agreed   B. already agreed

C. shall agree　　　　　　　　　　D. should have agreed
4. Any alteration in design would mean re-setting our machines, and the cost of this would be prohibitive _____ you could place an order for more than 5,000.
　　A. until　　　　　　　　　　　　B. with
　　C. unless　　　　　　　　　　　　D. when
5. Please see to it that the goods we ordered are shipped as soon as the covering letter of credit _____ you.
　　A. gets　　　　　　　　　　　　B. comes
　　C. arrives　　　　　　　　　　　D. reaches
6. According to the shipping _____, it will be impossible for us to ship the goods in October.
　　A. schedule　　　　　　　　　　B. timetable
　　C. plan　　　　　　　　　　　　D. scheme
7. We enclosed our Purchase Confirmation No. 4848 _____ duplicate.
　　A. in　　　　　　　　　　　　　B. for
　　C. with　　　　　　　　　　　　D. through
8. The shipment time is June or July at our _____ and the goods will be shipped in one _____.
　　A. option...for　　　　　　　　　B. option...consignment
　　C. choice...shipment　　　　　　D. decision...cargo
9. As it _____ only a small quantity, we hope you will have no difficulty in settling this matter.
　　A. involves　　　　　　　　　　　B. involved
　　C. has involved　　　　　　　　　D. may have involved
10. We are glad that we have _____ an agreement on this matter.
　　A. comes　　　　　　　　　　　　B. got
　　C. reached　　　　　　　　　　　D. arrived

Ⅲ. Fill in the blanks.
1. We have received with _____ your Quotation No. 668 and are pleased to send you the following order, which we trust will receive your best attention.
2. As this is a trial order, we trust you will attend _____ it with special care.
3. We look forward to receiving your advice _____ an early date.
4. Thank you very much for your _____ order and we hope that this may be the beginning of a long and a friendly connection with your firm.
5. Enclosed please find our Sales Contract No. 668 in duplicate. If you find everything in order, please sign and return one copy for our _____.
6. You will be advised _____ the time the machines are ready _____ shipment.
7. The relative L/C will be airmailed soon and you are requested to ship the above lot _____ the first available steamer _____ receipt _____ our L/C.
8. If the quality of your initial consignment turns _____ to be satisfactory, we can assure you _____ repeat orders.
9. We appreciate your recent efforts _____ prompting the sale _____ our products.
10. We are well experienced _____ this line and can place orders with you _____ large

quantities if your prices are attractive enough.
11. We confirm the sale _____ you of 100 tons groundnuts resulting _____ letters exchanged.
12. We hope we will have the pleasure _____ supplying you grain.
13. Please refer _____ the e-mails exchanged _____ us in April.
14. Contracts must be renewed one week _____ their expiration.
15. To avoid possible dispute _____ quality, both sides should describe the goods clearly in the contract.

Ⅳ. Translate the following sentences into Chinese.
1. We have received your letter of September 20, 2016 together with an order for 1,000 Sewing Machines. Enclose is our Sales Confirmation No. 346 in duplicate, one copy of which please sign and return to us for our file.
2. We'll certainly keep your requirement before us if we are able to get more goods next year.
3. If you want to purchase this product, we are able to supply as much as you require.
4. If you can persuade your end-user to accept this product, we can supply more.
5. We are pleased to give you an order for the following items on the understanding that they will be supplied from current stock at the prices named.
6. We expect to find a good market for these table linens and hope to place further and larger orders with you in the near future.
7. We appreciate your cooperation and look forward to receiving your further orders.
8. We'd like to cancel the order for the goods because of the change in the home market.
9. Your order is receiving our immediate attention and you can depend on us to effect delivery well within your time limit.
10. We shall greatly appreciate any order that you may have for us and feel confident that it will be filled to your satisfaction.

Ⅴ. Translate the following sentences into English.
1. 如果价格合理，质量满意，我们将大量订购。
2. 谢谢3月6日来信及所附的第123号订单。
3. 我们很高兴确认与你方达成了以下交易。
4. 请你方注意，信用证的条款必须与我方销售确认书的条款完全相符，以避免事后修改。
5. 随函附上试购订单一份。如果质量达到我们的要求，不久我们就会大量订购。
6. 如果能立即处理该订单，我们不胜感激。
7. 请注意做到货物必须在本月底运达我方。
8. 如果你方订购3 000箱以上，我们就削价2%。
9. 你方所报商品规格与我们所询不相符。
10. 由于大量承约，我们不能接受新订单。

Ⅵ. Writing task.
Write a letter to your customer, acknowledging receipt of his order, but regret being unable to accept it because the price leaves you very small profit. Make suggestion to them for approaching you in the future.

Chapter 6
第 6 章

支付方式
Terms of Payment

Learning Objectives

Enable the students to know about the importance of payment in the performance of business contract; to identify the modes of payment; to learn how to write the letter about payment.

使学生了解付款在商务合同履行中的重要性;熟悉各种支付模式;掌握有关支付的信函写作技巧。

6.1 背景知识
Background Information

支付方式的确定是国际货物买卖中必要的组成部分,也是主要的交易条款。国际支付方式与国内支付方式相比更加复杂、烦琐,主要原因为:

(1) 卖方并不了解买方,交易中涉及长距离运输和更多的程序;

(2) 完成付款需要的时间较长;

(3) 各国所采用的贸易制度和法律体系存在差异,使结算方式更为复杂;

(4) 货币和金融制度在各国存在差异,所采用的支付方式也存在差异。

Terms of payment are one of the main trading conditions as well as an indispensable part in the international sales of goods. International payment terms are much more complicated and difficult compared with domestic transaction payment arrangement for the following reasons:

(1) The seller usually does not know the buyer; long distance and more procedures are involved;

(2) Long time is needed in settling payments;

(3) Different regulations and systems of law that are applied further complicate the arrangements;

(4) The monetary and financial matters are different in the different countries and various methods are used.

根据支付时间安排的不同，付款方式可以分为以下几种：

（1）提前支付；

（2）货到付款；

（3）赊账。

一般来说，基本国际贸易支付方式有汇付、托收和信用证。

（1）汇付。汇付是指买方根据合同条款，通过银行或其他形式将货款转给卖方，汇付是最简单的国际结算方式，多适用于提前付款、订单付款及赊账等贸易模式。汇付方式涉及四个基本当事人：汇款人、收款人、汇出行和汇入行。根据不同的汇款方式，可分为：电汇、信汇和票汇。

（2）托收。托收是指债权人开出以买方为付款人的汇票，委托其所在地银行（托收行）通过其在买方所在地联行或代理行（代收行）向买方收取货款。托收的当事人包括委托人、托收行、代收行和付款人。托收分为付款交单（D/P）和承兑交单（D/A）两种形式。

（3）信用证。信用证作为当前广泛使用的国际结算方式，是指银行作出担保，只要出口商提交信用证要求的单据，就能拿到货款。信用证属于银行信用，银行充当进出口商的中间人，这不同于汇付和托收的商业信用。因此，信用证作为一种安全且可靠的支付方式，能促进卖方与不知名的买方之间的交易，保证买卖双方的利益。信用证的基本当

According to different payment time arrangements, the modes of payment can be divided into the following groups:

(1) Cash in advance (Advance payment/payment in advance/payment prior to delivery);

(2) Cash on delivery/Payment after arrival of the goods/Payment after delivery;

(3) O/A (Open account/Deferred payment).

Generally speaking, the basic methods of payment are remittance, collection and letter of credit.

(1) Remittance. It means the transfer of money through banks or other forms from the buyer to the seller according to the conditions stipulated in the contract. It's the simplest mode of payment in international trade and widely used for payment in advance, cash with order and open account business. There are four parties involved in the remittance operation: Remitter; Payee/Beneficiary; Remitting Bank and Paying Bank. It is divided into three forms of mail transfer; M/T, T/T and D/D.

(2) Collection. It means that the creditor (seller/principal/drawer) will issue the bill of exchange on the buyer and entrust the bank in the exporting country (remitting bank) to collect the payment of the shipment through the remitting bank's overseas branch or its correspondent bank in the buyer's country (Collecting Bank). The parties to a collection include: principal, remitting bank, collecting bank and payer. There are two types of collection: Documents against Payment (D/P) and Documents against Acceptance (D/A).

(3) Letter of Credit. Letter of Credit, as the most generally used method of international payment nowadays, is a banker's guarantee that payment will be made on presentation of all the required documents. It belongs to bank credit and the bank serves as the intermediary between the buyer and seller which is different from the commercial credit of remittance and collection. Thus L/C is a reliable and safe payment mode, facilitating trade with unknown buyers and giving protection to both sellers and buyers. The main parties involved in the L/C operations are Applicant, Issuing/Opening bank,

事人有：开证申请人、开证行、通知行、受益人、议付行和付款行。对于信用证的具体解释，我们可以参考国际商会第 600 号出版物《跟单信用证统一惯例》。

当撰写关于支付方式的信函时，首先应建议付款条件，可以销售合同为参考提出相关建议及惯例，然后要求对方接受。最后，应表达希望早日得到回复等期望。

而作为回信，首先应表明信函已经收到，同时对于所收到信函的内容再进行重述。

在回信中，表明接受或拒绝的态度并说明理由，若同意，应表达相互包容，充分考虑对方要求以及希望成功合作等愿望。若拒绝，则表明拒绝的必要性及理由，并表达愿意将来继续合作的意愿。

Advising/Notifying bank, Beneficiary, Negotiating Bank and Paying Bank. About detailed explanation to the L/C, we may refer to the Uniform Customs and Practice for Documentary Credit of International Chamber of Commerce Publication No. 600.

When writing letters about discussing the mode of payment, we should suggest the payment terms in the letter at first, so we can identify the reference such as S/C and suggest the terms of payment and usual practice, and then ask for acceptance. At last, we express our wish about early reply, etc.

As reply letter, the statement about that the last letter has been received should be written and then the main idea in the last letter should be repeated here.

Give your reply of agreeing or refusing and your reasons. If agreeing, express the wish to accommodate each other, consideration to the reader's request and the willingness of successful cooperation, etc; if refusing, stating the necessity and reasons; express your good will to further cooperation.

6.2 信例
Specimen Letters

Letter 6-1　Requesting easier terms of payment

> Dear Sirs,
>
> 　　In the past, our purchases of enamelware from you have normally been paid as a rule by confirmed, irrevocable letter of credit.
>
> 　　This arrangement has cost us a great deal of money. From the moment we open the credit to the time our buyers pay us, the tie-up of funds lasts about four months. This is currently a particularly serious problem for us in view of the difficult economic climate and the prevailing high interest rates.
>
> 　　If you could kindly offer us easier payment terms, it would probably lead to an increase in business between our companies. We propose either "cash against documents on arrival of goods", or "drawing on us at three months' sight".
>
> 　　Your kindness in giving priority to the consideration of our request and giving us early favorable reply will be appreciated.
>
> 　　　　　　　　　　　　　　　　　　　　　　　　　　　　　Yours faithfully,

Letter 6-2 Requesting modified payment terms

Dear Sirs,

We want to buy 800 casks iron nails at your price of USD 100.00 per cask CFRC3% London for shipment during July/August.

We would like to pay by 30 days L/C for this order. Involving about USD 80,000, this order is comparatively a big one. As we have only moderate means at hand, the tie-up of funds for three to four months is a big problem for our company.

We highly appreciate the support that you have extended us in the past. If you can do us a special favor this time, please send us your contract, upon receipt of which we will establish the relative L/C as soon as possible.

Yours faithfully,

Letter 6-3 Accepting the buyer's proposal to payment terms (Reply to letter 6-2)

Dear Mr. James,

Thank you for your order for 800 casks iron nails by your letter of January 15.

We have taken your proposal to pay a 30-day letter of credit into account. We do not usually accept time credit. However, in light of our long and mutually beneficial cooperation, we are willing to make an exception for you.

We must point out that this departure from our usual practice relates to this transaction only. We cannot regard it as setting a precedent for future transactions.

We enclose our Sales Contract No. 100 covering the order. We would be grateful if you would follow the usual procedure.

Yours sincerely,

Letter 6-4 Requesting D/P payment terms

Dear Mr. Smith,

With reference to your Sales Confirmation No. 256 dated May 8, covering lumber in the amount of GBP 900 and Contract No. 257 for iron pipe in the amount of USD 750.

As both of these contracts are each of a value of less than US$1,000, we shall be glad if you agree to ship the goods to us as before on Cash Against Documents (CAD) basis.

We hope that you will accommodate us in this respect and trust that this arrangement will meet with your approval.

We look forward to your early reply.

Yours sincerely,

Letter 6-5 Accepting the buyer's request of D/P payment terms

Dear Mr. Green,

We are in receipt of your letter of March 10, requesting Documents Against Payment for contract No. 374 and No. 375.

We agree to D/P payment terms for these two contracts. However, we consider it advisable to make it clear that in future transactions, direct payment will only be acceptable if the amount involved for each transaction is below USD1,000 or the equivalent in Renminbi (at the conversion rate then prevailing). Should the amount exceed that figure, payment by L/C would be required.

We would like to say that we extend you this accommodation only in view of our long and mutually beneficial cooperation.

Yours sincerely,

Letter 6-6 Advising the establishment of an L/C

Dear Sirs,

We would like to draw your attention to our Order No. 321 for 5,000 sets of Sony Color TV.

On 3 April, we sent you a letter of credit which expires on 30 June. This is our busy season and our buyers urgently need the goods. We shall therefore be very grateful if you ship the goods as soon as possible.

We must stress that any delay in shipping the order will involve us in problems with our buyers, which could affect our future business.

Your earliest reply will be highly appreciated.

Yours faithfully,

Letter 6-7 Urging the establishment of an L/C

Dear Sir,

<u>Our Sales Confirmation No. 518</u>

 Referring to the 10,000 pieces of blouses under our Sales Confirmation No. 518, we wish to call your attention to the fact that the date of delivery is drawing near, but up till now, we have not received the covering letter of credit. Please do your utmost to expedite its establishment, so that we may execute the order within the prescribed time.

 For your information, S. S. Peace is due to sail for your port around middle of next month, according to the shipping company here. If we have your L/C before the end of this month, we might catch that steamer.

 In order to avoid subsequent amendments, please see to it that the L/C stipulations are in strict conformity with the terms of the contract.

 We look forward to receiving your favorable response at an early date.

Yours faithfully,

Letter 6-8 Suggesting amendments to the L/C (1)

Dear Mr. Gray,

 Your letter of credit No. 2233 issued by the Bank of Barclays has arrived. On examination, we find that transshipment and partial shipment are not allowed.

 As direct sailings to Liverpool are infrequent, we have to ship via London more often than not. As a result, transshipment may be necessary. With regard to partial shipment, it would speed matters up if we could ship immediately the goods we have in stock instead of waiting for the whole shipment to be completed.

 With this in mind, we faxed you today, asking for the letter of credit to be amended to read: "partial shipment and transshipment allowed".

 We trust this amendment will meet with your approval and you will fax us to that effect without delay.

Yours sincerely,

Letter 6-9 Suggesting amendments to the L/C (2)

Dear Mr. Quek,

We have received your Letter of Credit No. 8788 with thanks, but we regret to say that there are some discrepancies between your L/C and the Sales Contract No. 0112 which are as follows:

Your L/C No. 8788

1) Transshipment not allowed
2) Equal part shipment in March and in April
3) No "more or less" clause

The S/C No. 0112

1) Transshipment allowed
2) Shipment not later than April 1
3) 5% more or less allowed

In order to effect shipment smoothly, please make necessary amendments to your L/C with the least possible delay.

Sincerely yours,

Letter 6-10 Requesting extension of the L/C

Dear Mr. Green,

Thank you for your letter of credit covering your order for 20 metric tons of frozen meat. We regret to say that, owing to a delay on the part of our suppliers, we will not be able to get the shipment ready before the end of this month. We faxed you earlier today to that effect.

We expect that the consignment will be ready for shipment in the early part of September. We are arranging to ship it on the S.S. May Flower sailing from Boston on 3 September.

We are looking forward to receiving your faxed extension to the letter of credit so that we can effect shipment of the goods.

We send our sincere apologies for the delay and trust that it will not unduly inconvenience you.

Yours sincerely,

Notes

1. tie-up funds

   占压资金

   The request for easier payment terms is compelled by their funds being tied up in numerous commitments.

   由于资金被许多业务占用,他们迫不得已要求较宽松的付款条件。

2. easy payment terms

   易于接受的支付条件；宽松的支付条件

   （1）They ask for easier payment terms because their funds are tight.

   他们要求较宽松的支付条件是因为他们资金紧张。

   （2）Easier payment terms would be conducive to our business with you.

   宽松的支付方式将有助于我们彼此间的业务。

3. draw

   v. 开出（汇票）

   draw（a draft）on sb. at…sight for an amount against sth. through…bank

   根据……向某人开出金额为……的……汇票

   （1）We regret to note that our 30 days draft drawn on you was dishonored.

   我们遗憾地得知以你方为付款人的 30 天汇票被拒付了。

   （2）We have drawn a sight draft on you against the documents for the amount of invoice through the Bank of Asia.

   我们已根据这些单据通过亚洲银行向你方开立了发票金额的即期汇票。

   （3）Please confirm that we can draw on you at 60 days after sight for US＄28,000.

   请确认我方可以向你方开出金额为 28 000 美元的 60 天远期汇票收款。

4. pay

   v. 付（款，费用）

   to pay in advance　预付

   to pay by installments　分期付款

   to pay on delivery　货到付款

   （1）We trust you will pay our draft on presentation.

   我们相信你方在见到我们的汇票时即照付。

   （2）The price of goods can be paid by installments.

   货款可以分期支付。

   payable　adj. 应付的（款项）；可付的

   bills payable　应付票据

   amount payable　应付金额

   account payable　应付账款

   a check payable at sight　见票即付的支票

   payment　n. （不可数）支付；（可数）支付的款项

   payment terms（terms of payment）　支付条件；付款条件

   payment in advance　预付货款

   deferred payment（payment on deferred terms）　延期付款

   cash payment　现金付款

   in payment of　付某种费用的款，如发票、费用、佣金等

   in payment for　付某种具体实物的款，如广告、商品、样品等

   （1）We enclose a check for US＄3,000 in payment of all commissions due to you up to date.

   随函附上 3 000 美元支票一张，以支付截至目前所欠你方的全部佣金。

(2) We have received your check for US $ 300 in payment for the samples we sent you last month.

收到你方 300 美元支票，支付我方上个月寄给贵公司的样品。

(3) Our payment terms are by a confirmed L/C payable by draft at sight.

我们的付款条件是以保兑的即期信用证支付。

(4) We have heavy payment to make before the end of this month.

本月底我们要支付一些巨额款项。

5. exception

n. 例外

make an exception to do sth. 破例

exceptional adj. 例外的；特殊的

as an exceptional case 作为例外；作为特例

exceptionally adv. 例外地；破例地

(1) In compliance with your request, we will accept delivery against D/P at sight as an exceptional case.

根据你方要求，我们破例同意以即期付款交单的方式交货。

(2) Demand for your products has been exceptionally heavy since last Christmas.

自去年圣诞节以来，对你方产品的需求一直格外地大。

6. departure

n. 背离；违背；离开（后接介词 from）

(1) It is a departure from your promise.

这违背了你方的诺言。

(2) We can get the goods ready before the ship's departure.

我们能在起航前将货物备妥。

7. usual practice

通常惯例；习惯

international business practice 国际商务惯例

customary practice 习惯做法；惯例

It is our usual practice to ask for sight L/C, no matter the order is large-sized or small-sized.

不管订单大小，我们的通常做法是要求即期信用证。

8. precedent

n. 创……的先例

set a precedent 开创先例

take/regard sth. as a precedent 将某事当作先例

(1) Our accommodation in this respect should not set a precedent for future transactions.

我们在这方面的通融不能为以后交易开创先例。

(2) It must be clearly understood that, in so doing, we are not establishing a precedent.

必须清楚地了解，我们这样做不是在建立一个先例。

(3) This way of settling the case would set an awkward precedent.

这样解决此案将开创一个尴尬的先例。

9. amount

   n./v. 数额；金额；总额；（金额）合计；达到

   for/in the amount of　金额计

   to the amount of　金额计（常指较大金额）

   amount to…　金额达到

   come to an amount of　金额达到

   amount due　到期应付金额

   outstanding amount　未付款

   amount in arrears　（过期未付的）欠款金额，拖欠金额

   （1）We have pleasure in sending you herewith our invoice for the amount of $1,000.

   我们高兴地随函寄上我方发票，金额为1 000美元。

   （2）We can assure you that these increases in price will not amount to an average of more than 5%.

   我们保证价格增长平均不会超过5%。

   （3）The total amount of your L/C should be US $15,000.

   你方信用证总金额应为15 000美元。

10. involve

    v. 涉及；包括；牵涉

    involve sb. in…把某人牵涉到……中

    （1）The extra premium involved will be for buyer's account.

    发生的额外保险费将由买方负担。

    （2）The matter involves a series of problems, such as patent, pricing of equipment and sales volume of the product.

    此事涉及专利、设备的作价及产品销售量等一系列问题。

    （3）To airmail the goods would involve a lot of expenses.

    航空邮寄此货，费用昂贵。

    （4）We don't want to involve you in any unnecessary trouble and expenses.

    我们不想给你方带来任何不必要的麻烦和费用。

11. equivalent

    n. 等值；等价；等价物　adj. 等值的；相当的

    be equivalent to

    （1）What is the equivalent of US $100 in pounds sterling at the current cross rate?

    按现行兑换率，100美元折合多少英镑？

    （2）One US dollar is equivalent to RMB ×× at the current conversion rate.

    按当前汇率，1美元相当于人民币××元。

12. conversion rate

    汇率

    conversion rate　通常指本币与外币之间的兑换率

    cross rate　通常指外币之间的汇率

    exchange rate　汇率

13. figure

    n. 数字（有时指价格） v. 计算；估计

    figure out   总计（at）；计算出；领会到；琢磨出

    (1) We cannot do business at your figure.
        我们不能按照你方价格成交。
    (2) The figure quoted by you is too high.
        你方报价太高。
    (3) Sales in the last three months figures out at about $230,000.
        前三个月的销售额合计23万元。
    (4) You can figure out the total amount according to the monthly sales volume.
        你可以根据月销售额计算出总额。
    (5) I can't figure out the exact meaning of the paragraph.
        我琢磨不透这段的确切含义。

14. draw one's attention to

    请……注意；提请……注意

    Similar expressions：

    invite/call/direct/bring one's attention to…

    (1) We would like to draw your attention to the fact that the validity of the L/C is drawing near. Please do your utmost to effect shipment without further delay.
        请你方注意这样一个事实，信用证的有效期已临近。请尽力完成装运，不得有进一步的延误。
    (2) We would like to call your attention to the quality of the goods.
        提请你方注意产品的质量。

15. expire

    v. 期满

    expiration   n. 期满；终止

    expiry   n. 期满；截止日期

    (1) The L/C expires on May 15.
        信用证于5月15日期满。
    (2) The shipment must arrive here before the expiration of the license.
        这批货物必须在许可证期满前运到。
    (3) The date of expiry of the L/C is May 15.
        信用证的截止日期是5月15日。

16. be in urgent need of sth

    急需

    Similar expressions：

    be badly in need of sth.

    be in great need of sth.

    Please do your utmost to expedite the shipment of our order as our buyers are in urgent need of the goods.

请尽快装运我方所订购货物，因为我方买主急需该货。
17. referring to

提及；关于；参阅

表示关于的其他介词短语：

with reference to

with regard to

as regards

regarding

as to

about

in connection with

respecting

in respect of

(1) With regard to the point you have just raised, we will have it investigated.

关于你方刚刚提出的问题，我们将进行调查。

(2) As to Item 3 in the contract, we have instructed our bank to open the covering L/C.

关于合同中的第三条款，我们已通知银行开立信用证。

(3) Kindly let us hear from you regarding the possibility of shipment to be made in June.

请来信告知你方能否在6月装船。

(4) In respect to the time of shipment, we want the goods to be delivered in October.

关于装运时间，我们希望十月交货。

refer to   v. 咨询；查询；参考；提及；谈及

refer sb. to 使某人向……请教；使某人向……查询（询问）

(1) As to our credit standing, you may refer to the Bank of China.

关于我方的资信状况，请向中国银行查询。

(2) You may refer to the Bank of China for today's exchange rate.

你可向中国银行咨询今日汇率情况。

(3) We wish to refer you to the recent exchange of faxes and are pleased to confirm having concluded with you a transaction of 500 m/ts of Bitter Apricot Kernels.

请参阅近日往来传真，并高兴地确认与你方达成了500吨苦杏仁的交易。

(4) We refer to your letter of December 6.

兹提及你方12月6日的来信。

18. expedite

v. 加快（进程等）；促进（措施等）；迅速处理（事务）

expedite/rush the establishment/opening/issuing of the L/C   加速开立信用证

Please try your best to expedite the establishment of the relative L/C.

请尽力加快有关信用证的开立。

19. execute

v. 执行

execution n 执行；履行

（1）We believe you will do your utmost to execute our first order as it will lead to a series of transactions between us.
我们认为你方会尽最大努力执行我方第一个订单，因为它将带来一系列交易。

（2）We assure you of our punctual execution of your order.
我们保证准时执行你方订单。

（3）Our best and prompt attention will be given to the execution of this order.
我方将妥善、迅速地处理这一订单。

（4）We cannot execute your order for lack of particulars.
没有详细说明，我们无法执行你方订单。

（5）All disputes in connection with this Contract or the execution thereof should be settled amicably by negotiation.
涉及本合同的争执或执行本合同过程中所发生的一切争执应通过友好协商予以解决。

（6）We always do our best to execute our contracts to the full.
我们始终是竭尽全力执行合同。

20. prescribe

v. 规定

within the prescribed/stipulated/agreed time（limit） 在规定的时间内

（1）We refer you to your L/C No. 2003 which prescribes that transshipment is not allowed.
请查阅你方第 2003 号信用证，该信用证规定不允许转船。

（2）We trust you will ship our order within the time prescribed.
我们相信你方会在规定的时间内装运我方订货。

21. due

a. 适当的；应有的；应得的

（1）After due consideration, we have decided to grant your request.
经过适当考虑，我们决定接受你方的要求。

（2）We trust the shipment will reach you in due course.
我们相信这批货将按期到达你处。

b. （票据等）到付款日期的；到期的

The draft will fall due on May 20.
汇票于 5 月 20 日到期。

c. 应当支付的；所欠的

The remittance is in payment of all commissions due to you up to date.
这笔汇款是支付迄今为止欠你方的各项佣金。

d. （预定）应到的；预期的

due to do 定于（某时做某事）

due for 应该得到

（1）The flight is due to arrive at Shanghai at noon.
航班预计中午到达上海。

（2）Both sides are due to sign a contract in the next week.

双方定于下周签订合同。

（3）Our salary scales are due for revision next year.

明年我们的薪水等级应该修改。

due to 由于（作状语）；应属于；应给予；应到的（作表语或定语）；欠……

The shipment was delayed due to bad weather.

装运延误是由于恶劣的天气。

22. see to it that

要注意使……；务必使……；保证使……

（1）Please see to it that the stipulations in the L/C should be in strict accordance with those of the contract.

务请你方确保信用证的条款要与合同的条款完全一致。

（2）Please see to it that the L/C is timed to reach here before the end of this month.

请注意安排使信用证在月内到达这里。

（3）Please see to it that the L/C is opened 30 days before the time of shipment.

请确保信用证在装运期前 30 天开出。

23. be in conformity with

与……一致；遵照

Similar expressions：

conform to

comply with

correspond with

abide by

in compliance with

in accordance with

in agreement with

as requested

at one's request

by request

24. examination

n. 检查；检验

examine　v. 检查；检验

upon/on examination　一经检验就……

after examination　经过检验后……

（1）Distributor shall permit examination by the producer at any time of such accounts and any contracts with his retailers.

经销商允许厂家随时检查他与零售商的账户和合同。

（2）Upon examination, we have found there are some discrepancies in your L/C.

经审核发现你方信用证有与合同规定不符的地方。

25. amend

v. 修改

amendment   n. 修改；修改书

amendment advice = advice of amendment   修改通知书

(1) The wording of the agreement calls for amendment.
协议书的措辞需要修改。

(2) Please rush the amendment to the L/C.
请对信用证速作修改。

(3) Please amend the amount of the L/C to read "5% more or less allowed".
请将信用证上的金额修改为"允许5%上下幅度"。

(4) Please amend the credit as allowing partial shipments.
请将信用证改为允许分批装运。

(5) Any and all amendments of this agreement shall be adhered to and binding upon the parties.
本协议的任何修改必须遵守，并对当事人具有约束力。

26. via

prep. 由；通过；取道

(1) The goods will go via Hong Kong.
这批货物将由香港转运。

(2) The goods are to be shipped to Vancouver, thence via Overland to Montreal.
货物由船运到温哥华，再由温哥华陆运至蒙特利尔。

(3) The sample you required were sent via airmail.
你方要求的样品已航空寄去。

27. to that effect

意思是……

to this effect

to the above effect

(1) We wrote you last week to the effect that we were inspecting the goods.
上周我们给你去信，大意是说我们正在检查这批货物。

(2) We are faxing you to this effect.
我们按这个意思传真给你方。

28. discrepancy

n. 异样；差异；不一致

(1) In case of any discrepancies between unit prices and total amount, unit prices shall govern.
如果单价与总金额之间有出入，应以单价为准。

(2) Please check the discrepancies between the original estimate of the cost and the actual bills.
请核查原有的成本估算表与实际账单之间的差额。

(3) We have received your L/C No. 555, but find it contains the following discrepancies.

我们已收到你方第 555 号信用证，但发现其中有下列不符之处。

29. without delay

    尽早地；早日的；立即

    Similar expressions：

    without any delay

    with the least possible delay

    at an early date

    at your earliest convenience

    at an early moment

    as soon as possible

    by return

    before long

    by (on, at) the earliest opportunity

    without fail

30. more or less

    溢短装条款；或多或少

    (1) We examined them one by one and found that each of them was leaking more or less.

    我们一个一个地检查，发现每个都有不同程度的渗漏。

    (2) Discount will more or less encourage us to make every effort to push sales of your products.

    折扣或多或少能给我们一些鼓励，能使我们更加努力地推销你方的产品。

31. on the part of sb.

    就……而言；在……方面

    (1) The fault is on the part of the shipping company.

    这是轮船公司方面的错误。

    (2) On our part, we always keep to our promise.

    就我们这方面来说，一贯遵守诺言。

    (3) We are sorry that owing to some delay on the part of our suppliers, we are unable to get the goods ready before the end of this month.

    很遗憾，由于我供货商的延误，我方无法在本月底前将货物备妥。

32. extension

    n. 延长；展期；分机

    extension advice   展期通知

    extension 101   101 号分机

    (1) We have to ask for a two-week extension of the validity of the L/C.

    我们不得不要求将信用证有效期延长两周。

    (2) Emphasis has to be laid that shipment must be made within the prescribed time limit, as further extension will be not considered (or will be out of the question).

    特别要强调一下，一定要在规定的期限内交货，再次延期是不容考虑的。

    extend   v. 延长；使展期；扩展；给予

(1) We hope you will extend your offer for two weeks.
我们希望贵方能将报盘延长两个星期。

(2) Please extend the validity of the L/C to September 1.
请将信用证的有效期延长至 9 月 1 日。

(3) We plan to extend our business to your area.
我们打算将业务扩展到你们地区。

(4) Let me extend warm welcome to our guest.
请让我向我们的客人表示热烈的欢迎。

(5) We shall appreciate the accommodation extended to us.
我们将感激你们给予的这一通融。

33. accommodate

v. 通融；照顾；容纳；接纳；提供；供给

accommodate sb. by doing sth. 提供照顾

accommodation n. 通融；照顾

accommodating adj. 通融的；照顾的

unaccommodating adj. 不肯通融的；不肯照顾的

(1) As a special accommodation, we will accept time L/C at 30 days.
作为一项特殊照顾，我们接受 30 天的远期信用证。

(2) We sincerely hope that you will not think us unaccommodating.
希望你方不要认为我们是不肯通融的。

(3) We hope you will accommodate us by allowing 5% commission.
望你方能通融，允许给我方 5% 佣金。

Words and Phrases

issuance	n. 出票
presentation	n. 提示
acceptance	n. 承兑
payment	n. 支付
endorsement	n. 背书
discount	v. 贴现
dishonor	v. 拒付
recourse	v. 追索
remittance	n. 汇付
remitter	n. 汇款人
payee	n. 收款人
collection	n. 托收
principal	n. 委托人
drawee	n. 付款人
applicant	n. 开证申请人

beneficiary	n.	受益人
fund	n.	资金；基金
currently	adv.	目前
particularly	adv.	特别是，尤其是
propose	v.	提议；建议
lumber	n.	木材
acceptable	adj.	可以接受的
prevailing	adj.	当前的
exceed	v.	超过
infrequent	adj.	稀少
association	n.	关系；协会
comparatively	adv.	比较地，相当地
present	v.	提出；出示
transshipment	n.	转船
unduly	adv.	过度地；不适当地

negotiating bank	议付行
paying bank	付款行
banker's demand draft	银行即期汇票
cash in advance	预付货款
cash on delivery	货到付款
open account	记账
lump sum payment	一次性付款
payment by installments	分期付款
remitting bank	汇出行；托收行
paying bank	汇入行
mail transfer（M/T）	信汇
telegraphic transfer（T/T）	电汇
demand draft（D/D）	票汇
collecting bank	代收行
Documents against Payment D/P	付款交单
Documents against Acceptance D/A	承兑交单
letter of credit	信用证
issuing bank	开证银行
advising/notifying bank	通知行
bill of exchange	汇票
the Uniform Customs and Practice for Documentary Credit of International Chamber of Commerce Publication No. 600.	国际商会第 600 号出版物《跟单信用证统一惯例》
Spinning Machine Parts	纺纱机部件
economic climate	经济气候；经济形势

interest rate	利率
lead to	导致
cash against documents on arrival of the goods	货到凭单付款（CAD）
time credit	远期信用证
mutually beneficial relationship	互利的合作关系
meet with your approval	得到某人许可
in the light of	根据；考虑到
moderate means at hand	手头有头寸
It goes without saying that	不用说；毋庸置疑
do a special favor	特别帮忙；优待
partial shipment	分批装运
direct steamer	直达轮船；直达船
more often than not	常常；多半
with this in mind	出于这种想法，考虑到
owing to	由于；因为
in the early part of May	五月初；五月上旬

6.3　外贸实战技巧
Techniques in Foreign Trade Practice

国际贸易中支付方式选择的影响因素

　　国际贸易的支付方式主要有汇付、托收和信用证三种，它们对出口人利益的保护程度是依次加强的，所以出口人很愿意采取 L/C 的支付方式来保证自己安全快捷地收汇。但是，我们必须正视的现实是：贸易双方是平等互利的，出口人在保护自身利益的同时也要兼顾进口人的利益。随着国际市场由卖方市场向买方市场的转变，出口人完全站在自己角度上单方面考虑回款安全性就显得障碍重重，很难实现。更现实的做法是兼顾进出口双方的利益，选择一种"双赢"的支付方式。

　　选择支付方式时应考虑的因素有以下五个方面：

　　（1）根据客户信用等级的高低而选择不同的支付方式。具体地讲，如果客户的信用等级很一般或是贸易双方是首次进行交易，应该选用 L/C 的方式；如果客户的信用等级较高，可以选用托收的方式，特别是用 D/P，这样既可以达到节省开证费的目的，也可以在一定程度上把握物权凭证的安全性；如果客户的信用等级非常高，可以选用 D/A 甚至是直接 T/T 的方式，这也是目前在西方国家的进出口贸易中大量使用 T/T 的根本原因之一。同时，客户的信用等级和客户所在地区有着密切的关系，一般而言，在金融运作体系正常的发达国家，就有可能更多地采取 T/T 和托收这样的属于商业信用的方式。另外，客户的信用资信是一个动态的概念，需要进行连续的跟踪，进行及时的评价，以便随时调整结算方式。

　　（2）根据经营意图的不同而选择不同的支付方式。具体地讲，如果是畅销的货品，卖方就有很大的余地选择对自身有利的支付方式，也许甚至要求买方预付货款，也可能要求买方必须用 L/C 的方式进行结算，否则，就以提高售价来威胁对方，逼迫买方做出妥协和让步；如果是滞销的货品，卖方极有可能会答应进口人的要求，选择一种节省进口总费用的支付方式，这时，出口方可能会违心地接受对自己的利益保障程度很小的支付方式。

（3）贸易术语的选用和合同金额的高低对支付方式的选择也有很大的影响。具体地讲，对于象征性交货组中的 CIF 和 CFR，就可以选用托收和 L/C 的方式；而对于 EXW 和实际交货的 D 组术语，一般就不会采取托收的方式进行结算；对于 FOB 和 FCA 等术语，由于运输的事宜是由买方安排，出口人很难控制货物，所以在一般情况下也不会选择托收的方式。另外，合同金额如果不大，就经常会考虑和选择速度较快、费用低廉的 T/T 方式。

（4）运输方式和运输单据种类的不同也是导致采用不同支付方式的重要原因。如果是采用海运，出口人可以得到作为物权凭证的提单，通常就可以采取托收和 L/C 方式，否则，不适宜采用托收，即使采用 L/C，也必须事先约定开证行是运输单据的收货人。

（5）贸易结算财务成本的高低也是重要的影响选择的因素。所谓贸易结算财务成本指的是使用某种支付方式时所必须承担的各项费用，主要包括财务费用和款项转移费用等。一般情况下，付款越早，出口商的财务费用越低，进口商的财务费用越高。采用 T/T 的成本是最低的，如果采用托收或 L/C，需要对银行支付较高的费用。

选择支付方式的最终目的是对贸易双方进行有效的监督，同时尽量降低结算的成本，促使进出口贸易的顺利进行。以上所列举的各个因素会在不同的时间、不同的国家和地区、不同的历史阶段、不同的具体客观情况而对货款的支付产生不同程度的影响。客观地讲，对支付方式的选择归根结底取决于进出口双方的力量对比的程度，而贸易各方总是会站在不同的角度看问题，他们最关心的是双方实力的较量。

6.4 有用的句子
Useful Sentences

6.4.1 选择付款方式
Choice of Terms of Payment

(1) We accept (adopt) payment by L/C.
我们采用信用证付款方式。

(2) We regret that we are unable to consider your request for payment under D/A terms.
对你方要求以承兑交单方式付款一事，我们歉难考虑。

(3) We are prepared to accept payment for your trail order on D/P basis.
对你方这批试订购的货物，我们准备接受付款交单方式付款。

(4) In view of our long business relations, we will make an exception to accept L/C at 30 days' sight.
鉴于我们长期的合作关系，我们破例接受 30 天的远期信用证。

(5) As a special accommodation, we agree to your proposal and accept payment by D/P at sight in compliance with your request, but this should not be regarded as a precedent.
应你方要求，作为特殊照顾，我们同意你方建议，接受即期付款交单，但是这不应视为先例。

(6) D/P is applicable only if the amount involved for each transaction is less than $1,000.
只有每笔金额不足 1 000 美元的交易才能采取付款交单的付款方式。

(7) In order to save a lot of expenses on opening the L/C, we will remit you the full amount by T/T when the goods purchased by us are ready for shipment and the freight space is booked.
为了节省开立信用证的大笔费用，我们会在我方购买的货物已经备妥待运，舱位已经订好时，电汇全部金额。

(8) It's expensive to open L/C and tie up the capital of a small company like us. So it's better for us to adopt D/P or D/A.
对我们这样的小公司来说，开信用证花费大，对资金周转影响很大。最好还是采用付款交单或承兑交单付款方式。

(9) In order to conclude this transaction, we are prepared to accept payment of 50% L/C and the balance by D/P at sight.
为了做成这笔交易，我方准备接受 50% 用信用证付款，余额部分用即期付款交单方式支付。

(10) We agree to adopt installment payment for this consignment and please remit 20% of the contract value to us before the end of next month as down payment.
对这批货我们同意采取分期付款的方式，请将合同金额的 20% 在下个月底前汇给我方作为首期付款。

6.4.2 开证
Establishment of an L/C

(1) We enclose an application form for documentary credit and shall be glad if you will arrange to open for our account an L/C for $40,000 in favor of ABC Company, the credit to be valid until June 15.
兹附寄跟单信用证申请表一份，请开立以 ABC 公司为受益人，金额为 4 万美元的信用证，有效期至 6 月 15 日止，由我方付款。

(2) We write to inform you that we have today established through Citi Bank a documentary L/C in your favor for the amount of $2,000 covering 100 sets of TV.
兹函告今天我们已由花旗银行开立以你方为受益人的跟单信用证，金额为 2 000 美元，用以支付 100 台电视机。

(3) This L/C will be confirmed by the First Commercial Bank and they will accept the draft on them at 60 days after sight for the amount of your invoice.
此信用证由第一商业银行保兑，该银行将承兑贵方开给他们的见票后 60 天付款的发票金额的汇票。

6.4.3 催证
Urging Establishment of an L/C

(1) We wish to draw your attention to the fact that the date of delivery is drawing near, but up to the present, we have not received the covering L/C.

我们希望提醒你方注意，交货期日益临近，但是截至目前，我方尚未收到相关的信用证。

(2) With reference to our Sales Confirmation No. … dated … , we regret to say that your letter of credit has not yet reached us up to the time of writing.
参阅我方……日的……号销售确认书，很遗憾你方的信用证到目前还没抵达我方。

(3) Please do your utmost to expedite the establishment of relevant L/C so that we may execute your order No. 012 smoothly within the prescribed time.
请加速开立相关信用证以便我方在规定的时间内顺利执行你方 012 号订单。

(4) The shipment date is approaching. It would be advisable for you to open the L/C covering your order No. 123 as early as possible so as to effect shipment within the stipulated time limit.
装运期日益临近，望你方尽早开立你方第 123 号订单的信用证，以便我方在规定时间内装运。

(5) Please see to it that the L/C stipulations conform strictly to the terms of the contract so as to avoid subsequent amendment.
请注意信用证的条款必须与合同条款完全一致，以避免日后修改。

6.4.4 改证
Amendment of an L/C

(1) We have received your L/C No. 555, but find it contains the following discrepancies.
我们已收到你方第 555 号信用证，但发现其中有下列不符之处。

(2) We are pleased to inform you that L/C No. 666 issued by the Chartered Bank of Liverpool for our S/C No. 111 has just been received. However, on examining the clauses, we regretfully find that certain points are not in conformity with the terms stipulated in the contract.
现高兴地通知你方，由利物浦麦加利银行开出的，用以支付有关我方第 111 号售货合同的第 666 号信用证刚刚到达我方。但经审核信用证条款后，我们遗憾地发现某些地方与合同规定的条款不符。

(3) We thank you for your L/C No. 999, but on checking its clauses, we find with regret that your L/C calls for shipment in October 2018, whereas our contract stipulates for November shipment.
感谢你方第 999 号信用证。经核对条款，我们遗憾地发现你方信用证要求 2018 年 10 月装船，但我方合同规定是 11 月装运。

(4) According to the L/C we received, payment is to be made at 60 days sight. But it should be made at sight as per the contract. Therefore please make amendment to the L/C as stated.
根据我方收到的信用证，应在见票后 60 天付款，但是合同规定见票即付，因此，请按以上意见修改信用证。

(5) The discrepancies are as follows:
  a. Commission should be 3%, not 5%.
  b. Shipment is to be made during June/July instead of "on or before June 30".
  c. Goods should be insured for 110% of the invoice value, not 150%.
不符之处如下：

a. 佣金应该是3%，而不是5%；

b. 货物应于6月或7月装运，而不是"6月30日当日或之前装运"；

c. 货物按发票金额的110%投保，而不是150%。

(6) Please amend your L/C No. 789 as follows：

a. Insert the word "about" between "quantity" and "100M/T".

b. Delete Items 1，3，5，7 and replace them by those stipulated in our S/C.

c. Increase the unit price from $0.78 to $87 and total amount to $12,345.00.

d. Delete the clause "Bankers expenses for beneficiary's account".

请将你方第789号信用证做如下修改：

a. 在"quantity"和"100M/T"之间加上"about"一词。

b. 删掉1、3、5、7项，用合同规定的内容取代。

c. 将单价从0.78美元增加到87美元，总金额增至12 345美元。

d. 取消"银行费用由受益人负担"的条款。

(7) Please amend the credit to allow transshipment/Please amend the L/C as allowing transshipment/Please amend the L/C as "transshipment is allowed".

请将信用证改为允许转船。

(8) Please amend L/C No. 898 to read "This credit will expire on December 31，2018 in China."

请将第898号信用证改为："该信用证将于2018年12月31日在中国到期"。

(9) As there is no direct sailing from Dalian to your port during April/May，it is imperative for you to delete the clause "by direct steamer" and insert the wording "Partial shipment and transshipment are allowed".

由于4月、5月没有从大连驶往你港的直达轮，请取消"用直达轮"条款，加上"允许分批和转船"字样。

6.4.5 展证

Extension of an L/C

(1) Please extend the shipment date and the validity of your L/C No. 518 to the end of October and November 15，2018 respectively and make arrangement for the amendment advice to reach us by September 30，2018.

请将你方第518号信用证的装运期和有效期分别展至2018年10月底和11月15日，并安排信用证的修改通知书于2018年9月30日到达我方。

(2) We have sent you by fax today asking for a two-week extension of the validity of the L/C covering your order No. 30 for 300 cases of frozen chicken.

我们已于今天发传真给你方，要求你方把订购300箱冻鸡肉的30号订单的信用证有效期延长两个星期。

(3) Please have the validity of your L/C No. 345 extended until June 9 so that we may make shipment without fail.

请把345号信用证的有效期延至6月9日，以便装运顺利进行。

6.5 补充商务信函
Letters for Further Reading

Letter 6-11

Dear Sirs,

　　We have received your letter of December 29, 2013 and appreciate your intention to promote the sales of our vacuum cleaner in your country.

　　We regret that we are unable to consider your request for payment on D/A terms. As a rule, we ask for payment by L/C. But in view of our friendly relations, we will, as an exceptional case, accept payment for your trial order on D/P basis. In other words, we will draw on you by documentary draft at sight through our bank, on collection basis, without L/C.

　　We hope the above payment terms will be acceptable to you and expect to receive your trial order in due course.

　　We look forward to your early reply.

Faithfully yours,

Letter 6-12

Dear Mr. Grover,

　　Thank you for your letter of May 10, 2014 asking for a change in payment terms.

　　There is nothing unusual in our current arrangement. From the time you open credit until the shipment reaches your port is normally about three months. In addition, your L/C is only opened when the goods are ready for shipment.

　　We regret to say that we must adhere to our usual practice and sincerely hope that this will not affect our future business relations.

　　We will contact you as soon as supplies of the steel pipes you require come into stock.

Yours sincerely,

6.6 练习
Exercises

Ⅰ. Translate the following phrases into Chinese.

1. mail transfer (M/T)
2. telegraphic transfer (T/T)
3. demand draft (D/D)
4. remitting bank
11. international business practice
12. customary practice
13. tie-up funds
14. easy payment terms

5. collecting Bank
6. Documents against Payment (D/P)
7. Documents against Acceptance (D/A)
8. letter of credit
9. issuing bank
10. extension advice
15. terms of payment
16. favorable reply
17. Sales Contract
18. mutually beneficial cooperation
19. date of shipment
20. port of shipment

Ⅱ. Choose the best answer.
1. We are faxing you this morning, asking you to amend the L/C _____ "Transshipment allowed".
   A. to read
   B. to reading
   C. as reads
   D. reads
2. We think it impossible to have the L/C _____ again.
   A. extended
   B. extending
   C. to extend
   D. extends
3. As we are _____ of these goods, please expedite shipment after receiving our L/C.
   A. in badly need
   B. in urgently need
   C. urgent in need
   D. badly in need
4. An L/C should be established _____ our favor available by documentary draft _____ six days' sight.
   A. in, after
   B. on, in
   C. in, for
   D. in, at
5. It _____ if you _____ the L/C for another 15 days.
   A. is appreciated, extend
   B. will be appreciated, could extend
   C. should be appreciated, could extend
   D. should be appreciated, can extend
6. _____ perusal of you L/C, we find that it calls _____ direct shipment which is not in conformity with the contract stipulations.
   A. With, to
   B. On, of
   C. On, for
   D. With, for
7. For future deal D/P will be acceptable if the amount _____ is not up to RMB ¥1,000.
   A. involved
   B. involve
   C. involving
   D. involves
8. As we must adhere to our customary practice, we hope that you will not think us _____.
   A. accommodate
   B. unaccommodate
   C. accommodating
   D. unaccommodating
9. We regret keenly this delay and can only hope it will not have seriously _____ you.
   A. trouble
   B. inconvenient
   C. inconvenienced
   D. convenienced
10. You're requested to make amendment _____ L/C No. 78 without delay.
    A. to
    B. in
    C. on
    D. at

11. We call your attention to the fact _____ the L/C covering your order No. 123 has not reached us.
    A. what B. that
    C. where D. it
12. It is possible to extend this Letter of Credit, which expires _____ January 25.
    A. on B. for
    C. of D. in
13. As regards our offer for Green Beans, we are anxious to know whether you _____ our request for D/A payment.
    A. agree upon B. agreeable to
    C. are agreeable to D. are agreeable with
14. We find that there is no stipulation of transshipment _____ in the relative L/C.
    A. which allowed B. being allowed
    C. allowing D. which allows
15. The relative L/C should be issued through a third country bank in Italy _____ the sellers.
    A. available by B. available to
    C. acceptable by D. acceptable to

Ⅲ. Fill in the blanks.
1. Payments should be made _____ sight draft.
2. 90% of the credit amount must be paid _____ the presentation of documents.
3. You don't say whether you wish the transaction to be _____ cash or _____ credit.
4. We shall be glad if you agree to ship the goods to us as before _____ cash against documents basis.
5. We have opened an L/C _____ your favor _____ the amount of RMB ¥20,000.
6. If the amount exceeds that figure, payment _____ L/C will be required.
7. From the enclosed copy of invoice you will see that price of US $1,800 is well _____ the maximum figure you stated.
8. We enclose a cheque for US $20,000 _____ payment of all commissions due _____ you up to date.
9. We will draw _____ you by our documentary draft at sight on collection basis.
10. We look forward _____ receiving your extension _____ an early date and assure you that your order will be shipped immediately _____ receipt of your amendment _____ the above L/C.

Ⅳ. Translate the following sentences into Chinese.
1. We have opened the L/C in your favor against No. GF805 available by documentary draft at sixty days' sight.
2. According to the shipment of S/C No. 2035, you should establish the covering L/C before April 20.
3. We have made arrangement with Bank of China to open a credit in your favor.
4. You must expedite the covering L/C, otherwise we shall be unable to effect shipment before

the end of this month.

5. With regard to L/C No. 705, we have already instructed the opening bank to extend the date of shipment and validity to May 15 and May 30 respectively.

6. According to the L/C we received, payment is to be made at 60 days' sight. But it should be made at sight as per the contract. Therefore, please make amendment to the L/C as stated.

7. We regret that we are unable to consider your request for payment under D/A terms.

8. It's expensive to open L/C and tie up the capital of a small company like us. So it's better for us to adopt D/P or D/A.

9. We are prepared to accept payment for your trail order on D/P basis.

10. In view of our long business relation, we will make an exception to accept L/C at 30 days' sight.

Ⅴ. Translate the following sentences into English.

1. 关于第 135 号合同，我们同意电汇的付款方式。
2. 装运期临近，请速开立相关信用证，以便我们在规定的时间内安排装船。
3. 作为特别照顾，我们接受 30 天的远期信用证。
4. 由于到你方港口的直达船稀少，我们不得不要求允许转运。
5. 这笔汇款是支付迄今为止欠你方的各项佣金。
6. 我们在这方面的通融不能为以后交易开创先例。
7. 请确认我们可以就你 325 号订单通过中国银行向你方开出金额为 48 000 美元的 30 天远期汇票收款。
8. 在今后的交易中，只是在每笔合同金额不超过 1 000 欧元或按当时的兑换率折算的等值人民币的情况下，才可以采用付款交单方式。
9. 附寄跟单信用证申请书一份，请开立以 ABC 公司为受益人，金额为 4 万美元的信用证，有效期截至 7 月 15 日为止，由我方付款。
10. 请注意信用证条款务必与合同条款严格一致，以免日后修改。

Ⅵ. Situational writing.

1. Write a letter according to the main points.

   （1）你方经中国银行开出的有关我 187 号销售确认书的信用证第 H-15 号刚刚收到。

   （2）经审查其中条款，我们遗憾地发现有些地方与合同的规定不符。

   （3）请将你方的信用证做如下修改：

   a. "吨" 前删去 "长" 字，加入 "公" 字

   b. 将数量减为 120 箱，而不是 1 200 箱。

   c. 删掉第 7 项的保险条款，用合同规定的内容取代。

   d. 展装运期和有效期分别至 10 月底和 11 月 15 日并准许分运、转船。

   （4）一收到你方的信用证修改书，我方立即安排装运。

2. Write a letter in English asking for amendments to the following letter of credit by checking it with the given contract.

   合同主要条款：

   卖方：广东宜原贸易有限公司

   买方：T. G. Salgo & Co., Melbourne, Australia

商品名称："雪花"（Snowflake）牌黄桃罐头
规格：450 克罐装
数量：50 000 罐
单价：CFR 墨尔本每罐 3 美元，含佣金 2%
总值：150 000 美元
装运期：2015 年 10 月自广州至墨尔本，在香港转船
付款条件：凭不可撤销即期信用证付款
合同号码：SP 05-1234

Commercial Bank

Melbourne, Australia

Irrevocable Documentary Credit No. F-12345

Date and place of issue: August 20, 2015, Melbourne

Date and place of expiry: November 15, 2015, Melbourne

Applicant: T. G. Salgo & Co., Melbourne, Australia

Beneficiary: Guangdong YiYuan Trading Corporation Limited

Advising Bank: The Bank of China, Guangzhou Branch

Amount: US＄15,000 (Say US Dollars Fifteen Thousand Only)

Partial shipment and transshipment are prohibited.

Shipment from Guangzhou to Melbourne, latest October 2015.

Credit available against presentation of the documents detailed herein and of your draft at sight for full invoice value.

Signed commercial invoice in quadruplicate.

Full set of clean on board ocean Bills of Lading made to order of Commercial Bank marked "Freight prepaid".

Insurance certificate or policy endorsed in blank for full invoice value plus 10%, covering All Risks and War Risk. Covering 50,000 tins of 500 grams of Snowflake Brand Canned Yellow Peaches at USD 3.00 per tin CFRC2% Melbourne.

As per Contract No. SP 05-1234

Chapter 7
第 7 章

包 装
Packing

Learning Objectives

Enable the students to know about the importance of packing in the international trade; to be familiar with the classification and the marks of packages; to master the structure and common expressions in this type of letters.

使学生了解包装在国际贸易中的重要性;熟悉包装的种类以及包装上的各种标志;掌握此类函件的结构以及常用的表达形式。

7.1 背景知识
Background Information

包装是国际贸易的必要组成部分,也是贸易双方进行贸易谈判的重要商务条件之一。包装的最终目的是使运输货物在到达目的地时保持完好,避免丢失。良好的包装必须能够承受住运输过程中出现的各种状况。因此,卖方要对包装的特点和外观特别注意。

就包装货物而言,一般有两种类型的包装:运输包装(外装)以及销售包装(内包装)。

运输包装

运输包装的主要特点:美观耐用;便于装卸;适合长途运输;

Packing is the necessary component part in the international trade. It is one of the most important business conditions to negotiate between the two trading parties. The ultimate purpose of packing is to keep the transported goods in perfect condition without missing on arrival. Good packing must be able to stand the roughest transportation. Therefore, the seller should pay attention to the features and appearance of packing.

As to packed cargo, there are usually two kinds of packing, transportation packing (outer packing) and packing for sales (inner packing).

Transportation Packing

The features of transportation packing should be: beautiful and durable; easy to load and unload; suited

防损、防盗；防水、防震；趋于标准化。运输包装主要用来保护货物以便于对其运输、装卸、存储以及清点等。

在国际贸易中主要使用以下几种类型的运输包装：

（1）瓦楞纸包装箱。瓦楞纸包装箱适用于许多出口货物的包装。与木箱相比，其具有弹性，故能防震。这种包装形式在使用金属集装箱运输时更加适合。

（2）胶合板箱。胶合板箱很坚固，因为它的框架可以承受放在上面的重物的压力。同时，胶合板箱实际上具有防撞和防盗的特点。

（3）袋装。包装袋可由纸、棉、塑料、麻等制成，是非常便宜的一种包装形式，而且适用于大部分类型的货物，如水泥、面粉、化肥、油渣、饲料等。

（4）胶木桶、圆桶及大桶。这种类型的包装主要由木、金属或塑料等材料制成。此类包装主要用于运输液体或者油脂类货物，如香肠。

（5）木质板条箱。木质板条箱主要适用于重型、散装的货物，可开启和关闭。木质板条箱的牢固框架对货物起到保护作用，避免装卸时吊索对箱子产生挤压。

（6）纸箱。随着集装箱运输的发展，纸箱包装比较常见，尤其适用于消费品的运输。

（7）集装箱。集装箱是在国际货物运输以及国际物流中被广泛使用的一种包装形式。

for long distance transportation; proof against damage; proof against pilferage; waterproof, shockproof; standardized. Transportation packing mainly protects the products so that they are conveniently transported, loaded and unloaded, stored, counted and so on.

The following are types of transportation packing usually used in the foreign trade.

（1）Corrugated Boxes. Corrugated boxes are used in the pack of many export goods. They are resilient and provide more shock absorbency than wooden boxes. Corrugated boxes are most suitable as out packing when carried within a metal container.

（2）Plywood Boxes. Plywood boxes are strong because of the framing and can withstand the pressure of heavy loads placed on top of them. And the plywood boxes are practically puncture-proof and theft-proof.

（3）Bags. Bags made of paper, cotton, plastic, or jute, are a cheap form of container and are ideal for a wide variety of products such as cement, flour, fertilizer, oil cakes, animal food and many other products.

（4）Barrels, Drums and Hogsheads. This type of containers is usually made of wood, metal or plastic. They are used for the conveyance of liquid or greasy cargos such as sausage.

（5）Wooden Crates. Wooden crates are used mainly for heavy, bulky goods and may be opened or closed. The strong frame of the wooden crate provides protection from the pinching effects of slings.

（6）Cartons. Cartons are now a very common way of packing with the development of containerization, particularly in international distribution of the type of consumer products.

（7）Containers. Containers are a form of packing extensively used in international cargo transportation and logistics.

销售包装

销售包装会随着商品进入零售网点并直接面对消费者。这种类型的包装不仅能保护商品，而且美观，利于产品宣传。当前销售包装被认为是影响家用消费品类或类似货物销售的关键因素。因此，销售包装的特征应为：新颖且具有美感、小巧精致、外观有吸引力、适合橱窗展示、易于宣传和销售货物。

包装标志

根据买方的包装要求完成包装后，在出口包装上面必须印制包装标志，包装标志主要包括：

（1）运输标志

运输标志是来识别货物的一种标志，可以使货物被轻松、快速地确认。在运输包装上应该标出进口商名称、目的港、货物原产国、订单号、重量以及体积等。

（2）指示性标志以及警告性标志

为了保障货物所有人以及承运人的利益，有关货物搬运、装卸以及起吊的指示性标志和警告性标志应印制在包装上。指示性标志提示人们在货物装卸、运输、存储等过程中应该注意的问题；而警告性标志是警告并保护货物和运输参与人的安全的标志。

当撰写与包装相关的信函时，一般应该包括以下几个部分：

（1）信函开始应表达对上一封信函的感谢，同时引入有关包装的事宜；

（2）信函的中间部分应该清晰、具体地阐述订单货物的包装

Sales Packing

Sales packing goes with the products to enter retailing network and faces the consumer directly. This kind of package not only protects the products, but also beautifies and publicizes the products. Sales packing now universally recognized as a decisive selling factor of household consumer goods and goods alike. So the features of sales packing should be: novel and pleasing to the eye; small and exquisite; look appealing; suitable for window display; easy to publicize and sell goods.

Marks of Package

After finishing packing, according to the packing requirements from the buyers, packing marks should be done on the export packages, which mainly include:

(1) Shipping Marks

The shipping mark is a mark to identify the goods and cargoes, so that goods can be identified easily and faster. It indicates the name of the importer, the port of destination, the country of origin of the goods, the order number, the weight and dimensions of the goods, etc.

(2) Indicative and Warning Marks

To ensure the benefit of both the owner and the carrier, indicative and warning marks regarding manner of handling, loading, unloading and lifting, etc. are to be stenciled on the package. The indicative mark is a mark to indicate what people should pay attention to the process of loading and unloading, transporting, and storage. A warning mark is a mark to warn and protect the safety of people and goods.

When writing letters about packing, the packing-related letter often includes the following parts:

(1) The opening sentence expresses thanks for the previous letter and introduces the matter of packing.

(2) The middle part should state clearly and concretely details concerning the packing instructions and

指示以及标志的细节。如果有必要，应进一步给出原因；

（3）信函的结束部分通常提出尽早得到回复的期望。

marks for the goods ordered. If necessary, the reasons are given.

(3) The closing sentence often raises the hope to make a response promptly.

7.2 信例
Specimen Letters

Letter 7-1　A buyer's requirement for packing

Dear Sirs,

　　　　　　Re：S/C NO. 90SP – 24988 Covering 2,000 Pallets Tea

We acknowledgeed receipt of your letter dated the 2nd March enclosing the above sales contract in duplicate, but wish to state that after going through the contract, we find that the packing clause in it is not clear enough. The relative clause reads as follows:

Packing: seaworthy export packing, suitable for long distance ocean transportation.

In order to eliminate possible future troubles, we would like to make clear beforehand our packing requirements as follows:

The Tea under the captioned contract should be packed in international standard tea boxes, 16 boxes on a pallet, 10 pallets in an FCL container. On the transportation packing, please mark our initials SCC in a diamond, under which the port of destination and our order number should be stenciled. In addition, warning marks like KEEP DRY, USE NO HOOK, etc., should be indicated.

We have made a footnote on the contract to that effect and are returning herein one copy of the contract after duly countersigning it. We hope you will find it in order and pay special attention to the packing.

We look forward to receiving your shipping advice and thank you in advance.

Yours faithfully,

Encl. S/C No. 90SP-24988

Letter 7-2　A negotiation on packing and marking

Dear Sirs,

We appreciate your packing instruction, but regret to inform you that we disagree with your request for packing.

In view of our long business relations and our amicable cooperation prospects, we suggest that you accept the following proposals:

> 1. The table cloth will be packed 8 dozen to a packet and 10 packets to a carton.
> 2. In addition to the gross and net weights, the shipping marks outside the carton should stencil the words "MADE IN CHINA".
>
> We look forward to your early reply.
>
> Yours faithfully,

Letter 7-3 A claim for improper packing

> Dear Sirs,
>
> We refer to Order No. 209 covering 500 tea sets.
>
> The consignment arrived here on May 14. After examination, we found 25 sets were badly damaged though the packages containing the tea sets appeared to be in good condition.
>
> Considering this damage was due to the rough handling by the shipping company, we are writing to claim on them for the loss, but an investigation made by the surveyor has revealed that the damages are attributable to improper packing. On the strength of the survey report, we hereby register our claim against you as follows:
>
> CIF value of 25 sets: USD 300.00
>
> Inspection fees: USD 200.00
>
> Total: USD 500.00
>
> We enclose one copy of Survey Report No. SR120 and look forward to your early settlement.
>
> Yours faithfully,

Letter 7-4 A reply to the packing instruction

> Dear Sirs,
>
> We appreciate your above order of May 10, 2014 and have pleasure in informing you that we can accept all the terms but the packing.
>
> We would like to provide you our latest package, which is economical and strong. The packing mentioned in your order was of the old method we adopted several years ago. Now we have improved it with the result that our recent goods have all turned out to the complete satisfaction of our clients.
>
> Our Women's Blouses are now packed in a poly-bag and then in a cardboard box, 5 dozen to a carton, with a gross weight about 25 kilograms. Each carton is lined with a polythene sheet, so that the content is protected from moisture.
>
> We are awaiting your prompt reply and wondering if our proposal meets your requirement.
>
> Yours faithfully,

Letter 7-5 Asking for improving packing

Dear Sirs,

   Thank you for your Quotation No. 22 about Round Steel Bars.

   We regret to inform you that among the five lots of Round Steel Bars arrived here per S. S. Mary on May 11, 2015 were six bundles of different grades, which were in scattered and mixed condition because their packing was not sufficiently strong and their iron hoops were broken in transit. Since it was very difficult to assort them, inconvenience and losses occurred. Although we had in time notified you of such unfortunate things occurred before, the present case has shown that our comments were ignored, for no improvement in packing has been made.

   Therefore, we must have your promise to take effective measures to improve your packing before we could book this new order with you.

   We are waiting for you early reply.

                                                                                    Yours faithfully,

Letter 7-6 An apology for improper packing

Dear Mr. Nelson,

   We have received your letter of March 15, together with one copy of survey report.

   Upon receipt of your letter, we have given this matter our immediate attention and made a thorough investigation. We are surprised that the findings are the same as the statement in the survey report. We regret to say that the damages were caused by improper packing which was due to the negligence of our warehouse staff.

   We wish to express our apologies for this matter. In order to maintain our long-standing trading relationship, we enclose a draft No. 1301 for USD 500.00 issued by Bank of China in full and final settlement of your claim.

   We trust that this unfortunate error will not adversely affect our future relations.

                                                                                    Yours sincerely,

Notes

1. pack

   vt. & vi. 包装

   (1) Pack the clothes into the trunk/suitcase. 把衣服装进箱里。

   (2) Have you packed yet? 你收拾好了吗?

   pack sth. (物品) in sth. (材料)　用……包装……

   Pack the glass in newspaper. 用报纸包装玻璃。

pack sth. into sth. 把……包装到……

Pack the books into boxes. 把书装到箱子里。

packing　n. 包装

The packing should be suitable for long distance shipment. 包装应适合长途运输。

包装材料：

cardboard box　硬纸箱

carton　软纸箱

wooden case　木箱

container　集装箱

2. eliminate

v. 排除；剔除

Eliminate possible future trouble　消除将来有可能发生的麻烦

3. FCL

FCL = Full Container Load　整箱货

container　n. 容器；集装箱

You may ship the goods in any suitable containers. 你可以用合适的集装箱装运货物。

container bill of lading　集装箱提单

container ship　集装箱船

containerize　用集装箱发运

We note your request for containerizing future shipment.

我方知道你方要求以后用集装箱发运货物。

containerization　n. 集装箱化

Containerization is regarded as a mode for more efficient shipment.

集装箱运输被认为是更有效的运输方式。

4. warning marks

警告性标志

Keep Dry　保持干燥

Use No Hooks　切勿用钩

With Care　小心搬运

Not to be laid flat　不能平放

To be kept upright　保持直立

This Side Up　这边向上

Fragile—with care　小心易碎

Keep Cool　不要靠热

Not to be thrown down　不可抛掷

5. effect

n. 效果；影响

The new development is likely to produce a favorable effect on the prices.

新的发展可能对价格产生有利的影响。

in effect　有效；实际上

take effect from/on　自/在……开始生效
come/go into effect from/on　自/在……开始生效
to this effect　大意是如此
to that effect　大意是那样
to the effect that　大意是……
We have not received information to the effect that the market has become brisk.
我没收到市场开始繁荣的信息。

6. comply with
   满足；依照
   We hope you will be able to comply with our request.
   希望你方能按我方要求办理。
   in compliance with　依从；按照
   Please make us a firm offer in compliance with our requirement.　请按我们的要求报实盘。

7. packet
   n. 小包
   package　n. 包件（指包、捆、束、箱等）
   The packages are intact. 包装完整无损。
   packaging　n. 包装方法
   We have improved the packaging. 我们改进了包装方法。

8. consignment
   n. 托运的货物
   consign　v. 托运
   consignor　n. 发货人
   consignee　n. 收货人

9. claim
   v. /n. 索赔
   claim against someone　向某人索赔
   claim on the goods　对该货物提出索赔
   claim for USD 2,000　索赔 2 000 美元
   claim for inferior quality　由于品质低劣而索赔
   lodge/raise/file/make/register a claim　提出索赔
   settle a claim　理赔
   reject a claim　拒绝索赔

10. be attributable to
    可归因于
    The damages are attributable to improper packing.
    货物受损是由于包装不当而造成的。

11. survey report
    检验报告，鉴定证书
    survey report on quality　品质鉴定证书

survey report on weight　重量鉴定证书

12. turn out

    结果是；产生……的结果

    （1）We hope everything will turn out (to be) satisfactory in the end.

    　　　我们希望最终一切都令人满意。

    （2）Everything turned out to be well.

    　　　结果一切都很好。

13. a thorough investigation

    彻底的调查

    a close (cursory, impartial) investigation　详细(草率，公正)的调查

    carry out (conduct/do/make) an investigation　进行调查

14. negligence

    n. 疏忽；挂失

    gross (ordinary, slight) negligence　严重(一般，轻微)的过失

    due to/through negligence　由于疏忽

15. maintain

    v. 保持；维持

    maintain one's friendship　保持友谊

    maintain one's reputation　维护名誉

16. S. S.

    S. S. = steam ship　汽船

    M. V. = motor vessel　机动船，两者通常译作"货轮"，后接船名。

Words and Phrases

seaworthy	adj. 适合海上航行的
pallet	n. 托盘；小货盘
amicable	adj. 友好的
economical	adj. 经济的；节约的
adopt	v. 采用；采纳
moisture	n. 潮湿；湿气
prompt	adj. 立即的；及时的
adversely	adv. 不利地；逆向地
specify	v. 明确说明；具体制定
measurement	n. 尺寸；大小
scheduled	adj. 预定的
invoice	n. 发票
consignment	n. 装运的货物；运送物
make clear	弄清楚
inside packing	内包装

outer packing	外包装
in a diamond	菱形
in a square	方形
packing instruction	包装要求；包装须知
gross weigh	毛重
net weight	净重
tare weight	皮重
protect…from…	保护……免遭……
rough handling	粗鲁搬运
on the strength of	因为；凭借
polythene sheet	塑料纸
portable computer	笔记本电脑
Bills of Lading	提单
Insurance Certificate	保险凭证
sight draft	即期汇票

7.3 外贸实战技巧
Techniques in Foreign Trade Practice

外贸包装信函的写作技巧

有关包装的信函应简洁明了。撰写这类信函时，出口方可以向进口方详细描述其习惯包装方式，同时也可说明可以接受进口方的包装要求，但额外费用应由进口方承担。进口方也可以通知出口方特别的包装要求或表示对包装的担心。如果要更改有关包装的任何条款，都必须在装运前经买卖双方商洽同意后确定。

包装信函的写作步骤和写作方式如下：

告知对方信函的目的（关于包装问题的洽谈），主要表达方式有：We thank you for your letter of…（感谢贵公司……日来函），We are pleased to inform you that…（很高兴告诉你方……），We are now writing to you in regard to the packing of…（我方来函告知关于……的包装问题）；说明包装方式、包装材料等包装要求，主要表达方式有：The relative clause should be…（相关条款应为……），Packing：…In addition, indicative marks should be…（包装材料（方式）：……，此外，指示性标志为……），We write to you in regard to the packing of…, and we would like you to have the goods packed in…（兹去函告知关于……的包装要求，我们希望采用……包装方式）；表示希望对方能够接受此包装要求并予以关注，盼早日回复，主要表达方式有：We hope you will find it in order and pay special attention to the packing.（希望你方会发现该包装方式是恰当的，并能给予特别关注），We should be grateful if you let us have your opinions about these requirements.（如果贵公司能告知我方对此包装要求的看法，我方将不胜感激）。

回复包装信函的写作步骤及常见的表达方式如下：

感谢对方来函并告知对方回信的目的，主要表达方式有：We have received your letter of…（我方已收到你方……日来函），We regret to inform you that…（很遗憾地告知你方……），

Thank you for your packing instructions, but regret our inability to comply with your request for special packing（感谢收到你方的包装指示，但很遗憾我们不能满足你方对特殊包装的要求）；提出有关包装的参考意见和解决办法，主要表达方式有：We shall pack…in…instead of in…as…（由于……我们将用……包装来代替……包装）；In order to…, we should like to make the following suggestions for your consideration.（为了……特提出以下意见供你方参考）；表示希望对方能够确认包装建议，We hope you will accept our packing and assure you of our sincere cooperation（希望你方能够接受我方包装，并向你方保证我方的合作诚意），We hope to have your confirmation on the packing（希望得到你方对此包装的确认）。

7.4　有用的句子
Useful Sentences

1. The surveyor maintains that the damage was due to insecure packing and not to any unduly rough handling.
   鉴定员认为损害是由于包装不牢固造成的，而非搬运不当所致。
2. On inspection, we found that 50 bags had burst due to the use of substandard bags and that the contents, estimated at 2,500kg, had been irretrievably lost.
   检查货物时，我们发现有 50 袋因使用不合标准的包装袋而破裂，里面的货物重达 2 500 千克，已无法挽回地丢失。
3. The instruments are damaged chiefly due to improper packing. They were packed too loose inside the wooden cases while not stuffed.
   仪器的损坏主要是由不良包装造成的。它们在木箱内装得太松又未做填充。
4. Our investigation shows damage was caused by improper packing. Therefore, we have to refer this matter to you.
   检验证明，货物受损是由于包装不当而造成的。因此，我们不得不将此事提交你方解决。
5. For the sake of precaution, the cartons must be secured with metal bands.
   为预防起见，纸箱必须用金属带捆绑以确保安全。
6. Please line the containers with waterproof material so that the goods can be protected against moisture.
   请用防水材料做容器里衬，以防货物受潮。
7. The suppliers should be held responsible for short weight resulting from improper packing.
   由于包装不当而引起的短重，供应商应该负责。
8. Cartons are comparatively light and compact, more convenient to handle in the course of the loading and unloading, quite fit for ocean transportation. As a kind of packing container, they have been extensively used in international trade.
   纸板箱比较轻巧，装卸搬运更为方便，很适合海洋运输。作为一种包装容器，纸板箱已在国际贸易中广泛使用。
9. The goods are to be marked with our initials in a diamond, and warning marks are to be clearly marked.
   货物唛头为菱形，内印我公司名称缩写，警告标志必须清楚标明。
10. In view of the fragile nature of the goods, they should be wrapped in soft material and firmly

packed in cardboard boxes so as to reduce damage in transit to a minimum.
鉴于此货物为易碎品，故应以软材料包装，再牢牢放置于纸板箱中，以尽量减少运输途中造成的损失。

11. In fact, this packing is both shockproof and waterproof. Nevertheless we have still marked the cartons with warnings like "FRAGILE" "USE NO HOOK" "DO NOT DROP".
实际上，这种包装既防震又防潮。尽管如此，我们仍在箱子上刷上了诸如"易碎""切勿用钩""轻搬轻放"等标志。

12. Our way of packing has been widely accepted by other clients, and we have received no complaints what so ever so far.
我们的包装方式已经被其他客户广泛接受，到目前为止，还没有任何投诉。

13. The packing must be seaworthy and strong enough to stand rough handling.
包装必须适合海运，足够牢固，经得住野蛮装运。

14. Each pair of socks is packed in a poly-bag and 12 pairs to a box.
每双袜子装入一个塑料袋里，12双袜子装入一个纸盒里。

15. The unique design of the packing will help you promote the sale of drugs.
独特的包装将有助于我们推销这些药品。

7.5 补充商务信函
Letters for Further Reading

Letter 7-7

Dear Sirs,

Thank you for your quotation of February 16. We are working on it and expect to come to a decision in about a fortnight.

As specified in our inquiry of Feb. 11, and also in our follow-up letter of the same date, the goods should be packed in sea-worthy cases suitable for a long voyage and well protected against dampness, shock, and rough handling. The seller should be liable for any damages to the goods and extra expenses due to improper packing and inadequate protective measures.

When you pack the goods, please see to it that the package number, measurement, gross weight, net weight, the words "KEEP AWAY FROM MOISTURE", and the following shipping mark shall be printed with fadeless paint on each package: SITC/PITC 12V 400ZC. The packing list in duplicate will indicate the gross weight, net weight, measurement and quantity of each item.

Upon receipt of the letter, please confirm by fax that you will fulfill these packing instructions.

Yours faithfully,

Letter 7-8

Dear Sirs,

We are writing to you to invite your attention to our order No. 43 covering 1,000 sets of chinaware for dinner service made in Jingdezhen. According to the Contract No. GH5878, this order should be due on November 30. Please pay attention to the delivery date and arrange the shipment as early as possible.

In addition, the chinaware is easily to be broken and is, especially, not capable of withstanding rough handling. Therefore, taking good care of proper packing is of great importance for reducing the losses in transporting. It is necessary for you to pack the goods in strong wooden cases bedded with foamed plastics for protection from being broken.

Your full cooperation will be expected.

Faithfully yours,

Letter 7-9

Dear Sirs,

We thank you for your letter of May 25, informing us of your clients' comments on our packing. We have discussed the matter with the competent department here and wish to explain as follows:

1. The cartons we use are up to standard and fit for ocean transportation. For years we have used these cartons in our shipments to many continental ports to the entire satisfaction of our clients. Moreover, the insurance companies have accepted such packing for WPA and TPND.

2. These cartons are well protected against moisture by plastic lining. Thus garments packed in them are not as susceptible to damage by moisture as those packed in wooden cases.

3. The cardboard used for making cartons is light but compact. It keeps down packaging costs and helps customers save on freight.

4. Your clients' anxieties over packing are presumed. We are confident that the insurance company can be made to pay the necessary compensation for any loss or losses from pilferage and breakage caused by using such cartons.

Please tell your clients that their fears are unwarranted. Nowadays, except for bulk cargo, nude cargo and huge machinery, most commodities are packed in cartons. To pack garments in wooden cases is obsolete. For future shipments, we are experimenting with special cartons, in which garments are hung on dress-hangers. These cartons can be containerized, so that the garments will not twist.

We highly value your comments, which will help improve our work. If you find any defect in our last shipment, please do not hesitate to let us know. We assure you of our cooperation and await your further orders.

Yours faithfully,

Letter 7-10

Dear Sirs,

On April 20, we received your consignment of 50 cardboard cartons of steel screws. We regret to inform you that 15 cartons were delivered damaged and the contents had spilled, leading to some losses.

We accept that the damage was not your fault but feel that we must modify our packing requirements to avoid future losses. We require that future packing be in wooden boxes of 25 kilos net, each wooden box containing 50 cardboard packs of 500 grams net.

Please let us know whether these specifications can be met by you and whether they will lead to an increase in your prices.

We look forward to your early confirmation.

Yours faithfully,

Letter 7-11

Dear Sirs,

We regret to inform you that the 200 cartons of nails you shipped to London on September 1, 2017 were badly damaged, of course through no fault of yours.

We are now writing to you in regard to the packing of these nails, which we feel necessary to explain for our future business.

The packing for London is to be in double gunny bags of 60 kilos each. For Rotterdam, we would like you to have the goods packed in wooden cases of 136 lbs net, each containing 8 lbs × 17 packets.

Kindly let us know whether these requirements could be met.

Yours faithfully,

Letter 7-12

> Dear Sirs,
>   We are pleased to inform you that the portable computers have now been shipped to you as specified below.
>   Packing: in 30 cartons, 20 portable computers to a carton.
>   Shipping marks: GC123 in diamond, London. Particulars of weight and measurement are given in the enclosed sheet.
>   Shipment: by S. S. "Fendou" of Sinotrans, which sailed from Shanghai on April 2, and is scheduled to arrive at London on April 23.
>   We have given a complete set of Bills of Lading, together with Invoice and Insurance Certificate, both in triplicates, to Citibank with a sight draft for US $50,000 under the terms of the L/C, and we have received the sum from the said bank.
>   We shall appreciate your information on the arrival of the consignment.
>   Yours faithfully,

7.6 练习

Exercises

Ⅰ. Translate the following phrases into Chinese.

1. packing
2. corrugated box
3. sales packing
4. indicative mark
5. gross weight
6. net weight
7. tare weight
8. wooden case
9. container
10. thorough examination
11. survey report
12. rough handling
13. shipping company
14. shipping advice
15. bill of lading
16. insurance certificate
17. sight draft
18. warning mark
19. inner packing
20. outer packing

Ⅱ. Choose the best answer.

1. _____ that it is necessary to take precautions to protect the goods from moisture, you should insure them against Fresh and Rain Water Damage Risks.
   A. Considering   B. To consider
   C. Consider   D. Considered

2. We are confident that our crate for the goods are not only _____ but also strong enough to protect the goods from any possible damage.
   A. seaworth   B. seaworthy

C. for sea D. fit for sea

3. The buyer suggested that the packing of this article _____ improved.
   A. be B. had to be
   C. was to be D. would be

4. You know that the appearance of the _____ contributes greatly to the sale of the consumer goods.
   A. packed B. package
   C. packing D. pack

5. Pens are packed 12 pieces _____ a box and 200 boxes _____ a wooden case.
   A. to, in B. in, to
   C. to, to D. to, of

6. Please see to it that the packing is suitable for a long sea _____ .
   A. travel B. trip
   C. voyage D. sail

7. We _____ our shirts in plastic-lined, waterproof cartons, reinforced with metal straps.
   A. put B. place
   C. pack D. fix

8. A thorough examination showed that the broken kegs were due to _____ packing for which the suppliers should definitely be responsible.
   A. proper B. improper
   C. unproper D. inproper

9. The packing must be strong enough _____ rough handling.
   A. withstand B. withstanding
   C. to withstand D. to be withstood

10. The report of survey revealed that the damage is _____ improper packing.
    A. contributed to B. because
    C. because of D. attributable to

Ⅲ. Fill in the blanks.

1. We look forward _____ receiving your shipping advice and thank you in advance.
2. In order to eliminate possible future troubles, we would like to make _____ beforehand our packing requirements as follows.
3. The packing should be suitable _____ long distance shipment.
4. The new development is likely to produce a favorable effect _____ the prices.
5. The shirts under the captioned contract should be packed _____ plastic bags, five dozen to one carton, 20 cartons on a pallet, 10 pallets in FCL container.
6. _____ reference to the coke under contract No. 162, we discovered that 11 drums are short of weight, each from 2kgs to 4kgs, totaling 30kgs.
7. We regret to inform you that your claim cannot be entertained as it is raised far _____ the time limit for claim set forth in the contract.
8. We sincerely apologize _____ the inconvenience caused to you.

9. We refer _____ Sales Contract No. 242 covering the purchase of 300 coffee sets.

10. _____ the strength of the survey report, we hereby register our claim against you as follows.

Ⅳ. Translate the following sentences into Chinese.
1. Kindly let us know whether these requirements could be met.
2. As glassware are extremely fragile, the goods must be wrapped in a poly-bag and packed in a standard export wooden case lined with foam capable of withstanding rough handling during transit.
3. Your fax of August 31st is greatly appreciated.
4. We are expecting a reply at your earliest convenience.
5. Pens are packed 12 pieces to a box and 200 boxes to a wooden case.
6. Please take necessary precautions that the packing can protect the goods from dampness or rain.
7. Referring to the shipment of our Order No. 123 for 200 cases of glassware, we wish to draw your attention to the following.
8. We hope you will be able to comply with our request.
9. The instruments are damaged chiefly due to improper packing. They were packed too loose inside the wooden cases while not stuffed.
10. We regret to inform you that we can not comply with your request for packing.

Ⅴ. Translate the following sentences into English.
1. 鉴定员认为损害是由于包装不牢固造成的，而非搬运不当所致。
2. 检查货物时，我们发现有50袋因使用不合标准的包装袋而破裂，里面货物重达2 500千克，已无法挽回地丢失。
3. 为答复你方9月2日询问我方彩色电视机包装之事的来函，现告知如下。
4. 我方同意贵方的包装要求。
5. 上述说明供你方参考。如在月底之前没有收到贵公司的不同意见，我们将照此执行。
6. 我们希望最终一切都令人满意。
7. 由于包装不当而引起的短重，供应商应该负责任。
8. 鉴于货物易碎的特点，你方需要采取特别的包装措施以预防破碎。
9. 我方检验证明，货物受损是由于包装不当造成的。因此，我们不得不将此事提交你处解决。
10. 作为一种包装容器，纸板箱已在国际贸易中广泛使用。

Ⅵ. Writing task.
Write a letter to ABC Co. with the following particulars.
（1）Importance of trustworthy packing;
（2）Requirements for machine parts packing;
（3）Request for confirming all other packing information before the shipment;
（4）Thanks in advance for the cooperation of ABC Co.

Chapter 8

第 8 章

装 运
Shipment

Learning Objectives

Enable the students to know about the necessity of choosing the correct mode of shipment; to be familiar with modes of shipment in the international trade; to master the structure and common expressions in this type of letters.

使学生了解选择正确运输方式的必要性；熟悉国际贸易中使用的主要运输方式；掌握撰写有关装运条款的函件结构以及常用的表达形式。

8.1 背景知识
Background Information

运输条款是销售合同中重要且不可缺少的部分。其涉及装船时间、装运港和目的港、运输方式、装船通知、装船指示以及装运单据等。

装船时间指卖方必须完成合同货物装船的时间期限或最后截止日期。因此在合同中必须恰当地规定装船时间。当买卖双方在签署合同之前商议装船时间时，应认真考虑几个重要因素，如货物及舱位的可用性、规定的灵活性和明确性、货物的性质等（尤其针对一些特殊的货物，如茶叶；季节性货物，如冷冻肉）。

The shipment clause is an integral and important part of a sales contract. It involves time of shipment, port of loading and destination, modes of transportation, shipping advice and instruction and shipping documents, etc.

Time of shipment refers to the time limit or deadline by which the seller must effect shipment of the contract goods. It is necessary to stipulate the time of shipment properly in the contract. When the buyer and seller discuss it before the contract is signed, several important factors should be taken into consideration carefully such as the availability of goods and shipping space, flexibility and clarity of stipulation, nature of cargoes (especially for some special goods like tea and seasonal goods like frozen meat).

对于出口商来说，选择正确的交货方式十分重要，因为其涉及货物的安全、运费、到达时间、货物的销售以及业务的拓展。一般情况下，天气状况、时间、生产能力、风险、货物类型、速度、灵活性、成本以及服务等因素都会或多或少地影响运输方式的选择。运输方式主要包括海洋运输、铁路运输、航空运输、集装箱运输、内陆运输、邮政运输、内河运输以及国际多式联运等。

每种运输方式都有其优点和缺点，然而在国际货物运输中，海洋运输是最重要的运输方式。根据船舶的经营方式，海洋运输可以分为两种形式：班轮运输和租船运输；同时，根据货物运送方式又可以将海洋运输分为直接运输、分批运输以及转船运输。

海洋货物运输单据通常包括提单、商业发票、保险单、装箱单、检验证书、原产地证书、重量单等，这些单据作为出口汇票的随附单据，其中前三项单据最为重要。一般来讲，运输单据应在装运后由出口方或者卖方交与银行用于议付货款。有时，在向买方发出告知其做好接船准备的装船通知时，相关货运单据的副本也会相应附上。

在撰写货物运输相关的信函时，信函的写作目的主要有以下几个方面：催促尽早装运、修改装运条件，给予装船指示或发出装船通知以及提供装运单据等。除了上述目的外，若我们已掌握

It's very important for the exporter to choose a correct method of delivery, because this concerns the safety of goods, freight, time of arrival, sales of goods and development of the business. And usually such terms as weather condition, time, capacity, risks, cargo types, speed, flexibility, cost, service and so on will influence the decision more or less. Modes of transport include marine transport, railway transport, air transport, container transport, inland transport, postal transport, inland waterway transport, international multi-modal transport, etc.

And each has its advantages and drawbacks. While in international cargo transportation, ocean transport is the most important one. According to its mode of operation, ocean transport can be divided into two types: Liner Shipping and Chartering Shipping/Tramp Shipping. At the meanwhile, means of conveyance can also be divided into direct shipment, partial shipment and transhipment.

Shipping documents usually include the B/L, commercial invoice, insurance policy, packing list, certificate of inspection, certificate of origin, weight memo, etc, which are along with the export bill of exchange, and among them the first three documents are necessary. Generally speaking, shipping documents should be given by the exporter or the seller to the bank for negotiating the payment of the goods after shipment. And sometimes when sending the shipping advice to the buyer for getting ready for the acceptance of the shipment, the copies of duplicates of theses should be given, too.

When writing letters regarding shipment, the letters should be written for the following purposes: to urge an early shipment; to amend shipping terms; to give shipping instruction or advice; to dispatch shipping documents and so on. And we also can succeed in availing the writing opportunity to convey the good will of fulfilling

适当的写作技巧，也可以在信中表达能够圆满履行合同，拓展业务关系的良好意愿。

1. 关于装船通知信函的写作步骤：

（1）通知买方×××合同项下的货物已经在×××日期装上×××船只；

（2）通知买方按照合同规定已寄出的相关运输单据；

（3）希望货物能够完好无损地到达买方，并使买方满意；

（4）感谢买方的订单，希望继续收到订单。

2. 撰写催促/提前装船信函的写作步骤：

（1）提及相关事项及货物，并强调信用证已经开出；

（2）指出催促/提前装船的必要性及原因；

（3）提示对方若延迟装船会对交易带来的危害；感谢卖方为满足我方要求而给予的配合。

3. 关于通知分批装运以及转船运输信函的写作步骤：

（1）提及上一封信函及主要内容；

（2）建议采取分批运输或者转船运输，并说明提出此建议的原因；

（3）建议买方接受、确认并相应修改相关信用证；

（4）希望尽快收到信用证修改通知。

the contract and expanding business relations besides the original purposes if handling the proper writing skills.

1. Writing steps of shipping advice letters.

(1) Inform the buyer that the goods under ××× contract have been shipped via S. S. ××× on ××× date.

(2) Advise the buyer what shipping documents have been sent according to the contract stipulations.

(3) Wish the goods to arrive in sound condition and make the buyers satisfactory.

(4) Thank the buyer's order and wish to receive his repeat orders.

2. Writing steps of urging/advancing shipment letters.

(1) Identify the reference and the goods, and state that the relative L/C has been opened.

(2) State the necessity and reasons of urging/advancing shipment.

(3) Hint the harm to business if shipping is delayed and thank the seller for cooperation by meeting with the request.

3. Writing steps of partial shipment/transshipment advice letters.

(1) Refer to the last letter and its main idea.

(2) Advise to adopt partial shipment or transshipment mode, and give the reasons why theses modes will be adopted.

(3) Request the buyer to accept, confirm and amend the relative L/C accordingly.

(4) Look forward to receiving the amendment advice.

8.2 信例
Specimen Letters

Letter 8-1 Urging immediate or punctual shipment

Dear Sirs,

We wish to invite your attention to our Order No. 3781 covering 50,000 dozen socks, for which we sent to you about 30 days ago an irrevocable L/C No. BA288.

The shipment should be effected by the date as contracted. However, up to present, we have not received any information about it. As the season is rapidly approaching and our buyers are badly in need of these socks, we shall be very much obliged if you will effect shipment of the goods as soon as possible, thus enabling them to catch the brisk demand at the start of the season.

We would like to emphasize that any delay in shipping our booked order will undoubtedly involve us in great difficulty.

Should this trial order prove satisfactory to our clients, we are fully confident that repeat orders will follow soon. We thank you in advance for your cooperation in this respect and await your shipping advice by fax.

We are looking forward to your early reply.

Faithfully yours,

Letter 8-2 Insisting on shipments by designated steamer

Dear Sirs,

With reference to our Order No. 99 for 400 metric tons of peanut oil, we have today received a fax from our buyer, Black and White Company Ltd., regarding delivery of the order.

We wish to draw your attention once again to our letter of October 8, in which we have given you our instructions as to how Order No. 99 should be shipped. To meet their requirements, it is of great importance to our buyers that the arrival dates of the order should be confirmed as early as possible. The main reason for our insisting on shipments being carried by steamers of K-Liners is that their steamers offer the shortest time for the journey between Hong Kong and Hamburg. We shall appreciate it if you will endeavor to ship the consignments as follows:

> Order No. 99 by S. S. Montreal due to sail from Hong Kong on October 16, arriving at Hamburg on October 28.
>
> We shall appreciate very much your close cooperation in this respect and shall always find opportunities to reciprocate.
>
> Yours faithfully,

Letter 8-3 Sending a shipping advice (1)

> Gentlemen:
> RE: L/C No. M06125, S/C No. MED06188
>
> We are pleased to inform you that we have shipped the covering goods according to your instruction by M. S. "Dongfeng", which shipped from Shanghai yesterday and is due to arrive at Hamburg on June 8. The details are given below:
>
> Name of Commodity: Soy beans
>
> Enclosed please find copies of the following relevant shipping documents:
> - Commercial Invoice No. ARD8199 in duplicate
> - Packing list No. 24566 in duplicate
> - Non-negotiable Bill of Lading No. AD458 in duplicate
> - Insurance Policy No. SHO2/PYCK20158988
> - Inspection Certificate No. CH201566289
>
> As desired, we have drawn a draft at sight for USD 65,500.00 to cover the shipment and negotiated it through Bank of China Hangzhou Sub-branch under your L/C No. M06125.
>
> We trust the above shipment will reach you in good condition and expect to receive your further order before long. We appreciate the business you have been able to secure for us and assure you that all your future correspondence, enquires and orders will continue to receive our careful attention.
>
> Truly yours,

Letter 8-4 Sending a shipping advice (2)

> Dear Sirs,
>
> We take pleasure to notify you that the wine you ordered under S/C No. 445 has been shipped on board S/S Elizabeth which is sailing from Hong Kong to New York via Panama Canal on March 6, 2015 and is due to arrive at New York on or about April 15.

Further details, regarding the consignment including packing and shipping marks, are contained in our Invoice No. 112 enclosed in three copies. In order to cover this shipment, we have drawn on you a draft for the amount of US $29,000 under L/C No. 321 and negotiated it through the Bank of China with the relative shipping documents. Enclosed please find one set of duplicate shipping documents for the goods, the originals of which are being sent to you through our bankers.

We trust that this consignment will turn out to your entire satisfaction, and hope that we shall have many opportunities in future to demonstrate our ability to handle orders promptly and carefully.

Yours faithfully,

Letter 8-5 Introduction to the shipment container

Dear Sirs,

Thank you for your inquiry of June 5. The shipping containers we provide are of two sizes, namely 10ft. and 20ft. They can be opened at both ends, thus making it possible to load and unload at the same time. They are both water-tight and air-tight and can be loaded and locked at the factory, if necessary.

When separate consignments are carried in one container, and if their port of destination is same, there will be a saving on freight charges, and an additional saving on insurance because of the lower premium charges for container-shipped goods.

We enclose a copy of our tariff and look forward to receiving your instructions.

Yours faithfully,

Letter 8-6 Requesting advancing shipment

Dear Sirs,

With reference to our Order No. 333 for 20 sets spinning machines, under the terms of the order, shipment is scheduled during June/July. We would now like to bring shipment forward to March/April.

We realize that the change of shipment date will probably bring you inconvenience and we offer sincere apologies. We know that you will understand that we would not ask for earlier shipment if we did not have compelling reasons for doing so.

> In view of our longstanding, cordial business relationship, we shall appreciate it very much if you would make a special effort to comply with our request.
> We look forward to your early reply.
> Yours faithfully,

Notes

1. invite your attention to...
   提醒贵方注意的是……
   invite 还可以替换为 draw, direct, call 等。
2. shipment
   n. 装运
   Partial shipment is not allowed. 不允许分批装运。
   船货；到货
   Our customers are satisfied with your last shipment.
   我方客户对贵方上次货物表示满意。
   装船期限
   Please extend the shipment for 20 days.
   请将装运期展延 20 天。
   常见短语：
   make/effect/handle/arrange shipment 装运
   expedite/rush/hasten/speed up shipment 加速装运
   shipment time/date 装运期
   advance shipment/bring shipment forward 提前装运
   postpone shipment 延迟装运
   （1）It is stipulated that shipment is to be made in October. However, we shall appreciate the shipment to September to enable us to catch the busy season.
   按规定应于 10 月装运，但是如蒙贵方设法提前于 9 月交货以使我方赶上旺季，则不胜感激。
   （2）As the market is sluggish, please postpone the shipment of our ordered goods to March.
   由于市场萧条，请将我方所订购货物延迟至 3 月。
   表示平均装运：
   to make shipment in three equal lots
   分三次平均装运
   The contract stipulated that the shipment should be made in two equal lots.
   合同规定需分两批等量装运。
   表示某月份装运：
   shipment in May
   for shipment during June and July

shipment May

for May shipment

(1) Shipment is to be made during April to June in three equal lots.

装运在 4 月至 6 月期间，分三次平均装运。

(2) We will do our best to expedite shipment to meet your requirements in time.

我们将尽力早装，及时满足你方所需。

(3) Please ship the three lots on a single bill of lading.

请将这三批货用一张提单装出。

3. up to present

到目前为止，等同于 up to now，up to date，up till now，up to the moment，so far。

4. be drawing near

日益临近，等同于 be approaching。

5. involve sb. in no small difficulty

把某人牵涉到大麻烦中，还可以说 involve sb. in trouble。

6. shipping

n. 海运

shipping company　轮船公司

shipping agent　货运代理人

shipping instruction　装运指示；装运须知

shipping advice　装运通知

shipping document　装运单据

shipping mark　装运标志

shipping container　船运集装箱

shipping order　装货纸；装货单

shipping space　舱位；船位

shipping date　装船日期

shipping day　开船日期

Shipping documents may include：

运输单据包括：

(1) commercial invoice　商业发票

(2) bill of lading　提单

(3) insurance policy　保险单

(4) packing list　装箱单

(5) weight memo　重量单；磅码单

(6) certificate of origin　原产地证明

(7) certificate of inspection　检验证明

7. reserve

v. 预订；保留

(1) It is difficult to reserve shipping space on account of heavy congestion.

由于货运拥挤，很难订到舱位。

(2) The final control and management of the factory shall be reserved to the first party.
   甲方保留对工厂的最终控制权和经营权。

8. forwarding

   n. 货运代理业；发送

   forwarding agency/house   货运代理行

   forwarding agent   货运代理人

   forwarding country   发送国

   forwarding operation   代运业务

   forward

   adj. 在前部的；远期的；期货的；预约的

   forward rates   远期汇率

   forward exchange transaction   远期外汇交易

   adv. 向前；出来；提前地；今后地

   (1) We look forward to hearing from you. 盼望得到你方回复。

   (2) Put forward your proposal. 提出你方建议

   freight forward = freight to collect   运费到付

   date forward   预填日期

   v. 寄送；发送

   Your order No. 123 can be forwarded early next month.

   你的订单123号最早下个月发货。

9. seaworthy

   adj. 适合海运的

   (1) The goods under Order No. 321 shall be packed in seaworthy wooden cases.
      第321号订单项下的货物须用适于海运的木箱包装。

   (2) Our cartons for canned food are not only seaworthy, but also strong enough to protect the goods from possible damage.
      我方罐头食品纸箱包装不仅适合海运，而且很结实，能防止货物受损。

10. withstand

    v. 抵挡；顶得住；经受住

    (1) The goods must be packed in seaworthy wooden cases capable of withstanding rough handling.
       货物必须用适于海运的木箱包装，能经受住粗鲁搬运。

    (2) Seaworthy packing is necessary to protect the goods from the strains of long sea voyage.
       若使货物能经受长途海运，必须要用适合海运的包装。

    (3) The contract stipulates that the packing should be strong enough to withstand rough handling.
       合同规定包装必须牢固，足以承受野蛮装卸。

11. rough handling

    粗鲁搬运；野蛮装运

    Any damage resulted from rough handling must be compensated by the seller.

任何由装卸不慎引起的损坏由卖方赔偿。

12. shipping mark

    装运标志；唛头

    to mark　刷上；刷唛

    (1) On the outer packing, please mark our initials SCC in a diamond.

    　　在外包装上，请刷上一菱形，内刷我公司首字母 SCC。

    (2) The cases are to be marked with the lot number as given in the order sheet.

    　　箱子上应按订单所示刷上批号。

    to have the marking　标上……；有……标记

    Each package should have the marking "fragile".

    每个包装上应标上"易碎"字样。

    to be stenciled or printed（with…）　被印上……

    Please mark our initials SCC in a diamond, under which the port of destination and our order number should be stenciled or printed.

    请刷上一菱形，内刷我公司首字母 SCC，其下刷目的港及我方订单号。

    to indicate　显示；标出

    It's not necessary to indicate the name and address of the consignee on each package, as shipping marks comprises the initials of the buyer's name.

    不需要在每个包装上标出收货人名称和地址，因为装运唛头包含了买方名称的首字母。

13. negotiate

    v. 谈判；商谈；兑换（支票）

    negotiating bank　议付银行

    (1) The Trade Union negotiated a new contract with the owner.

    　　工会与厂家商订了一份新合同。

    (2) We are sorry that our bank does not negotiate foreign cheques.

    　　抱歉我方银行不兑换外国支票。

14. sailing

    n. 航行；航程

    (1) There are no more sailings this month.

    　　本月不再有船。

    (2) There are six sailings a day.

    　　每天有 6 个船运航班。

    adj. 航行的

    (1) The next sailing opportunity is September 10.

    　　下次船是 9 月 10 日。

    (2) Please fax name and approximate sailing date of vessel on which space is booked.

    　　请传真告知预订舱位轮船的船名以及大约起航的日期。

15. liable

    adj. 易于……的；有……倾向的（后接介词 to）；有责任的（后接介词 for）

    (1) She's liable to airsickness.

她容易晕机。

(2) Without careful investigation, we are liable to come to wrong conclusions.
不仔细调查研究，我们就很容易得出错误结论。

(3) Other buyers are liable to misunderstand if we allow you a special discount.
如果我们给你们特别折扣，其他买主容易产生误解。

(4) We are not liable for the delay in shipment.
我们对装运延误不承担责任。

(5) All the canned fruits and meats are to be packed in cartons. If the cartons are not strong enough, most of them will be liable to go broken on arrival. We would suggest that you strengthen the cartons with double straps.
所有水果和肉罐头都用纸板箱包装。如果纸板箱不够结实，货到时大多数纸板箱很容易破损。因此，我方建议用两根包装带加固纸板箱。

16. freight

    n. 运费；货物

    freight list   运价表

    freight charges   运费

    freight rate   运费率

    freight rebate   运费回扣

    freight space   舱位；船位

    freight tariff   运费表

    freight ton   运费吨

    freight to collect   运费到付

    freight prepaid   运费预付

17. tariff

    n. 价目表；关税；关税率；运费费率表

    conventional tariff   协定税率

    preferential tariff   特惠税率

    tariff barrier   关税壁垒

    (1) There is a very high tariff on this kind of merchandise.
    对这种商品所征收的关税税率很高。

    (2) We shall appreciate it if you could send us your latest tariffs.
    如蒙寄给最新运费费率表将不胜感激。

Words and Phrases

carton	n. 纸板箱
contract	v. 签合同
punctual	adj. 严守时刻的；守时的
Montreal	n. 蒙特利尔（加拿大的港口城市）
via	prep. 通过；经由

duplicate	n. 复制品；副本
original	n. 正本
compelling	adj. 强制的；令人信服的
cordial	adj. 诚挚的
remaining	adj. 剩余的
as contracted	按合同约定
be badly in need of	急需
be obliged to	对……感激
catch the selling season	赶上销售旺季
trial order	试订单
repeat orders	续订单
be susceptible to shock	易受震损的
capable of	能够……
in transit	在运输途中
give the users entire satisfaction	使用户完全满意
Panama Canal	巴拿马运河
spinning machines	纺纱机
comply with	照做；符合
best selling	畅销的
supply…from stock	现货供应
meet with one's approval	得到……的认可，同意

8.3 外贸实战技巧
Techniques in Foreign Trade Practice

分批装运风险及防范

分批装运是国际贸易货物运输中十分常见的做法。其原因包括卖方货源不足，市场需求有限，运载工具有限等。卖方在根据合同和信用证规定办理分批装运时，将面临以下风险：

第一，是否允许分批装运的风险。正确理解信用证条款和审核信用证是一项重要工作，单证严格一致是安全收汇的绝对保证。

第二，分批装运次数方面的风险。

第三，每批装运数量方面的风险。尽管合同和信用证规定了每一批装运货物的数量，但由于货源、船舶以及其他方面的原因，卖方可能无法按既定要求分批装运。

第四，分批装运时间方面的风险。《跟单信用证统一惯例》第41条规定："如信用证规定在指定的时期内分期装运，任何一期未按信用证所规定期限装运时，信用证对该期及以后各期均告失效，除非信用证另有规定。"

从防范风险的角度来看，卖方在办理分批装运时，应做到以下几点：

第一，严格按照合同或信用证规定确定是否分批装运。一般来说，无论是否允许分批装运，合同和信用证中都应明确说明。在允许分批装运时，还应进一步明确分批装运的时间、次数、货物种类和数量。当合同和信用证中未明确规定禁止分批装运时,按照惯例,应视为可以分批装运,且卖方有决定权。

第二,对于分批装运的时间、批次、货物种类和数量等细节性问题,如果合同和信用证中已做出规定,卖方应严格按规定行事;如果因为港口、船舶或货源等方面的原因而无法执行合同和信用证的规定时,卖方应及时与买方联系,请求变通;如属受不可抗力事件影响,卖方应从双方利益出发,自行调整履约行为、时间和内容,并将不可抗力事实及时通告对方,争取免责。

第三,提高国际贸易业务人员的业务素质。在国际贸易中,审证工作是一项非常重要而又细致的工作,需要对信用证条款有一定理解能力的人员担任此项工作,才能对企业起到把关的作用。在审证时,要严格审查信用证条款,逐字逐句地严格审核。如遇到不了解、不清楚的条款,不能自以为是,应及时与有关方面核实、商讨,最后落实。

8.4 有用的句子
Useful Sentences

1. We are glad to inform you that the goods you ordered are ready for shipment. Please let us have your instructions for packing and dispatch.
   我方高兴地通知,贵方所订购的货物已备妥待运,请告知包装及装运要求。
2. Please book the necessary shipping space in advance to insure timely dispatch of the goods ordered.
   请预订所需的舱位以保证及时装运所订购的货物。
3. The order No. 306 is so urgently required that we have to ask you to speed up shipment.
   第 306 号订单所需货物我们急用,请你们加快装船速度。
4. The goods must be shipped before October, or we won't catch the season.
   货物必须在 10 月之前装船,否则我们就赶不上销售旺季。
5. You may rest assured that we will expedite/hasten/rush the shipment as soon as possible.
   请放心我们一定会尽快装运。
6. As the purchase is made under FOB terms, you should ship the goods from Liverpool on a steamer to be designated by us.
   由于采用 FOB 价购货,贵方应在利物浦港将货物装上我方指定的船只。
7. Our customer request the shipment should be made in three equal lots, during January to June (each every two months).
   我方客户要求从 1 月到 6 月分三批等量运输(每两个月装一批)。
8. As our users are in urgent need of the consignment, please get the goods dispatched within the stipulated time.
   由于我方客户急需此货物,请按规定的时间发运。
9. It is stipulated that shipment is to be made in October. However, we shall appreciate the shipment to September to enable us to catch the busy season.
   按规定应于 10 月装运,但是如蒙贵方设法提前于 9 月交货以使我方赶上旺季,则不胜感激。
10. Something unexpected compels us to seek your cooperation by advancing shipment of the goods

under S/C No. 730 from Aug./Sep. to July.

意外的情况迫使我们寻求贵方配合，请将第 730 号售货确认书项下货物装运期由 8、9 月提前到 7 月。

11. We take pleasure in advising you that we have today shipped the goods under your Order No. 756 on board S/S "Peace" which sails for your port tomorrow.

我方高兴地通知贵方，756 号订单项下货物已于今日装上"和平"号轮，该轮将于明日驶往贵方港口。

12. We are pleased to inform you that Contract No. 332 for 5,000 sets Haier DVD Players has been dispatched by S.S. Mayflower which sailed from Shanghai yesterday and is due to arrive at London on March 6, 2018.

我方高兴地通知贵方，332 号合同项下的 5 000 台海尔 DVD 由五月花轮运出，该轮昨天从上海起航，定于 2018 年 3 月 6 日抵达伦敦。

13. We have pleasure in notifying you that we have shipped you today by M.V. "Yellow River" 200 cartons of alarm clocks. They are to be transshipped at Hongkong and are expected to reach your port early next month.

我方高兴地通知贵方，已由"黄河"号轮将 200 箱闹钟运往贵处。此货物将在香港转船，预计于下月初到达贵方港口。

14. In compliance with the terms of the contract, a full set of non-negotiable documents were airmailed to you immediately after the goods were shipped.

按照合同条款，在货物装船后即将全套单据副本空邮给贵方。

15. The Commercial Invoice and Insurance Policy together with clean on board Ocean Bill of Lading have been sent through the National Bank.

商业发票、保险单和清洁、已装船海运提单已交国家银行转送。

8.5 补充商务信函
Letters for Further Reading

Letter 8-7

Dear Sirs,

We are in the receipt of your letter of January 21 with thanks, regarding your order No. PA 459 for 35 sets of X324 spinning machines, in which you ask for earlier shipment of the whole order.

We are sorry that we are unable to comply with your request because the article you ordered is our best selling product and we have a lot of orders to fulfill, so that we cannot supply 35 sets machines from stock at the same time.

> If you wish to get the products earlier, we would like to make a partial shipment of 18 sets in April and ship the remaining 17 sets in June. We hope this arrangement will meet with your approval.
>
> If you agree with the new arrangement, please fax an amendment of the relevant L/C, then we will effect partial shipment.
>
> We look forward to your prompt reply so that we can ask the manufacturer to effect the shipment.
>
> Yours faithfully,

Letter 8-8

> Dear Sirs,
>
> Referring to our letters in respect to Order No. 2170 for 1,000 metric tons of Tin Foil Sheets, so far we have no definite information from you about delivery time, although these goods are contracted for shipment before the end of last month, and our L/C was opened with the Bank of China as early as in March 2018.
>
> We have been inconvenienced by the delay. You should fax us immediately of the earliest possible date of shipment for our consideration without prejudicing our right to cancel the order and/or lodge claims for our losses.
>
> Please look into the matter and give us your definite reply without further delay.
>
> Yours faithfully,

Letter 8-9

> Dear Sirs,
>
> Re: Your L/C No. 5757 covering your Order No. 134
>
> Thank you for your extension of your L/C No. 5757. Today we shipped the above consignment on board S.S. "Nellore" which sails for your port tomorrow.
>
> Enclosed please find one set of the shipping documents covering this consignment, as follows:
>
> (1) One copy of B/L
> (2) Invoice in duplicate
> (3) Packing List in triplicate
> (4) One copy of Manufacturer's Certificate of Quality
> (5) One copy of Insurance Policy

We are glad to have filled your order after long delay and trust that the goods will reach you in time to meet your urgent need and that they will turn out to your complete satisfaction.

We will fill your future orders promptly and carefully.

Yours faithfully,

Letter 8-10

Dear Sirs,

We confirm having received your letter of October 5, for which we thank you.

With respect to the 50,000 metric tons wheat, 5% more or less at buyer's option, we would like to say that the loading rate is 5,000 metric tons per weather working day of 24 consecutive hours, Sundays and holidays at port of loading included. In case it exceeds this figure, the time will count pro rata. We have to point out that you must submit your final confirmation for lay days to us so that proper arrangements for loading can be made by us as we have other loading commitments.

We also agree demurrage and dispatch money shall be settled directly between the sellers and the ship owners and insist that you should advise us of the estimated time of arrival 15 days prior to the arrival of the carrying vessel at the port of loading. Please confirm and reply.

Yours faithfully,

Letter 8-11

Dear Sirs,

We refer to your Order No. 456 for 1,000 DVD players. Owing to the problem at the port, we will not be able to meet the agreed delivery date of October 1.

We are doing everything possible to ship your order, but the contracted date has now become unrealistic. We believe, however, that we will be able to meet the December 1 delivery deadline.

We apologize for the inconvenience, but the delay is due to circumstances beyond our control. It would be much appreciated if you could understand our position and do hope that will not influence our future cooperation.

Yours faithfully,

Letter 8-12

> Dear Sirs,
>
> Referring to Contract No. 201 covering 31 metric tons of mild steel flat bars, we believe that amendment to the relative L/C has reached you already. We should like to solicit your cooperation to expedite shipment.
>
> Yesterday, our clients came to us with the request that 21 M/Ts of the bars be shipped during February and the remainder in March, as they are in urgent need of them.
>
> We presume that you must have received a lot of bookings for this commodity abroad, resulting in a tight shipping schedule. Nevertheless, we venture to write to you, hoping you will see your way to accommodate us. Thank you in advance for your kind cooperation.
>
> Yours faithfully,

8.6 练习
Exercises

Ⅰ. Translate the following phrases into Chinese.
1. packing list
2. rough handling
3. discharge port
4. loading port
5. partial shipment
6. freight prepaid
7. liner terms
8. bill of lading
9. shipping space
10. forwarding company
11. trial order
12. repeat order
13. freight list
14. freight charges
15. freight rate
16. forwarding country
17. forwarding operation
18. safe and sound
19. Panama Canal
20. spinning machines

Ⅱ. Choose the best answer.
1. Please make sure that our order will be executed to the entire _____ of our customers.
   A. satisfactory   B. satisfaction
   C. satisfy   D. satisfied
2. We regret keenly this delay and can only hope it will not have seriously _____ you.
   A. trouble   B. inconvenient
   C. inconvenienced   D. convenienced
3. The goods _____ if your L/C had arrived by the end of June.
   A. would be shipped already   B. must have been shipped already
   C. had been shipped already   D. have been shipped already
4. Unless otherwise _____, we wish to arrange to take out a TPND insurance policy for you on

the shipment.
   A. instructed　　　　　　　　　　B. instructions
   C. instructs　　　　　　　　　　　D. instructing
5. You may be aware that any further delay _____ shipment will bring about adverse effect on our future business.
   A. on　　　　　　　　　　　　　　B. for
   C. with　　　　　　　　　　　　　D. in
6. Please try your best to ship our order _____ that steamer.
   A. by　　　　　　　　　　　　　　B. for
   C. in　　　　　　　　　　　　　　D. with
7. Direct steamers to your port are few _____ winter season.
   A. with　　　　　　　　　　　　　B. on
   C. against　　　　　　　　　　　　D. during
8. We find _____ transshipment and partial shipment of the Men's Shirts are not possible.
   A. that　　　　　　　　　　　　　B. what
   C. where　　　　　　　　　　　　D. if
9. For the goods under S/C No. 234, we _____ space on S. S. East Wind due to arrive at London around May 3.
   A. have booked　　　　　　　　　B. have bought
   C. have hired　　　　　　　　　　D. have retained
10. We were surprised to learn from your fax today that the rice has not reached you. It _____ on November 2, and should have reached you by the end of the month.
    A. dispatched　　　　　　　　　　B. has been dispatched
    C. will dispatch　　　　　　　　　D. was dispatched

Ⅲ. Fill in the blanks.
   1. Owing _____ the delay _____ the part of the suppliers, we must ask you to extend the date _____ shipment _____ September 15 _____ October 15.
   2. We wish to draw your attention _____ the fact that the date _____ delivery is approaching, but up _____ the present moment we have not received any news _____ you.
   3. Today we shipped the above consignment _____ board S. S. "Xinghai" which sails _____ your port tomorrow.
   4. Please take the matter _____ consideration at once and see to it that the goods are delivered _____ the least possible delay.
   5. We shall appreciate it if you will inform us _____ the condition of packing as soon as the consignment arrives _____ your end.
   6. We could not deliver the total quantity _____ one shipment.
   7. Shipment is _____ _____ made from April to June _____ three equal lots.
   8. As the manufacturers cannot get all the quantity ready at the same time, it is necessary _____ the contract stipulations to be so worded as to _____ partial shipment.
   9. We hope you will make every effort to effect shipment _____ the stipulated time as any

delay would cause us much trouble and financial loss.

10. Kindly advise us of the steamer that call _____ your port every month.

Ⅳ. Translate the following sentences into Chinese.
1. The goods ordered are all in stock and we assure you that the first steamer will make the shipment available in November.
2. Please be informed that the shipment of the cargo was sent yesterday, airway bill No. 123.
3. In case you do not receive the goods on or before December 23, please let us know.
4. The facilities for shipping goods to Southeast Asia countries have changed a lot.
5. Sometimes, we have to make a transshipment because there is no suitable loading port in the producing country.
6. So far as I know, there are risks of pilferage or damage to the goods during transshipment in Hong Kong.
7. If the cargo space must be reserved, please send us the necessary application forms.
8. We think it necessary to move the articles by way of combined transportation.
9. If the goods are to be transshipped from one means of transportation to another during the course of the entire voyage, it's called "combined transport".
10. When the goods have been loaded, you can get the B/L signed by the master of the vessel.

Ⅴ. Translate the following sentences into English.
1. 装运应从6月开始分三次平均装，在哥本哈根转船。
2. 因此笔交易按装运港船上交货价成交，你方必须在我方港口装船。
3. 由于从上海到你方港口没有直达船，此货必须在香港转船。
4. 我方已订妥"风庆"轮舱位，该轮将于3月20日左右到达汉堡。
5. 兹通知你方，第2008号订单500辆自行车已于本月20日装"王子"轮运出，并预订于下月初到达你方港口。
6. 由于开证推迟，无法按合同于5月发货，将延迟至6月。
7. 由于采用FOB价购货，贵方应在利物浦港将货物装在我方指定的船上。
8. 货已备妥待运多时，请告知所派船名、船次及预计到达时间，以便我方及时安排装运。
9. 很遗憾，我们无法满足你方要求将交货期提前到7月，因为工厂订单太多。
10. 我们相信306号订单项下的货物将会完好无损地到达你方。

Ⅵ. Situational writing.
　　As an exporter of colour TV sets, you are asked to send an email to a forwarding agent for service. In your email, the following points should be covered.
（1）货物正等候发往吉隆坡（Kula Lumpur）的Messrs Clements公司；
（2）要求用第一艘便船将货物运往吉隆坡；
（3）货物分三箱装运，随附发票表明数量和总值1 800美元；
（4）货物发送后，要求寄提单正本及副本各一份并附保险单及其他必要单据。

Chapter 9
第 9 章

保 险
Insurance

Learning Objectives

Enable the students to know about the importance of insurance in the international trade practice; to be familiar with the basic terms related to insurance and the insurance policies; to master the structure and common expressions in this type of letters.

使学生了解国际贸易实践中保险的重要性；熟悉与保险及保险单相关的基本术语；掌握撰写此类函件的结构以及常用的表达形式。

9.1 背景知识
Background Information

保险与对外贸易关系密切。在国际商务中，货物从卖方到买方通常要通过长距离的航空、陆路及海路等运输方式，经历装卸、存储环节。在此过程中，会涉及各种风险，从而导致货物损坏或损失，给买卖双方带来不便，甚至经济上的损失。为了避免货物遭受可能的损失，买方或卖方经常在装船前对有关货物向保险公司投保。

国际货物运输保险是指投保人在装运前针对货物向承保人，即保险公司进行投保。投保人根

Insurance is closely related to foreign trade. In international business, the transportation of the goods from the seller to the buyer by air, by land, or by sea is usually over a long distance and has to undergo the procedures of loading, unloading and warehousing. This process involves various risks which may result in the damage or loss of the goods, and thus the inconveniences or even financial losses to both the seller and the buyer. To protect the goods against possible losses, the buyer or the seller usually applies to an insurance company for insurance covering the goods to be transported prior shipment.

International cargo transportation insurance refers to the fact that the insured covers insurance for the shipment with the insurer, i.e. the insurance company before

据投保金额、保险责任范围、保险费率向保险公司支付保险费并获得保险单。承保人应对货物在运输过程中遭受的承保范围内的损失或损坏给予赔偿。

为国际贸易货物购买保险的责任一般由卖方决定。在 FOB 和 CFR 条件下由买方负责办理保险，在 CIF 条件下则由卖方办理保险。

承保人的责任决定于投保人购买的保险种类。当选择保险种类时，投保人应考虑保险费金额以及承保的风险。当选择承保风险时，应考虑投保货物的性质、包装、运输以及季节等因素。

国际货物买卖保险包括陆路运输保险、航空运输保险、邮包险以及海运险。然而，在大多数情况下，海运险最为重要，因为国际贸易货物大部分都是采用海洋运输方式。海洋运输货物保险所承保的风险、发生风险所造成的损失和费用，一般分为下列几类：

1. 海上风险
（1）一般海上风险
a. 自然灾害
b. 意外事故
（2）外来风险
a. 一般外来风险
b. 特殊外来风险
2. 海上损失
（1）全部损失
a. 实际全损
b. 推定全损
（2）部分损失
a. 共同海损

shipment. The insured pays insurance premiums to the insurance company on the basis of the insured amount, level of coverage as well as the premium rate, in order to obtain an insurance policy. The insurer shall compensate the insured for the losses of, and damage to the goods, if any, during the transportation within the scope of insurance coverage.

The responsibility for buying insurance for internationally traded goods is generally decided by the seller. The buyer pays for insurance in FOB and CFR contracts and the seller pays for it in CIF contracts.

The responsibility of the insurer is defined by the kind of insurance purchased. When choosing the kind of insurance, the insured should take into account both the amount of insurance premium and the risks to be covered. When choosing the risks to be covered, such factors as the nature of the goods, packing, transportation and season should be considered.

Insurance for international trading include overland transportation insurance, air transportation insurance, parcel post insurance and marine insurance. However, in most cases, marine insurance is of prime importance because most of international trading cargoes are delivered by sea. Risks covered under marine insurance, losses and charges resulted from the happening risks are generally classified into the following categories:

1. Perils on the Sea
（1）General Perils of the Sea
a. Nature Calamities
b. Fortuitous Accidents
（2）Extraneous Risks
a. General Extraneous Risks
b. Special Extraneous Risks
2. Marine Loss
（1）Total Loss
a. Actual Total Loss
b. Constructive Total Loss
（2）Partial Loss
a. General Average

b. 单独海损
　3. 海上费用
　（1）施救费用
　（2）救助费用
　　对于海上货物运输保险，目前被世界上大多数国家采用的是伦敦保险协会制定的《协会货物条款》（ICC）。ICC 主要包括六个条款：协会货物条款 A、协会货物条款 B、协会货物条款 C、协会战争险条款、协会罢工险条款以及恶意损害险条款。

　　中国人民保险公司（PICC）有自己的保险条款，被称为中国保险条款（CIC），其不同于 ICC。中国人民保险公司根据其海洋运输货物保险条款所承保的海洋运输基本险的险别有：平安险（FPA）、水渍险（WPA）和一切险。除了以上三种险别，还承保一些附加险：一般附加险和特殊附加险。在投保平安险或水渍险的基础上，可以额外投保一种或几种附加险。

　　在撰写关于保险的信函时，例如买方提出保险要求的信函，应遵循以下步骤：
　　（1）提及合同或者订单中所涉及的货物；
　　（2）建议具体的保险内容，例如：保险金额、保险险别、保费以及可能涉及的额外保险费及保险险别；
　　（3）希望卖方能够接受保险要求并尽快发货。

　　作为卖方的回信，应包括以下内容：
　　（1）表明来信已收到并重述买方来信的要点；

　　b. Particular Average
　（3）Marine Charges
　a. Sue and Labor Expenses
　b. Salvage Charges

　　As to the coverage of marine insurance, the Institute Cargo Clauses (ICC), which were set forth by the Institute of London Underwriters, are adopted by most countries in the world. Insurance under ICC falls into six clauses: Institute Cargo Clauses A; Institute Cargo Clauses B; Institute Cargo Clauses C; Institute War Clauses—Cargo; Institute Strike Clauses—Cargo; Malicious Damage Clauses.

　　The People's Insurance Company of China (PICC) has its own insurance clauses, known as China Insurance Clauses (CIC), which are different from ICC. The principal perils which the basic marine policy of the PICC insured against under its Ocean Marine Cargo Clause are: Free from Particular Average (FPA), With Particular Average (WPA) and All Risks. In addition to the three forms mentioned above, there are some additional risks, which are also coverable and classified into two forms. There are General Additional Risks and Special Additional Risks. In case of FPA or WPA, one or several kinds of Extraneous Risks may be covered in addition.

　　When you write letters about the insurance, such as buyers' insurance request letter, the letter should be finished as follows:

　　(1) Mention the goods of contract or order.

　　(2) Suggest the detailed terms of insurance such as insurance amount, coverage, premium as well as relative extra premium and coverage, if possible.

　　(3) Wish the seller to accept and ship the goods without delay.

　　As sellers' reply letter, the letter should be finished as follows:

　　(1) State that the letter has been received duly and retell the emphasis of the buyer's last letter.

（2）给出接受或拒绝的回复并说明原因（有时可介绍保险条件和通常做法）；

（3）说明若保险条款能够达成一致，货物会尽快发出等。

(2) Give the reply of agreeing or refusing and the reasons. (Sometimes introduce the insurance conditions and usual practice).

(3) State the goods will be sent soon, etc. if they will agree with each other on insurance terms.

9.2 信例
Specimen Letters

Letter 9-1　Asking for insurance arrangement

Dear Sirs,

　　　　　　Re: Our Order No. 101 covering 209 cases Electronic Toys

We wish to refer you to our Order No. 101 for 209 cases electronic toys, from which you will see that this order was placed on CFR basis.

As we now desire to have the consignment insured at your end, we shall be much pleased if you will kindly arrange to insure the goods on our behalf against All Risks at invoice value plus 10%, that is, USD 2,000.

We shall of course refund the premium to you upon receipt of your debit note, or if you like, you may draw on us at sight for the amount required.

We sincerely hope that our request will meet with your approval.

　　　　　　　　　　　　　　　　　　　　　　　　　　　　Yours faithfully,

Letter 9-2　Advising insurance effected

Dear Sirs,

　　　　　　Re: S/C No. 623 for 400 Cases Pottery

We have acknowledged receipt of your letter dated June 23 asking for effecting insurance on the captioned shipment for your account.

We now take pleasure in informing you that we have covered the above shipment with the People's Insurance Company of China against All Risks for USD 13,000. The policy is being prepared accordingly and will be forwarded to you by the end of this week together with our debit note for the premium.

For your information, we are making arrangements to ship the 400 cases of pottery by S/S Tai Hu, sailing on or about July 13.

　　　　　　　　　　　　　　　　　　　　　　　　　　　　Yours faithfully,

Letter 9-3　Informing the customer of insurance rate

Dear Mr. White,

　　In reply to your inquiry dated June 12, we are prepared to insure the consignment in question. Considering that you will be our regular customer, out rate for US$ 200,000 All Risks policy on 2,000 sets of Sony Color TV from Dalian to London is 1% of declared value.

　　This is an exceptionally low rate and we trust you will be satisfied with it and give us the opportunity to handle your insurance business. We are ready to assist you at any time on all future insurance contracts.

Yours sincerely,

Letter 9-4　Requirement about covering insurance on CFR basis

Dear Sir,

　　We are in receipt of your letter dated November 11, quoting us for 400 cases of electronic toys on CIF basis. However, we are regretful to say that we prefer to have your quotation on CFR basis.

　　For your information, we have taken out an open policy with the Lloyd Insurance Company, London. When a shipment is made, we shall inform the company of the particulars for certain. Furthermore, we usually receive from our underwriter quite a handsome premium rebate at regular intervals.

　　In the meantime, would you please supply us with full details regarding the scope of cover handled by the People's Insurance Company of China for our reference?

　　We look forward to receiving your early reply.

Yours faithfully,

Letter 9-5　Giving information on insurance arrangement

Dear Sirs,

Re: Insurance

　　We appreciate your letter of February 24 regarding insurance. In reply, we would like to inform you the relative details as follows:

　　All Risks: Generally, we cover insurance WPA and War Risk in the absence of definite instructions from our clients. If you want to cover All Risks, we can provide such coverage at a slightly higher premium.

> Breakage: Breakage is a special risk, for which an extra premium will have to be charged. The present rate is about 0.7%. Claims are payable only for that part of the loss that is over 5%.
>
> Value to be insured: We note that you wish us to insure shipments to you for 10% above invoice value, which is having our due attention.
>
> We trust the above information can serve your purpose and await your further news.
>
> Faithfully yours,

Letter 9-6 Request the seller to make a claim

> Dear Sirs,
>
> Thank you for your prompt shipment of our order No. 2299 by S.S. "Prince".
>
> After unloading the goods, it was noticed that one side of Case No. 8 containing the "Haier" DVD players was split. We therefore had the case opened and the contents examined by a local insurance surveyor in the presence of the shipping company's agents. Six of the 30 DVD players were found to be badly damaged.
>
> We enclose the surveyor's report and the shipping agents' statement. As you hold the insurance policy, we should be grateful if you would take the matter up for us with the insurer.
>
> Meanwhile, six replacement DVD players will be required. Please arrange to supply these and charge to our account.
>
> We hope no difficulty will arise in our insurance claim and thank you in advance for your trouble on our behalf.
>
> Yours faithfully,

Notes

1. Phrases about insurance in common use.

    Parties involved

    insurer/underwriter/insurance company   承保人；保险人；保险公司

    the insured/insurant/assured   被保险人；投保人

    insured cargo/goods   投保货物

    insurance agent   保险代理人

    insurant broker   保险经纪人

    Money involved

    insurance amount/value   投保金额

    insurance coverage   承保范围；险别

    insurance premium   保费

    insurance (premium) rate   保费率

    Documents involved

insurance policy　大保单；正规保单
insurance certificate　分保单；小保单
open policy　预约保单
insurance declaration　保险声明书；保险通知书
insurance receipt　保险收据
Clauses involved
ICC（Institute Cargo Clauses）　协会货物保险条款
CIC（China Insurance Clauses）　中国保险条款
OMCC（Ocean Marine Cargo Clauses）　中国海洋运输货物保险条款

2. insurance coverage of CIC
　　Basic Risks　基本险
　　FPA（Free from Particular Average）　平安险
　　WA or WPA（With Average or With Particular Average）　水渍险
　　All Risks　一切险；综合险
　　General Additional Risk　一般附加险
　　Theft，Pilferage & Non-Delivery Risks（TPND）　偷窃、提货不着险
　　Fresh and/or Rain Water Damage Risks（FRWD）　淡水雨淋险
　　Shortage Risk = Risk of Shortage　短量险
　　Intermixture & Contamination Risks　混杂沾污险
　　Leakage Risk = Risk of Leakage　渗漏险
　　Clash & Breakage Risks　碰损破碎险
　　Taint of Odor Risk　串味险
　　Sweating & Heating Risk　受潮受热险
　　Hook Damage Risk　钩损险
　　Rust Risk = Risk of Rust　锈损险
　　Breakage of Packing Risk　包装破损险
　　Special Additional Risk　特殊附加险
　　War Risk　战争险
　　SRCC（Strikes，Riots，Civil Commotions）　罢工、暴动、民变险
　　Import Duty Risk　进口关税险
　　Rejection Risk　拒收险
　　Failure to Delivery Risk　交货不到险

3. insure
　　vt. 投保，相当于 cover
　　insure + sb.
　　insure + sth.
　　insure +（against）　险别
　　insurance　n.
　　cover/effect/arrange/take out/provide/issue + insurance + prep.
　　insurance 后面接介词的一般用法

a. on + 投保货物
b. against + 投保险别（WPA 和 FPA 险别前不用 against）
c. for + 投保金额
d. at + 保险费率
e. with + 保险公司
f. by + 投保人

(1) Please insure against All Risks. 请投保一切险。
(2) Please insure FPA. 请投保平安险。
(3) We noted that you wish to insure the shipment for 10% above invoice value, which is having our due attention.
我们已注意到你方希望按发票金额的 110% 投保，我们正在洽办中。
(4) We shall cover insurance against TPND on your order.
我们将为你方所订货物投保偷窃、提货不着险。
(5) WPA plus Risk of Breakage suit your consignment.
你方货物适合投保水渍险和破碎险。
(6) Do you cover risks other than WPA and War Risk?
除了水渍险和战争险外，你们还保其他险吗？
(7) On FOB and CFR sales, insurance is to be covered by buyers.
对离岸价格及成本加运费价格条件成交的货物，保险由买方办理。
(8) Insurance is to be made on the goods by the seller against All Risks for 110% of the invoice value with PICC at the rate of 0.3%.
由卖方按发票金额 110% 向中国人民保险公司以 0.3% 的保费率投保一切险。

4. for one's account
由……支付
类似的表达法还有：
to be borne by
to be responsible by
to be charged to one's account

(1) The extra freight is to be for the buyer's account.
额外运费由买方负担。
(2) We bought the goods for the account of our branch office.
这批货物是我们代我分公司购买的。
(3) As a rule, the extra premium involved will be for buyers' account.
按常规，额外保险费应由买方负责。

5. debit note
借方通知；索款通知单
debit　v. 把……记入借方
debit an amount to one's account（debit one's account with an amount）把一笔金额记入某人账户的借方
His account with the Bank of China had been debited with the sum of $5 for half-yearly bank

charges.

中国银行把一笔五美元的账记入他账户的借方,作为半年的银行手续费。

6. open policy

    预约保单

    effect an open policy with　　与……洽办预约保单

7. the particulars

    细节;详细情况

    the particulars of…(the full details of…)　　……的全部细节;……的详细情况

8. premium

    n. 保险费

    premium rebate　　保险费回扣

    premium tariff　　保险费率表

    extra premium　　额外保险费

    (1) The premium is calculated according to the premium rate or rates for risks to be covered.

    保险费是根据投保险别的保险费率计算的。

    (2) This risk is coverable at a premium of 1%.

    此种险别的保险费率是1%。

    (3) Insurance of the goods is to be covered by us for 110% of the CIF value, and any extra premium for additional insurance, if required, shall be borne by the buyers.

    货物的保险将由我方按照CIF价的110%投保。如果需要投保附加险,额外的保险费将由买方承担。

9. coverage

    n. 承保范围;险别

    (1) Our insurance coverage is for 110% of invoice value up to the port of destination only.

    我方按发票金额的110%投保,仅至目的港。

    (2) Kindly note that the insurance covers FPA and War Risk only. Should additional insurance coverage be required, the extra premium incurred would be for the buyers' account.

    请注意,保险只包括平安险和战争险。如果要求投保附加险,所需额外保险费将由买方支付。

    (3) WPA coverage is too narrow for a shipment of this nature. Please extend the coverage to include TPND.

    对这种性质的货物只投保水渍险是不够的,请加保偷窃、提货不着险。

10. in the absence of

    在没有……(的情况下);在缺乏……(的情况下)

    We usually cover insurance WPA and against War Risk in the absence of the buyers' detailed requirements.

    在买方没有具体要求的情况下,我们一般投保水渍险和战争险。

11. invoice value

    发票金额

    按发票金额的110%的表达方法:

for 110% of invoice value　发票金额的110%
for 10% above invoice value　在发票价值上加10%
at invoice value plus 10%　按发票价值另加10%

Words and Phrases

pottery	n. 陶器
regarding	prep. 关于
validity	n. 有效期
extra	adj. 额外的
shipment	n. 一批货物
forward	v. 转寄；运送
sail	v. 启航
certify	v. 证明
branch	n. 分行
survey	n. 调查；鉴定
claim	n. 索赔
issue	v. 出具；开立
handsome	adj. 相当大的；可观的
unload	v. 卸货
split	v. 裂开
meanwhile	adv. 在此期间；与此同时
amount to	总计；金额达
see to	确保
shipping advice	装运通知
acknowledge receipt of	收到
make arrangement	安排
in the event of	如果……发生
the Lloyd Insurance Company	劳埃德保险公司
definite instructions	明确指示
at a slightly higher premium	略高的保险费

9.3　外贸实战技巧
Techniques in Foreign Trade Practice

保险类信函写作技巧

在撰写保险类信函时，应做到简洁、清晰、明了，应明确投保要求及保险费的支付办法，以便对方及时办理投保手续。回复保险信函时，应做到及时而有礼貌，并清楚地表明己方的保险要求或提出合理的建议。在填制货运保险保单时需要注意以下事项：

被保险人：被保险人即保单的受益人，因此需要具有可保利益的抬头（对货物有经济买卖关系的）。以 CIF 术语成交时，可以将发货人作为被保险人，后期通过背书转让保单给收货人，也可以直接将收货人作为被保险人。由于被保险人的唯一性，个人抬头的需提供身份证号码或者护照号码。注意：如果物流公司只是承运人，不能将其设为被保险人。

通信地址：在出口保单中通信地址通常不用填写，因为保单作为流转单据，可以被连续背书转让，故通信地址是否标明影响不大。进口保单和国内保单，一般要写上联系人和联系方式，以便出险时方便保险公司联系此人协助提交单据。因此联系人和联系方式与被保险人的抬头没有必需的对应关系，可以写代理物流公司的通信地址。

运输工具：采用出口散货、出口集装箱运输时，可以填船名、航次。如果一票货的集装箱数量比较少，则可以直接标注海运。如果是整船、散货船运输，需要提供船名来预先申报。如果是空运，填航班号；如果是国内陆运，填车牌号码。

发票号码或者提单号码：两个号码至少提供一个，也可以两个都写上。如果想做到真正意义上的仓至仓，就可以用发票号码投保，因为提单号码一般都比较迟才能得到，而发票号码可以自己编写。进出口填写形式发票号码的较多。如果是国内保单，此处可以填写运单号码，也可以填车牌号码。

起运日期：如是国内保单，运输工具没有发出，起运日期可以写起运日或投保日。如果是国际货物运输，应写装船日期当天或者投保日期当天。需要特别注意的是保单注明的起运日期不能迟于运单上的起运日期，否则会影响理赔。

起运地：起运地通常以城市行政区域为最小单位。起运地如果写城市，则包括这个城市的所有行政区域，不能只写国家。有些客户在填写起运地时，直接填写具体地址，这样虽然没有错误，但是就不包括整个城市的行政区域，使保险范围缩小。

中转地：直达运输不需要填写中转地，如果需要中转，按照实际发生填写。可能有一个或多个中转地，按实际中转地填写。

目的地：保单中的目的地往往是保险责任终止的地方。一般应填写收货人仓库所在的城市。

保险金额：保险金额是理赔的上限。进出口贸易保单，由于物流成本等其他成本比较高，通常会按国际惯例加成 10% 投保，保险公司允许对合理的运费和利润投保。当然，也可以不加成投保，或者低比例投保。国内水、陆运保单中，保险金额一般就是实际货值。

保险货物项目：此处应写清楚货物的名称，不能过于笼统。如货物是金属冲压机，不能只填写"机器"。货物是月饼，不能只写"食品"。因为不同的货物具有不同的特性，保险公司往往是根据货物的特性来判定风险。

标记：这里默认是写货物的唛头，如果有多个唛头，也可以填写。

包装：保险公司非常注重货物的运输包装，会根据不同的包装情况设定不同的承保条件。如果包装不适航，保险公司还可以以"包装不善"拒赔。因此，应如实、具体地填写货物的包装情况。

数量：保单默认为投保货物的总数量，应准确填写，尤其理赔时，需要清点货物数量。对于某些特殊的货物，可以用重量或体积来计算。

赔款偿付地点：一般默认为目的地，以保单上注明的货物成交币种赔付。由于当前全球转账非常便捷，赔付地的概念逐渐淡化，如果信用证对赔款偿付地点有要求，就按信用证要求执行。

查勘代理人：确定查勘代理人的原则是就近原则，保单默认为离目的地最近的查勘代理人。进口保单默认为保险公司的联系方式，由保险公司去找第三方机构查勘。出口保单默认为目的港的查勘代理人联系方式，客户也可以自己找具有国际检验机构劳埃德认证资格的查勘代理人。

承保条件：CIF 价格一般要求的是最低险别，例如，平安险或其他基本险。在实际操作中，客户都偏向投保一切险，而二手货、旧货类不能承保一切险。

其他要求：比如信用证要求、除外责任、免赔额条件等。

9.4 有用的句子
Useful Sentences

1. Please insure FPA at your end.
   请在贵地投保平安险。
2. We generally insure WPA on CIF sales.
   按 CIF 价出售的货物，我们一般投保水渍险。
3. Please cover the goods against War Risk.
   请将货物投保战争险。
4. We have insured the goods FPA and against All Risk.
   我们已将货物投保平安险和一切险。
5. As our order was placed on a CIF basis, the insurance is to be arranged by you.
   由于我方是按 CIF 价订货的，应由你方投保。
6. We will effect/cover/take out/arrange insurance on your behalf.
   我方愿代贵方投保。
7. Please insure us on the following goods.
   请为我方投保下列货物。
8. Insurance is to be made on the goods by the seller against All Risks for 110% of the invoice value with PICC at the rate of 0.3%.
   由卖方按发票金额 110% 向中国人民保险公司以 0.3% 的保费率投保一切险。
9. The usual insurance amount is 110% of the invoice value. If you require a higher percentage, you'll have to bear the extra premium (the extra premium will be for your account/at your cost/charged to your account).
   通常的保险金额为发票金额的 110%。如果贵方要求更高的加成比例，就得承担额外的保费。
10. Our quotation is on CIF basis. If you prefer to have the insurance to be covered at your end, please let us know, so that we may quote you CFR prices.
    我方报价是 CIF 价，如果你方想自己投保，请告知，以便我方给你按 CFR 报价。
11. We request you to extend the insurance coverage to include leakage.
    我方要求你方把保险范围扩大到包括渗漏险。

12. If any damage to the goods occurs, a claim may be filed with the insurance agent at your end, who will undertake to compensate for the loss sustained.
货物如果发生损坏,可向贵地的保险代理提出索赔,他们将赔偿你方遭受的损失。
13. We enclose an inspection certificate issued by the Beijing Commodity Inspection Bureau and the Shipping Agent's Statement as well as the original Insurance Policy.
现附上北京商品检验局签发的检验证明、轮船代理人的报告书以及保险单原件。
14. An insurance claim should be submitted to the insurance company or its agents within 30 days after the arrival of the consignment at the port of destination.
保险索赔应在货物到达目的港 30 天内提交保险公司或其代理商。
15. Should any damage be incurred, you may approach the insurance agents at your end and submit an insurance claim supported by a survey report.
如果货物发生损坏,贵方可凭检验报告与贵处保险代理联系并提出保险索赔。

9.5　补充商务信函
Letters for Further Reading

Letter 9-7

Dear Sirs,

　　In reply to your letter of November 13 enquiring about the insurance on our CIF offer for Traveling Scissors made to you on October 20, we wish to give you the following information:

　　For transactions concluded on CIF basis, we usually effect insurance with PICC against All Risks as per Ocean Marine Cargo Clauses of PICC dated 1 January, 1981. Should you require the insurance to be covered as per Institute Cargo Clauses (ICC), we would be glad to comply, but if there is any difference in premium between the two, it will be charged to your account.

　　We are also in a position to insure the shipment against any additional risks if you do desire, and the extra premium is to be borne by you. In this case, we shall send you the premium receipt issued by the relative underwriter.

　　Usually, the amount insured is 110% of the total invoice value. However, if a higher percentage is required, we may do accordingly, but you have to bear the extra premium as well.

　　We hope our above information will provide you with all the information you wish to know and we are now looking forward to receiving your order.

Yours faithfully,

Letter 9-8

Gentlemen:

We wish to call your attention to our order No. 418 for 100 M/Ts canned meat placed on CFR basis.

As we now desire to have the shipment insured on your side, we shall appreciate it very much if you will kindly arrange to insure the same on our behalf against All Risks at invoice value plus 10%. Upon receipt of your debit note, we will refund the premium to you at once.

It is our sincere hope that our request will meet with your approval.

We are looking forward to your early reply.

Truly yours,

Letter 9-9

Dear Sirs,

We take pleasure in acknowledging your letter dated May 4, requesting us to effect insurance on the 100 M/Ts canned meat under Order No. 418 for your account.

Now we take pleasure in advising you that we have today covered the shipment with the People's Insurance Company of China against All Risks for US $3,000. In one week you will get the policy together with our debit note for the premium, for which kindly send us a remittance at an early date.

We would like to mention that the insurance is to be arranged from warehouse to warehouse. The insurance shall terminate when the goods are delivered to the consignee's warehouse at the destination named in the policy. The cover, however, is limited to 60 days upon discharge of the insured goods from the carrying vessel at the final port of discharge before the insured goods reach the consignee's warehouse.

For your information, this consignment will be shipped by s/s "Red Star" due to sail on or about June 15. We shall send you shipping advice in due course.

Faithfully yours,

Letter 9-10

Dear Sirs,

<u>Additional Risk of Breakage</u>

We refer to your L/C No. 157 covering Glazed Wall Tiles, which we have just received.

Please note for this article we do not cover Breakage. You have to, therefore, delete the word "Breakage" from the insurance clause in the credit.

Furthermore, we wish to point out that for such articles as window glass, porcelains, etc., even if additional Risk of Breakage has been insured, the cover is subject to a franchise of 5%. In other words, if the breakage is surveyed to be less than 5%, no claims for damage will be entertained.

We trust that the position is now clear. Please make the amendment at once.

Yours faithfully,

Letter 9-11

Dear Sirs,

<u>Re: Your Order No. 338</u>

We acknowledge the receipt of our letter of December 15, inquiring about the insurance on the above-mentioned order.

As to the goods sold on CIF basis, we would say, our company will insure against All Risks & War Risk for 110% of the invoice value. If you want to insure broader coverage, the extra premium involved will be for buyer's account.

Should any damage to the goods occur, a claim may be filed with the insurance agent of PICC at your end, who will undertake to compensate for the loss sustained.

In presenting a claim to the Insurance Company or its agent, the insured is usually required to submit the following documents:

(1) Original Policy or Certificate of Insurance, original or copy of Bill of Lading, Invoices, Packing List;

(2) Certificate of Loss or Damage and/or Short-landed Memo, Survey Report;

(3) Statement of Claims.

An insurance claim should be submitted to the Insurance Company or its agent as promptly as possible so as to provide them with ample time to pursue recovery from the relative party in fault. Claims against the Ocean Carriers usually become time-barred one year after discharge of the cargo from the sea-going vessel.

The PICC enjoys high prestige in settling claims promptly and equitably. For further particulars, please contact the PICC or its agent at your end.

Yours faithfully,

Letter 9-12

> Dear Mr. Black,
> Re: Our S/C No. 1023 for 600 Cases Pottery
>
>   Regarding our S/C No. 1023 covering 600 cases pottery, we would like to inform you that we have established with the Bank of China an L/C No. 2132 amounting to $10,000 with validity until June 30.
>
>   Please see to it that the above-mentioned goods are shipped before June 30 and insured against All Risks for 130% of the invoice value. We know that according to your usual practice, you insure the goods only for 110% of the invoice value, therefore, the extra premium will be for our account.
>
>   Please arrange the insurance as requested and in the meanwhile, we await your shipping advice.
>
> Yours sincerely,

9.6 练习
Exercises

Ⅰ. Translate the following phrases into Chinese.

1. Basic Risks
2. General Additional Risk
3. invoice value
4. shipping advice
5. insurance amount/value
6. insurance coverage
7. insurance premium
8. insurance (premium) rate
9. insured cargo/goods
10. insurance agent
11. insurant broker
12. insurance policy
13. insurance certificate
14. open policy
15. FPA
16. WPA
17. All Risks
18. premium rebate
19. premium tariff
20. extra premium

Ⅱ. Choose the best answer.

1. Please _____ the article WPA.
   A. assure   B. ensure
   C. insure   D. be sure

2. The goods should be insured against breakage _____ your cost.
   A. in   B. for
   C. on   D. at

3. Unless otherwise _____, we wish to arrange to take out an All Risks insurance policy for you _____ the shipment.

  A. instructed, on   B. instructions, for

  C. instructed, for   D. instruction, on

4. Please _____ insurance on your side.

  A. effect   B. make

  C. do   D. take

5. We note that you expect us to insure the shipments for you for the invoice value _____ 10%.

  A. add   B. less

  C. plus   D. minus

6. Under the FPA terms, the insurance company is liable for any loss, whether total or partial, _____ other external causes, i.e. theft and pilferage.

  A. arise from   B. arose

  C. rising from   D. arising from

7. You may _____ assured that your wishes will be carried out.

  A. resting   B. be rest

  C. be   D. rested

8. Insurance is to be _____ by the buyer if a transaction is concluded on FOB or CFR basis.

  A. taken   B. covered

  C. done   D. made

9. Breakage is a (an) _____ risk, for which an extra premium will have to be charged.

  A. average   B. special

  C. extraneous   D. basic

10. We had to have the goods warehoused _____ insuring against usual risks.

  A. on your own account   B. on account of

  C. for your account   D. for the account of

Ⅲ. Fill in the blanks.

1. Generally we cover insurance _____ War Risk and WA _____ the absence _____ definite instructions _____ our clients.

2. Insurance _____ the goods shall be covered _____ us _____ 110% _____ the CIF value, and any extra premium _____ additional coverage, if required, shall be borne _____ the buyers.

3. We are pleased to inform you that we have booked shipping space _____ your Order No. 3322 _____ 30 cases _____ captioned goods _____ S.S. Swan which sails _____ your port _____ or _____ March 25.

4. Insurance is very closely related _____ foreign trade. People _____ international trade should have a thorough knowledge _____ it.

5. It is stipulated _____ the S/C that insurance is to be covered _____ Sellers _____ the amount of 30% _____ the invoice value _____ TPND, Fresh and/or Rain Water Damage _____ addition to WPA.

6. We regret our inability to _____ with the buyer's request for covering insurance for 150% of the invoice value, because our contract stipulated that _____ should be covered for 110%

of invoice value.

7. Since the premium varies with the extent of _____, extra premium is for buyer's account, should additional risks be _____ .

8. Should any damage occur, you may, within 30 days after the arrival of the consignment, approach the insurance agent at your end and raise a claim with him to be _____ by a survey report.

9. Regarding insurance, the _____ is for 110% of invoice value up to the port of destination only.

10. The buyer's request for insurance to be covered up to the Island city can be accepted on condition that such extra premium is for the _____ account.

Ⅳ. Translate the following sentences into Chinese.
1. The premium is calculated according to the premium rate or rates for risks to be covered.
2. We won't have such a risk included, as it is not stipulated in the Ocean Marine Cargo Clauses.
3. We adopt the "Warehouse to Warehouse" clause that is commonly used in international insurance.
4. According to international practice, we do not insure against such risks unless the buyers call for them.
5. The underwriters are responsible for the claim as far as it is within the scope of cover.
6. May I ask what exactly insurance covers according to your usual CIF terms?
7. It's important for you to read the "fine print" in any insurance policy so that you know what kind of coverage you are buying.
8. The rates quoted by us are very moderate. Of course, the premium varies with the range of insurance.
9. You should study not only the benefits, but also the terms and limitations of an insurance agreement that appears best suited to your needs.
10. As our usual practice, insurance covers basic risks only, at 110 percent of the invoice value. If coverage against other risks is required, such as breakage, leakage, TPND, hook and contamination damages, the extra premium involved would be for the buyer's account.

Ⅴ. Translate the following sentences into English.
1. 根据你方要求，我们将按发票金额的110% 投保。
2. 因为保险费随保险范围的不同而不同，如果买方要求投保附加险，额外的保险费则应该由买方负担。
3. 由于这些货物是在CIF 价格基础上购买的，我们想了解您是否接受对货物投保一切险。
4. 如果贵方要求我方投保偷窃、提货不着险，非常容易办到，只要支付附加保险费即可。
5. 由于合同规定按发票金额的110% 投保，如你方要求按130% 投保，额外保费应由你方负担。

6. 我们常从保险公司那里定期拿到一笔可观的保险费回扣。
7. 如果没有你们的明确指示，我们将按一般惯例投水渍险和战争险。
8. 至于第345号合约项下的300台缝纫机，我们将自行办理保险。
9. 破碎险的保费率是1.2%，如你方愿意投保破碎险，我们可以代为办理。
10. 很遗憾，我们不能接受这一索赔，因为你们的保险没有包括"破碎险"。

VI. Situational writing.

Your company has just ordered 500 cases of black tea. Now you are asked to send the following notice to the seller telling him how to insure the goods.

关于你方第777号的500箱红茶的售货合约，兹通知你方，我们已由伦敦中国银行开立了第999号信用证，共计金额2 000欧元，有效期至7月15日为止。

请注意上述货物必须在7月15日前装出，保险必须按发票价的130%投保一切险。我们知道，按照我们一般惯例，你们只按发票价另加10%投保，因此额外保险费由我们负责。

请按我们的要求办理保险，同时我们等候你方的装运通知。

Chapter 10
第 10 章

索 赔
Claims

Learning Objectives

Enable the students to know about the reasons that will bring out a claim; to be familiar with the basic terms related to claims in the international trade; to master the writing method and the style of claim letters.

使学生了解产生索赔的原因；熟悉国际贸易中涉及的索赔条款；掌握撰写索赔类函件的写作方式以及写作风格。

10.1 背景知识
Background Information

在执行国际商务合同的过程中，合同双方都应严格遵循合同条款，履行各自的责任和义务。如果合同一方不能全部或部分履行合同义务就会给另一方带来麻烦，有时甚至会使另一方蒙受经济损失。在这种情况下，受损失的一方有权根据合同规定的相关条款要求责任方弥补其损失或者采取其他补救措施，这种行为被称为"索赔"。而责任方应采取行动对受损方提出的索赔要求进行处理，即"理赔"。

在国际商务交易中，常见的买方对卖方进行索赔的原因有：

During the course of carrying out a sales contract, the two parties which have signed the contract should strictly fulfill the duties stipulated in the terms and conditions of the contract. If one of the parties failed to do that wholly or partially, the other will be involved in troubles and even suffer great financial losses consequently. Under this circumstance, the affected party has the right to request the defaulter to make up his losses or take some other remedial measures according to the relevant provisions under the contract, which is called a "claim". And the liable party will take action to deal with the request put forward by the affected party, which is called "settlement of a claim".

In the international business transaction, it's more often that the buyer lodge claims against the seller for the

（1）错发货物；
（2）货物品质低劣或品质不符；
（3）规格不符；
（4）数量不符；
（5）包装不当；
（6）唛头不详；
（7）延迟交货；
（8）货物损坏或短量；
（9）货物损失；
（10）未交付货物；
（11）未提供完整、正确的单据等。

然而，有时买方会试图找到货物存在的瑕疵，并以此为借口逃脱履约责任，其原因是买方不再想要这批货物，或者买方发现能以更低廉的价格买到货物。这时买方的索赔并不是基于事实或充足的证据，在这种情况下卖方有理由也有权利拒绝买方的索赔。

卖方也可以基于以下原因向买方提出索赔：
（1）没有及时开出信用证；
（2）没有及时派船运载合同货物；
（3）无理拒收货物等。

当撰写关于索赔的信函时，通常遵循以下步骤：
（1）阐述问题及事实情况；
（2）强调对方违约带来的损失或不便；
（3）给出合理的解决方法，换句话说，明确提出希望对方如何解决问题，或直接把解决问题的主动权交由对方。

在撰写解决索赔信函时，主要步骤如下：

reasons such as：
（1）wrong delivery；
（2）inferior quality or quality discrepancy；
（3）specification discrepancy；
（4）quantity discrepancy；
（5）poor packing；
（6）unclear mark；
（7）delayed delivery；
（8）damage or shortage of the goods；
（9）loss of the goods；
（10）failure to make delivery；
（11）without complete or correct documents, etc.

Sometimes, however, the buyer may intend to find fault with the goods as an excuse to escape from his contractual obligations, either because they no longer want the goods or because they have found that they can get them cheaper and make claims not based on facts or based on the abundant evidence, on the condition of that, the seller has the reasons and right to reject the claim.

While, the seller may also put up claim against the buyer for the following reasons：
（1）failure to open an L/C in time；
（2）failure to dispatch a vessel to carry the goods；
（3）unreasonable rejection of the goods, etc.

When writing letters about claims, a claim letter usually follows the procedures as follows：
（1）Explaining the problem and the facts；
（2）Emphasis on the loss or inconvenience resulted from the faults；
（3）Statement of a reasonable adjustment, in another word, making clear how you wish the reader to solve the problem or just leave it to the reader.

Writing steps of the claim settlement letters should be as follows：

（1）提及相关事项及货物，对给对方带来的不便表示歉意；

（2）提供勘验报告，解释问题产生的原因并接受索赔；

（3）针对索赔解决方案提出建议；

（4）向对方保证会采取必要的措施避免此类情况再次发生，并希望合作继续。

当撰写拒绝索赔信函时，主要步骤如下：

（1）提及相关事项，对给对方带来的不便表示歉意；

（2）说明问题，解释问题产生的原因并表明自己的立场；

（3）给出拒绝索赔的证据及原因，或者建议可能的解决方案；

（4）希望和对方继续合作。

(1) Identify the reference and the goods, regret for the inconvenience caused to the reader;

(2) Submit the survey report, explain the reasons of the problems and acknowledge to accept the claim;

(3) Advise the recipient of the way of settling claim;

(4) Assure the recipient that necessary steps will be taken to avoid recurrence, and wish to cooperate with the reader again.

Writing steps of letters of declining claims should be as follows:

(1) Identify the reference and regret for the inconvenience caused to the reader;

(2) State the problems, explain the reasons for the problem and make clear your position;

(3) Give the evidences and reasons for declining claims or suggest possible settlement;

(4) Wish to cooperate with the reader again.

10.2 信例
Specimen Letters

Letter 10-1　A claim for low quality

Dear Sirs,

　　The green beans under the Order No. 22 dispatched on September 12, 2014 have arrived at our port yesterday. The Commodity Inspection Bureau has carefully examined the quality of the beans, and we regret to say that the goods were far below the standard stipulated in the contract. The covering Inspection Certificate is going to be airmailed to you as soon as it comes to hand.

　　We think you will look into the matter as soon as possible and take some immediate and effective measures to avoid the mistakes in the future.

　　The low quality of these goods has brought us much more difficulties to exploit market and it is hard for us to dispose of them, even at a rather low price. We think you should be responsible for the low quality and we hold the claim against you for the compensation for the loss thus incurred.

　　We are awaiting your prompt reply.

Yours faithfully,

Letter 10-2 A claim for short-delivery and inferior quality

Dear Sirs,

<u>S. S. "Blue Sky" —Rice</u>

We have just received the Survey Report from Dalian Commodity Inspection Bureau evidencing that the captioned goods unloaded here yesterday was a short-weight of 1.3 M/T. From the survey report, you will see that it is beyond doubt that the shortage occurred prior to shipment, as the packing remains intact. Meanwhile the goods are much inferior to the samples you submitted to us before. Under the circumstances, we have to lodge claims with you as follows:

Claim Number	Claim for	Amount
DL01	Short-weight	US $1,368.60
DL02	Inferior quality	US $1,532.31
	Plus survey charges	US $50
	Total amount	US $2,950.91

In order to support our claims, we are sending you herewith one copy of each of Inspection Certificate Nos. DCIB01011 and DCIB01012 together with our Statement of Claims which amounts to US $2,950.91.

Please give our claims your most favorable consideration and let us have your settlement at an early date.

Yours faithfully,

Letter 10-3 Settlement of the claim

Dear Sirs,

<u>Contract No. AB0109—Rice</u>

We have just received your letter of May 16, with enclosures, claiming for short-weight and inferior quality on the consignment of Rice shipped per S. S. "Blue Sky".

Upon receipt of your letter, we have given this matter our immediate attention. We have found that our Rice was properly weighed at the time of loading and the quality was up to standard. We really cannot account for the reason of your complaint. But since the goods were examined by Dalian Commodity Inspection Bureau upon arrival at Dalian, we have no choice but to accept your claims as tendered.

We therefore enclose our check No. 12345 for US $2,950.91 in full and final settlement of your Claims DL01 and DL02.

We trust that the arrangement we have made will satisfy you and look forward to receiving your further order.

Yours faithfully,

Letter 10-4 The reply to the claim

Dear Mr. Smith,

We are very surprised to learn from your letter of October 20, 2014 that the green beans dispatched on September 4, 2014 were below the standard stipulated in the contract and that you are reserving the right to lodge a claim against us.

Naturally we hope that the transaction will be concluded to your satisfaction. Now that you have found the quality of the beans does not comply with the stipulated in the contract, we want to have the problem clarified without any delay. So we have sent our representative to your end to investigate the matter in detail. We would not give any comment before our representative inspects the goods. We will soon let you know the date of this visit and hope you will give him your best cooperation.

You may be assured that the matter will be settled in a reasonable manner to our mutual benefits.

Yours sincerely,

Letter 10-5 Declining a claim for deteriorated Herbs

Dear Sirs,

We feel deeply sorry that 40 cartons of Herbs supplied to your Order No. DF-3 were found deteriorated on arrival at the port of destination.

You may be aware that our Herbs have been sold in a number of markets abroad for many years. All our goods were carefully inspected before shipment by China Commodity Inspection Bureau and were found to be of standard quality, and enjoy a good reputation on international markets. But for any possible deterioration for which we are found rain liable, we shall always be ready to compensate.

For this particular transaction, however, we have to point out that the goods were in good condition when shipped, which was clearly stated in the clean Bill of Lading. We, therefore, are certain they were damaged or stained through careless handling while in transit, or they were put in the open and damaged by rain.

For this reason, we regret that we cannot agree to your request for a replacement.

Yours faithfully,

Letter 10-6 Making a complaint for wrong delivery

Dear Sirs,

Re: Our Order No. 123 for Toys

We are glad to have received the documents and took delivery of the goods on arrival of s/s "Prince" at Antwerp. We are much obliged for your prompt execution of this order.

Upon examination of the order, we regret to inform you that everything appears to be correct and in good condition except in case No. 22. After opening this case, we found it contained completely different articles. We can only presume that the contents of this case were for another order.

As we are in urgent need of the items, we must ask you to substitute them with right goods immediately. We attach a list of the contents of case No. 22. Please check this with our order and the copy of your invoice.

In the meantime, we are holding the above-mentioned case at your disposal. Please fax us to let us know what to do with it.

Please treat the matter as urgent. We trust you will find no difficulty in settling this matter and bring the case to a satisfactory close soon.

Yours faithfully,

Notes

1. arrive in such an unsatisfactory condition that…
   到达时的情况如此令人不满以至于……
   in good/perfect/sound condition 状况良好
   in an unsatisfactory condition 状况令人不满意
   in bad/poor condition 状况不良
   in a damaged condition 破损状况
   We regret to inform you that the goods shipped per S. S. "Victory" arrived in an unsatisfactory condition that we cannot but lodge a claim against you.
   我们遗憾地告知你方，由"胜利"轮运来的货物情况令人十分不满，我们不得不向你方提出索赔。

2. claim
   n./v. 索赔；声称；断言；要求
   to lodge/file/make/raise/submit/register/put forward/place a claim on sth. against sb. for some reasons for the amount of money
   因……而对……向……提出金额为……的索赔
   accept/entertain a claim 接受索赔
   settle a claim 解决索赔

reject a claim　拒绝索赔

claim on account of damage　因损坏而索赔

claim for financial loss　要求经济损失的诉权

claim for inferior quality　因质量低劣而索赔

claim for payment　要求付款的诉权

claim for short delivery　因短装而索赔

(1) Buyers have lodged a claim on this shipment for RMB¥1,300 for short weight.

因短重买方对这批货物提出人民币 1 300 元的索赔。

(2) The quality of your shipment for our order is not in conformity with the agreed specifications. We must therefore lodge a claim against you for the amount of $15,800.

你方为我订单提供的货物与双方商定的规格不符。因此，我们必须向你方提出索赔，金额为 15 800 美元。

(3) The evidence you have provided is inadequate, therefore, we cannot consider your claim as requested.

你方提供的证据不充分，因此我方不能考虑你方的索赔要求。

(4) As regards inferior quality of your goods, we claim a compensation of $15,000.

关于你方产品质量低劣的问题，我方要求你方赔偿 15 000 美元。

(5) We shall lodge a claim for all the losses incurred as a consequence of your failure to ship our order in time.

由于你方未能按时交货，我方将向你方提出由此而遭受的全部损失的索赔。

3. complaint

n. 抱怨；控告

complain　v. 抱怨；投诉

(1) The buyer has lodged a complaint against the seller about the quality of the precision grinding machine.

买方已就精密磨床的质量向卖方提出异议。

(2) The store has a special department to handle customer complaints.

这家商店有专门的部门处理顾客的投诉。

(3) She complained that the exam was hard.

她抱怨考试太难。

(4) The buyer complained of the delay in shipment.

买家投诉货物迟发。

(5) Our users have complained to us about the damage of the goods.

我们的客户因货物破损向我们投诉。

(6) They complained that our shipment was not up to the agreed specification.

他们投诉我们的货物没有达到合同规定的规格要求。

4. insufficient packing

有缺陷的包装

类似的表达法还有：

improper packing　包装不当

poor packing　包装不良

defective packing　有欠缺的包装

faulty packing　有缺陷的包装

insecure packing　不可靠的包装

We cannot acknowledge your claim for damage due to defective packing.

我方无法接受贵公司因包装欠缺而提出的索赔。

5. recourse

n. 求助于（to）；追索权（法律）

（1）In this case, it may be necessary for us to have recourse to arbitration.

这种情况下，我们有必要求助仲裁。

（2）If the issuing bank does not pay the draft, the negotiating bank has recourse to the beneficiary.

开证行若不付款，议付行可向受益人行使追索权。

6. in consequence

因此；结果是

（1）The sellers shall not be held responsible for failure or delay in shipment in consequence of Force Majeure incidents.

卖方对由不可抗力原因造成的不能或延迟交货不负责任。

（2）We have not received the covering L/C yet, and in consequence, we did not effect the shipment in time.

我们尚未收到有关的信用证，因此我们没能按时装运。

（3）Most buyers have withdrawn from the market in consequence of unstable prices.

由于价格不稳定的缘故，大多数买主已退出市场。

7. take special care

特别注意

（1）Special care has been taken to its packing, which we trust will prove satisfactory to your clients in every respect.

该货物的包装已予以特别注意，相信在各方面都能使你方客户满意。

（2）We shall take particular care to keep strictly to your specification.

我们应特别注意严格遵照你们的规格要求。

8. per

prep. 由……装运走（从出口商的角度是"运走"）

ex. prep. 由……装运来（从进口商的角度是"运来"）

（1）We have shipped the 100 tons of wool per S. S. "Rose".

我们已将100吨羊毛由"玫瑰"轮运走。

（2）我们已收到了由"玫瑰"轮运来的100吨羊毛。

We have received the shipment of 100 tons of wool ex S. S. "Rose".

9. discharge

v./n. 卸货；履行；清偿；解雇

discharge cargo from a ship　从船上卸下货物

discharge a ship of the cargo　把货卸下船

discharge receipt　卸货收据

port of discharge　卸货港

discharge sb. from an obligation　免除某人的义务

discharge（oneself of）one's duty　履行职责

discharge one's debt　清偿债务

(1) They discharged the cargo at New York.

他们在纽约港卸货。

(2) The boss discharged him because of habitual absenteeism.

因为他习惯性旷工，老板解雇了他。

(3) The judge found him not guilty and discharged him.

法官认为他无罪而释放了他。

10. short-weight

n. 短重

short delivery　n. 短交；缺交

short shipment　n. 短装；装载不足

short-calculated　adj. 少算的

short-delivered　adj. 短交；缺交

short-established/opened　adj. 少开

short-invoiced　adj. 发票少开

short-landed　adj. 短卸

short-paid　adj. 少付

short-shipped　adj. 短装

(1) We have to lodge a claim against you for a short-weight of 5 tons.

由于短重 5 吨，我们必须向你们提出索赔。

(2) After taking delivery of the goods, we find a short delivery of 130 lbs in weight.

提货后发现货物短交 130 磅。

(3) Our commission on this order is short-calculated.

本次订货的佣金少算了。

(4) Your L/C is short-opened to the amount of $125.

你方信用证少开了 125 美元。

(5) The shipment is short-invoiced by $315.

此批货物的发票少开了 315 美元。

(6) Since the loss is not negligible, we request that you make up the short-landed goods promptly.

由于这笔损失较大，我们要求你方立即补偿短卸的货物。

(7) Enclosed is our Credit Note No. 818 for the short-paid amount of $315.

随函附上我方少付 315 美元的第 818 号贷方通知。

(8) The short-shipped goods will be forwarded together with your next order.

短装的货物将与你方下批订货一起发运。

11. Inspection Certificate

    n. 检验证明

    Survey Report　检验报告

    Survey Report on Examination of Damage or Shortage　检验残损证明书

    Survey Report on Inspection of Tank Hold　船舱鉴定证明书

    Survey Report on Quality　品质鉴定证明书

    Survey Report of Weight　重量鉴定证明书

12. settlement

    n. 解决；清偿

    settle v. 解决；清偿

    settlement by amicable arrangement　以友好的方式解决

    settlement by arbitration　以仲裁方式解决

    settlement of balance　结清余额

    settlement of account　结账

    settlement of claims　理赔；解决索赔

    settlement of loss　偿付损失

    settlement of exchange　结汇

    settlement currency　结算货币

    （1）The question has been settled.

    这个问题已经解决。

    （2）Please settle this long outstanding account without further delay.

    请清偿这笔长期未清的账目，勿再拖延。

    （3）We enclose a check in settlement of all commissions owing.

    我们附上支票一张，清偿所欠全部佣金。

    （4）We have arrived at a compromise settlement with our customer.

    我们已经和客户折中和解。

    （5）We'll make a remittance within a week in full settlement of our purchase of fertilizer.

    我们会在一周之内将购买化肥的全部款项汇给你方。

13. at the time of loading　装货时

    load　v. 装货

    unload　v. 卸货

    port of loading = port of shipment　装货港

    port of unloading = port of discharging　卸货港

    loading rate　装运率

14. account for

    解释；说明……的原因

    （1）He could not account for his absence from school.

    他不能解释旷课的原因。

    （2）We cannot account for the delay in shipment.

    我们无法解释延迟装运的原因。

15. presume

    v. 猜想；认为；推测

    （1） We presume you can make us attractive prices.
    我们认为你方能给我们一个具有吸引力的价格。

    （2） Since you did not reply to our fax in time, we presume you're not interested in the offer.
    由于未及时答复我方传真，我们认为你们对此报盘不感兴趣。

16. substitute

    v. 代替；以……代替

    substitution　　n. 代替

    replacement　　n. 调换；替换

    replace　　v. 代替；替换

    replace A with/by B　　用 B 替换 A

    （1） We cannot agree to the proposed substitution because the substitute suggested does not suit the purpose.
    我们不同意提议的替换办法，因为它不能达到目的。

    （2） We request your replacement of the goods as stipulated in the contract.
    我们要求你方按合同规定换货。

17. at one's proposal

    由某人使用（支配、处理等）

    （1） We will try our every means at our proposal to turn out the goods in a month.
    我们将竭尽全力在一个月内完成这批货物的生产。

    （2） We are holding the goods wrongly delivered at your disposal.
    我们将保留错发的货物由你方处理。

    （3） The whole parcel is quite useless to us and we hold the goods at your disposal pending your reply. Meanwhile, we are warehousing them at your expense.
    整批货物都已无用处，你方回复前，我方将代为保存该货，等候处理。现在已仓储，费用由你方负担。

Words and Phrases

misjudge	v. 误判
intact	adj. 完好无损的；未受损害的
submit	v. 提供
full	n. 全额
tender	v. 提供
recurrence	n. 再发生
New Orleans	n. 新奥尔良（美国海港城市）
herbs	n. 草药
deteriorated	adj. 腐烂的；变质的
stained	adj. 沾污的；玷污的

batch	n. 一批（货）
Survey Report	检验报告
Commodity Inspection Bureau	商检局
prior to	在……之前
Statement of Claims	索赔清单
look into	观察；调查
be up to standard	合乎标准；达到标准
in settlement of	结清
white crystal sugar	白砂糖
unfortunate incident	不幸事件
meet one's orders	满足某人的订单
5-ply	五层
strong paper bag	坚固的纸袋
due entirely to negligence	完全归咎于疏忽
tender one's apologies	表示歉意
be of standard quality	质量符合标准
clean bill of lading	清洁提单
put in the open	把……置于露天
make up	包装
take delivery	提货
execution of the order	执行订单
treat the matter as urgent	把此事视为紧急事件
bring the case a satisfactory close	给此事一个满意的结局

10.3 外贸实战技巧
Techniques in Foreign Trade Practice

索赔信函写作注意事项

在合同的执行过程中，签约双方应该严格履行合同义务。任何一方如果不能履约就会给另一方带来麻烦，有时还会使另一方遭受经济损失。一旦发生这种情况，受损方有权根据合同规定要求责任方赔偿或采取补救措施。受损方所采取的这种行动称为"索赔"；责任方就受损失一方提出的要求进行处理，叫作"理赔"。

索赔时，应根据事实和有关证明分清责任，向责任方、轮船公司或保险公司提出索赔。理赔时，应根据事实和有关证明，该赔就赔，不该赔就拒绝赔偿。在国际贸易业务中，经常因进口方拒开或迟开信用证、不按时派船或无理毁约使出口方提出索赔。例如，当进口方在收货时发现货物破损或者货物的质量不符合合同规定的要求时，进口方就会向出口方提出索赔。

在撰写索赔及理赔信函时，应注意以下几点：
（1）迅速及时。索赔必须在（合同规定的）索赔期限内提出，否则对方有权不予受理。

理赔方对索赔期内提出的索赔要求应予重视，按照国际惯例迅速进行调查研究，弄清事实，并及时给予答复。

（2）详细明确。索赔时往往会信函与电子邮件或传真并用。为争取时间，首先发出电子邮件或传真，明确提出要求，紧接着通过发送信函来详细申述理由以使对方信服，必要时应根据合同规定，附以有关证件（如检验证明等）来支持信函中提出的观点和要求。提出的要求或解决办法一定要明确，切忌含糊其词。

（3）语气婉转。书写索赔信函时，说理要充分，信心要坚定，语气要客气，婉转而不失礼貌。处理索赔事件时，要防止感情用事，避免情绪激动。激动的情绪非但无助于问题的解决，而且还会起反作用。

10.4 有用的句子
Useful Sentences

10.4.1
Useful Sentences for Complaint and Claim

(1) The importer made/filed/laid a complaint with our corporation about poor packing of the goods.
进口商因货物的不良包装向我公司提出申诉。

(2) The buyer complain to the seller of the breakage of the goods.
买方因货物破损向卖方提出申诉。

(3) Not only have you been unpunctual in effecting shipment, but the goods you supplied are not up to the standard as well. We think it necessary for you to make up the defects.
你方不但没有准时交货，而且所供货物没有达到标准。我们认为你方必须采取措施以弥补这些缺陷。

(4) On examination, we feel regretful that the consignment is not in accordance/conformity with the original sample.
检查后，我们感到很遗憾，这批货与原来的样品不符。

(5) We regret to complain that your consignment of clothes shipped by M. V. "Fengqing" is not of the quality and color of the samples.
你方由"风庆"号轮所装的服装的质量和颜色与样品不符，我们遗憾地对此表示不满。

(6) Much to our regret, upon opening the container, we found that there were only 2,980 kegs instead of the 3,000 kegs shipped by you/the goods were short by 20 kegs, and we hope you will do your utmost to remedy it.
打开集装箱后，令我们遗憾的是，你方只发了2 980桶而不是应发的3 000桶，我们希望你们能全力补救。

(7) Your shipment of our Order No. 630 has been found short weight by 220 kilos.
现发现你方所发运的我方630号订单货物短重220公斤。

(8) Much to our regret, after inspection of the consignment, we found Art. No. A63 missing.
我们检查后，很遗憾地发现缺少货号A63的商品。

（9）On opening the cases, we found that 25 sets of video recorders had been damaged by sea water, and seemed to be a complete write-off.

打开箱子后,我们发现 25 台录影机被海水损坏,看起来完全报废了。

（10）We shall lodge(file/make/raise/submit/register/put forward/place) a claim against you on this shipment for RMB¥1,300 for short weight./We shall claim on you on this shipment for RMB¥1,300 for short weight.

我方将向你方因短重对这批货物提出人民币 1 300 元的索赔。

（11）We regret to inform you that the goods shipped per S. S. Peace arrived in such an unsatisfactory condition that we cannot but lodge a claim against you.

我们遗憾地告知你方,由"和平"轮运来的货物情况令人十分不满意,我们不得不向你提出索赔。

（12）On the basis of the SCIB's survey report, we lodge a claim against you for inferior quality of the goods.

根据商品检验检疫局的检验报告,我们对你方货物低劣的质量提出索赔。

（13）In order to settle the problem, we have to ask for/demand compensation from you for the loss we suffered.

为了解决问题,我们要求你方赔偿我们所遭受的损失。

10.4.2

Useful Sentences for Settlement of Claims

（1）In view of our friendly business relations, we are prepared to meet (accept/entertain) your claim for the 100 cases.

考虑到双方友好的合作关系,我们准备满足/接受你方索赔 100 箱货物的要求。

（2）According to the contract, we are responsible/liable for repairing or replacing those inferior goods.

根据合同,我们会负责修复或替换那些品质不良的货物。

（3）We regret that we have sent you LP-300 instead of the LP-301 Laser Printers that you ordered, and we will ship the correct items to you immediately at our expense.

很遗憾我们给你方发送的是 LP-300 而不是你们订的 LP-301 激光打印机。我们将立即装运正确的货物,费用由我方承担。

（4）We are sorry for the confusion and delays and will take effective measurers to have your orders fulfilled correctly in the future.

我们对混乱和拖延表示抱歉,并将采取有效的措施正确执行你方订单。

（5）Please accept our sincere apologies for the inconvenience that has caused you and we hope this will not affect our friendly relationship.

对我们给你方造成的不便,请接受我们真诚的道歉。我们希望这不会影响我们的友好关系。

10.4.3
Useful Sentences for Rejection of Claims

(1) We must repudiate our liability for the claim on account of lack of evidence to support your statement.
由于缺乏证据来证实你方的申诉,我们拒绝对你方索赔负责。
(2) We regret we cannot entertain your claim which is without any foundation.
很遗憾我们不能接受你方索赔,它没有任何根据。
(3) It is a case of Force Majeure which is beyond our control.
这是我方无法控制的不可抗力事件。
(4) We can't entertain your claim for loss incurred in transit.
运输途中产生的损失我们不负责赔偿。
(5) As the goods have been insured, you may refer the matter to the insurance company or their agents at your end.
由于此批货已办理保险,你可以将此事提交保险公司或其在你地的代理人处理。
(6) Such color deviation existing between the products and the samples is normal and permissible, therefore, the claim for compensation is unacceptable.
产品和样品之间的这种色差是正常的,也是允许的。所以,索赔不能接受。
(7) This is the maximum concession we can afford. Should you not agree to accept our proposal, we would like to settle by arbitration.
这是我们所能做的最大让步。如你方不同意接受我方建议,我们建议通过仲裁解决。

10.5 补充商务信函
Letters for Further Reading

Letter 10-7

Dear Sirs,

<u>Re: Claim on Sewing Machines</u>

The captioned goods you shipped per S.S. "Yellow River" on May 14 arrived here yesterday.

On examination, we have found that many of the sewing machines are severely damaged, though the cases themselves show no trace of damage.

Considering this damage was due to the rough handling by the steamship company, we claimed on them for recovery of the loss, but an investigation made by the surveyor has revealed the fact that the damage is attributable to improper packing. For further particulars, we refer you to the surveyor's report enclosed.

We are therefore, compelled to claim on you to compensate us for the loss, $27,500, which we have sustained by the damage to the goods.

> We trust that you will be kind enough to accept this claim and deduct the sum from the amount of your next invoice to us.
>
> Yours faithfully,

Letter 10-8

> Dear Sirs,
>
> Thank you for your letter of April 5 referring to the consignment of Sewing Machines sent to you per S. S. "Yellow River". We regret that we can not accept your claim.
>
> We have investigated the matter thoroughly. As far as we can ascertain, the goods were in first class condition when they left here. The bill of lading is evidence for this. It is obvious that the damage you complain of must have taken place during transit. It follows, therefore, that we cannot be held responsible for the damage. We therefore advise you to make a claim on the shipping company, Johnson Line, who should be liable for that.
>
> We are grateful that you have brought the matter to our attention. If you wish, we would be happy to take the issue up with the shipping company on your behalf.
>
> We look forward to resolving this matter as soon as possible.
>
> Yours faithfully,

Letter 10-9

> Gentlemen:
>
> After carefully examining the blouses supplied to our order No. Z115 of June 8, we must express surprise and disappointment at their quality. They certainly do not match the samples you sent to us. Some of them are so poor that we cannot help feeling there must have been some mistakes in making up this order.
>
> You will remember that in our previous exchange of correspondences, I stressed time and again that the delivery must be in exact accordance with the samples.
>
> As the parcel is quite unsuited to the needs of our customers, we have no choice but to ask you to take them back and replace them by materials of the quality ordered. If this is not possible, then I am afraid we shall have to ask you to cancel our order.
>
> Please look into the matter and let us know your solution as soon as possible.
>
> Truly yours,

Letter 10-10

Dear Sirs,

We are very sorry indeed to learn from your letter of July 15 that you are not satisfied with the blouses supplied to your order No. Z115.

From what you say, it seems possible that some mistake has been made in our selection of the materials meant for you. We are arranging for our sales manager Mr. Wilson, who is now in Hong Kong on a business trip, to call on you later this week to compare the goods supplied with the previous samples.

If it is found that our selection was faulty, then you can most certainly rely on us to replace them. In any case, we are willing to take the goods back and, if we can not supply what you want, to cancel your order.

We hope the above arrangements will satisfy you.

Faithfully yours,

Letter 10-11

Gentlemen:

We thank for your letter dated October 15, with the enclosure of Survey Report No. F556.

Your claim that the quality of the goods shipped per S. S. "East Wind" is not up to the standard of the original sample and request to make a 10% reduction in the contracted price. This does not appear to us to be reasonable, as we sent you a shipping sample prior to shipment, and not hearing from you to the contrary, presumed it to be acceptable to you. Meanwhile, this is a quality we have sold for years without receiving any complaints from other customers. It is made in our own mills, and the source of raw materials has not been changed.

However, considering our long-standing business relations and since the goods were examined by a Public Survey upon arrival, we will meet you halfway by offering a discount of 5%.

We hope that our proposal will be entertained by you for the settlement of the pending case so that we may continue doing business with you shortly.

We look forward to your early reply.

Truly yours,

Letter 10-12

Dear Sirs,

We are surprised to note from your letter of June 10 that you are not prepared to consider our offering a 15% discount to compensate you for the defects in the goods supplied in execution of your order No. 998 of June 1.

Though we consider our solution workable, and even generous, we are afraid that it is not be shared by you. However, we regard with disfavor your threat to resort to litigation, and we suggest that the dispute should be settled just as effectively and far more economically by arbitration.

We would recommend on the grounds of economy a joint arbitrator, but should you prefer to have one appointed by each of us, and a third called in with a casting vote in the event of disagreement, we should be prepared to fall in with your wishes.

Yours faithfully,

10.6 练习
Exercises

Ⅰ. Translate the following phrases into Chinese.
1. effective measure
2. economic compensation
3. exploit market
4. lodge a claim
5. international business transaction
6. quantity discrepancy
7. unclear mark
8. loss of the goods
9. wrong delivery
10. faulty packing
11. insecure packing
12. port of discharge
13. discharge one's debt
14. short delivery
15. short shipment
16. settlement of claims
17. settlement of exchange
18. port of shipment
19. unfortunate incident
20. meet one's orders

Ⅱ. Choose the best answer.
1. The goods under Contract No. 12345 left here _____ .
   A. in a good condition
   B. in good condition
   C. in good conditions
   D. in the good condition
2. We have lodged a claim _____ ABC & Co. _____ the quality of the goods shipped _____ m. v. "Peace".
   A. against, for, by
   B. with, for, under
   C. on, against, as per
   D. to, for, per
3. As the goods are ready for shipment, we _____ your L/C to be opened immediately.

    A. hope   B. anticipate

    C. await   D. expect

4. As arranged, we have effected insurance _____ the goods _____ 110% of the invoice value _____ All Risks.

    A. of, at, with   B. for, in, against

    C. on, for against   D. to, at, over

5. The goods _____ shipped already if your L/C had arrived by the end of December last.

    A. would be   B. must have been

    C. had been   D. would have been

6. It is important that your client _____ the relevant L/C not later than April 12, 2018.

    A. must open   B. has to open

    C. open   D. opens

7. The buyer suggested that the packing of this article _____ improved.

    A. be   B. was to be

    C. would be   D. had to be

8. If we had a sample in hand, we _____ to negotiate business with our end-users now.

    A. would be able   B. should have

    C. had been able   D. should have been able

9. Your claim for the damage is to be _____ with the insurance company

    A. met   B. filed

    C. satisfied   D. compensated

10. Will you please let us know details of any lines of goods which you think are _____ for your market?

    A. interesting   B. suitable

    C. proper   D. desirable

Ⅲ. Fill in the blanks.

1. We are lodging a claim _____ the shipment _____ s/s "Red Star" _____ short delivery.

2. We hope you will _____ our analysis acceptable.

3. After inspection _____ the port of destination, the quality _____ the goods shipped _____ s/s "Red Star" under No. AB2345 was found not _____ conformity _____ the contract stipulations.

4. Please give our claim your _____ attention and _____ us have your reply immediately.

5. We regret _____ hear that several bags of the last _____ were broken during transit.

6. The shipment was _____ by insurance _____ All Risks.

7. We have _____ choice _____ to ask you to take them back.

8. We are very sorry to hear that goods you received are not _____ _____ the quality expected.

9. We are sorry to inform you that your claim _____ us _____ short weight is unsuited to the international insurance claim standards.

10. We have already raised a claim _____ the insurance company _____ $ 350 _____

damage in transit.

IV. Translate the following sentences into Chinese.
1. I'm afraid you should compensate us by 5% of the total amount of the contract.
2. We regret for the loss you have suffered and agree to compensate you by US $500.
3. Please examine the matter and send us the goods to meet the shortage as soon as possible.
4. We shall lodge a claim for all the losses incurred as a consequence of your failure to ship our order in time.
5. This seems to be a very clear case and we hope you will see your way to make a prompt settlement.
6. Our investigation shows that improper packing caused damage. Therefore we have to refer this matter to you.
7. As the goods are inferior in quality, we are returning the whole of the 20 cases and must ask you to replace them.
8. We hope this unfortunate incident will not affect the relationship between us.
9. Enclosed is the surveyor's report on the three damaged cases.
10. Claim on delayed shipment is that sellers fail to make the delivery according to time schedule.

V. Translate the following sentences into English.
1. 我们很遗憾地告诉你们,贵方索赔不能被受理,因为它已远远超过合同规定的索赔期限。
2. 关于你方产品的品质低劣的问题,我方要求你方赔偿1万美元。
3. 由于你方未能按时交货,我方将向你方提出由此而遭受的全部损失的索赔。
4. 任何有关该产品质量问题的申诉应在货物到达后15天内提出。
5. 很遗憾我们无法接受你方关于货物短交的索赔。
6. 因为双方均有责任,单方面要求我方对全部损失承担责任是不公平的。我方只准备赔偿50%的损失。
7. 错发的货物可以由下一班可利用的轮船退回,但最好在你市场处理(卖掉)。
8. 你方提出的短缺很可能发生在运输途中,而对此我方无能为力。
9. 通过双方的合作,这一事件得以友好解决。我方将寄上¥3 546用于赔偿由此而产生的全部损失。
10. 由于没有足够的证据,你方的索赔无法立足,我方认为进一步追究此事是毫无意义的。

VI. Translate the following passage into English.
执事先生:
    现随函寄去上海商检局开具的第SH(89)135号检验报告。该报告证明上述货物的品质比以前送来的样品差得多。由于这批货物对我们完全无用,因此要求你方归还这批货的发票金额和检验费用共计25 000美元。
    谅必你们会迅速处理此项索赔。一俟索赔解决,我方当立即将货物退回,一切费用由你方负担。

谨上

Chapter 11

第 11 章

国际商务合同
International Business Contract

Learning Objectives

Enable the students to know about the varieties of contracts; to be acquainted with the format of business English contract, the writing requirements, language features; to be able to skillfully translate related contract; and master the main points regarding business contracts translation.

使学生了解商务合同的种类；熟悉商务英文合同的格式及写作要求、语言特色；能较熟练地翻译相关合同；掌握商务合同翻译的要点。

11.1 背景知识
Background Information

在国际商务中，如果卖方作出发盘，而买方接受该发盘，则意味着交易达成，接下来，通常需要撰写书面合同或销售确认书。合同是规定有关当事人的权利和义务的正式书面协议。合同一经订立，即具有法律约束力和强制执行力。未履行义务的一方必须赔偿对方因此带来的损失。合同或销售确认书必须包含谈判过程中针对所涉及的具体交易细节而达成的所有条款和条件。

In international business, if the seller makes an offer and the buyer accepts that offer, it means a deal. A written contract or sales confirmation is usually made out. A contract is a formal written agreement, which sets forth rights and obligations of the parties concerned. Once entered into, a contract is binding and enforceable by law. Any party who fails to fulfill his obligations must make compensation for the other party's losses. A contract or sales confirmation must contain all the terms and conditions agree upon during the negotiation in full details.

11.1.1 合同的定义
Definition of A Contract

合同是由两个或两个以上当事人为了达成交易而订立的协议,它是对有关当事人规定约束性责任的一种协议。

A contract is an agreement between two or more competent parties for the purpose of transacting business. It is an agreement which sets forth binding obligations of the relevant parties.

11.1.2 合同的种类
The types of Contracts

在国际贸易中,出口和进口合同的名称和形式各不相同,主要有协议书、售货单、销售协议、销售合同、销售确认书、订货确认书、购货合同、购货单、订单、购货确认书、贸易协议、双边贸易协议、多边贸易协议、进口合同、出口合同、寄售合同、代理协议、代理合同、补偿贸易合同等,但是常见的合同形式为合同、确认书、协议书和备忘录。合同或确认书可以由卖方或买方起草,分别被称为销售合同/确认书或购货合同/确认书。销售或购货合同比销售或购货确认书更正式。

In international trade, export and import contracts vary in both names and forms, which mainly include: Agreement, Sales Note, Sales Agreement, Sales Contract, Sales Confirmation, Confirmation of Order, Purchase Contract, Purchase Note, Order Sheet, Purchase Confirmation, Trade Agreement, Bilateral Trade Agreement, Multilateral Trade Agreement, Import Contract, Export Contract, Consignment Contract, Agency Agreement, Agency Contract and Compensation Trade Contract. But the names that often appear are contract, confirmation, agreement and memorandum. A contract or confirmation can be drawn up either by the seller or the buyer. Respectively, they are called a sales contract/confirmation or a purchase contract/confirmation. The sales or purchase contract is more formal than the sales or purchase confirmation.

11.1.3 合同的原则
Principles of Contracts

——合同或协议的内容应当遵循平等互利原则,通过共同协商确定。

——合同或协议中的条款应完整、具体、明确、不得有遗漏。

——准确地使用词语和表达方式,妥善安排内容,使其合乎逻辑,没有任何错误。

——The contents of contracts or agreements should conform to the principle of equality and mutual benefit and through common negotiation.

——The stipulations of contracts or agreements should be complete, concrete, clear and without careless omissions.

——Using words and expressions accurately, arranging the contents properly, logically and without mistakes.

11.1.4 合同的格式
Formation of Contracts

正式书面合同通常包括以下几个部分：

1. 合同的名称
2. 前文
（1）签订日期、地点；
（2）合同当事人及其国籍、主要的经营场所或住所；
（3）当事方权限；
（4）订约的缘由/说明条款。
3. 正文
（1）定义条款

用于解释合同或协议中重复出现的关键词，这些词有特殊含义或容易引起误解或争议。

（2）基本条款

如商品名称及规格、数量、单价、总价、包装、装运期、装运港、目的港、付款条件、保险、检验、索赔、仲裁、不可抗力等。

（3）一般条款

包括合同有效期、合同的终止、合同的让与、适用的法律、诉讼管辖、通知手续、完整条款、合同的修改以及其他。

4. 结尾条款
（1）结尾语；
（2）订约人签字；
（3）盖章。

Generally, a formal written contract includes the following parts:

1. Title
2. Preamble
（1）Date and place of signing;
（2）Signing parties and their nationalities, principal place of business or residence address;
（3）Each party's authority;
（4）Recitals or whereas clause.
3. Body
（1）Definition clause

To give specific explanation to the key words repeatedly appearing in a contract or agreement, which have special meanings or easily cause misunderstanding and controversy.

（2）Basic conditions

Such as the name and the specification of the commodity, quantity, unit price and total value, packing, the time of shipment, the port of shipment, the port of destination, terms of payment, insurance, inspection, claim, arbitration and force majeure, etc.

（3）General terms and conditions

Including duration, termination, assignment, governing law, jurisdiction, notice," Entire agreement " clause, amendment and others.

4. Witness clause
（1）Concluding Sentence;
（2）Signature;
（3）Seal.

11.1.5 国际商务合同的语言特色
Language Features in International Business Contract

（1）使用正式的法律用词

由于重要的国际商务合同是具有法律约束力的文件，合同各方通常采用书面形式，使用法律

（1）Formal legal term

Because an important international business contract is a legally binding document, it generally takes the writing form, written, uses the legal words to show the

词汇，以体现合同的正规性、庄严性。国际商务合同具有准确、规范以及严谨的语言特色。

（2）使用古体词

商务合同中大量使用古体词汇。古英语词汇的使用可以避免用词重复、文句冗余，使合同更加简练、准确、有说服力。古体词经常以合成副词形式出现，如hereto、herein、hereby、hereof、whereby、thereafter等。"here"代表"this"，"there"代表"that"，"where"代表"which"，以引出从句。由于古体词在日常用语中很少出现，古体词的使用增加了理解合同的难度。

（3）情态动词的使用频率高

"shall""shall not""may"在合同中经常出现，但含义与日常表达有所不同，多用"shall"代替"will"或"should"以加强语气和增强强制性。在合同中，"shall"并非单纯表示将来，而通常用来表示法律上具有约束力，可强制执行的义务，宜译为"应该""必须"。"shall"是指当事人的义务，即应该做什么；"shall not"是指禁止做的事情；"may"指当事人的权利，即可以做什么。

（4）用短语替代从句

有时为了使英语商务合同中的句子更加简洁，会使用一些短语代替某些定语从句、状语从句和主语从句。

（5）长句多

在一些国际商务合同条款中，常能见到数以百计的词以及复杂结构句子，每个句子的信息量大，

formality, solemnity of the contract and it has the language features of accuracy, normalization and preciseness.

(2) Use archaic words

Extensive archaic words are used in business contracts. The use of these Old English words so as to avoid repetition and redundancy, makes the contract concise, accurate and persuasive. Archaic words often appear in the form of synthetic adverbs, such as hereto, herein, hereby, hereof, whereby, thereafter etc. "here" stands for "this", "there" stands for "that", "where" stands for "which" and leads clause. As archaic words rarely appear in everyday language, the use of archaic words increases the difficulty of understanding contracts.

(3) Modal verbs are used frequently

"shall" "shall not" "may" are often used and have different meanings in contracts. Use "shall" instead of "will" or "should" to enhance tone and coercion. In the contract, "shall" does not simply mean the future, but often used to indicate a legally enforceable obligation that is binding, should be translated as "should" "must" "shall" refers to the parties obligations, that is, what to do; "shall not" mean prohibited; "may" refers to the rights of the parties, what can be done.

(4) Replace clauses with phrases

Sometimes in order to make the sentence simple in the English business contract, some phrases will be used instead of certain attributive, adverbial and subject clause.

(5) Long sentences

It is easy to find that hundreds of words and complex structure sentences constitute some clauses in the international business contract. The content information of

信息表达完整且严密。为了不被曲解、误读,选择使用长句是必要的。要想成功使用长句,不仅要有严密的逻辑思维和法律基础,还需具备英语语法和词法功底。

(6) 基本句式为陈述句

合同是用来确定双方当事人的法律关系,规定双方当事人权利和义务的具有法律性质的正式文件,因此为了突出其法律特性,在草拟合同时习惯采用陈述句。

each sentence in the contract is large and the information is complete and strict. In order not to be distorted, misread, choose to use a long sentence is necessary. In order to successfully use long sentences, not only must there be strict logical thinking and legal basis, but also English grammar and lexical skills.

(6) The basic sentence is the statement

A contract is an official document that determines the legal relationship between the parties and provides for the legal character of the rights and obligations of both parties. Therefore, in order to highlight its legal characteristics, it is customary to adopt a statement at the time of drafting.

11.2 合同及信例
Specimen Contracts and Letters

销售合同样例
Sample sales contract

销售合同
SALES CONTRACT

合同编号:
Contract No.:
签订日期:
Date:
签订地点:
Signed at:

卖方:
Sellers:

买方:
Buyers:

经买卖双方同意成交下列商品,订立条款如下:
This contract is made by and agreed between the Buyers and Sellers in accordance with the terms and conditions stipulated below.

唛头 Marks and numbers	名称及规格 Description of goods	数量 Quantity	单价 Unit price	金额 Amount

总值 Total value：

包装条件：
Packing：

转运：
Transshipment：
☐ 允许　　☐ 不允许
　 Allowed　　 Not allowed

分批装运：
Partial shipments：
☐ 允许　　☐ 不允许
　 Allowed　　 Not allowed

装运期：
Shipment date：

保险条款：
Insurance：
由_____按发票金额110%投保_____险，另加保_____险至_____为止。
To be covered by the _____ for 110% of the invoice value covering _____ additional _____ from _____ to _____ .

付款条件：
Terms of payment：

☐ 买方不迟于_____年_____月_____日前将100%的货款用即期汇票/电汇送抵卖方。
　 The buyers shall pay 100% of the sales proceeds through sight (demand) draft/by T/T remittance to the sellers not later than _____ .

☐ 买方须于_____年_____月_____日前通过_____银行开出以卖方为受益人的不可撤销_____天期信用证，并注明在上述装运日期后_____天内在中国议付有效，信用证须注明合同编号。
　 The buyers shall issue an irrevocable L/C at _____ sight through _____ in favor of the sellers prior to _____ indicating L/C shall be valid in China through negotiation within _____ day after the shipment effected, the L/C must mention the Contract Number.

☐ 付款交单：买方应对卖方开具的以买方为付款人的跟单汇票在见票后_____天付款，付款后交单。
　 Documents against payment (D/P): The buyers shall duly make the payment against documentary draft made out to the buyers at _____ sight by the sellers against presentation of the documents.

□ 承兑交单：买方应对卖方开具的以买方为付款人_____天的跟单汇票进行承兑，承兑后交单。
   Documents against acceptance (D/A): The buyers shall duly accept the documentary draft made out to the buyers at _____ days by the sellers against presentation of the documents.

单据：
Documents required：

卖方应将下列单据提交银行议付/托收。
The sellers shall present the following documents required for negotiation/collection to the banks.

□ 整套正本清洁提单。
   Full set of clean on board ocean bills of lading.

□ 商业发票一式_____份。
   Signed commercial invoice in _____ copies.

□ 装箱单或重量单一式_____份。
   Packing list/weight memo in _____ copies.

□ 由_____签发的数量与质量与证明书一式_____份。
   Certificate of quantity and quality in _____ copies issued by _____.

□ 保险单一式_____份。
   Insurance policy in _____ copies.

□ 由_____签发的产地证一式_____份。
   Certificate of Origin in _____ copies issued by _____.

装运通知：
Shipping advice：

　　一旦装运完毕，卖方应即电告买方合同号、商品名称、已装载数量、发票总金额、毛重、运输工具名称及启运日期等。
　　The sellers shall immediately, upon the completion of the loading of the goods, advise the buyers of the Contract No., names of commodity, loaded quantity, invoice value, gross weight, names of vessel and shipment date by Fax.

检验与索赔：
Inspection and claims：

（1）卖方在发货前由_____检验机构对货物的品质、规格和数量进行检验，并出具检验证明书。
　　The buyers shall have the qualities, specifications, quantities of the goods carefully inspected by the _____ inspection authority, which shall issue Inspection Certificate before shipment.

（2）货物到达目的口岸后，买方可委托当地的商品检验机构对货物进行复检。如果发现货物有损坏、残缺或规格、数量与合同规定不符，买方须于货到目的口岸的_____天内凭_____检验机构出具的检验证明书向卖方索赔。
　　The buyers have right to have the goods inspected by the local commodity inspection authority after the arrival of the goods at the port of destination if the goods are found damaged/short/their specifications and quantities not in compliance with that specified in the contract, the buyers shall lodge claims against the sellers based on the inspection certificate issued by the

_____ Commodity Inspection Authority within _____ days after the goods arrival at the destination.

(3) 如买方提出索赔，凡属品质异议须于货到目的口岸之起_____天内提出；凡属数量异议须于货到目的口岸之日起_____天内提出。对所装货物所提任何异议应由保险公司、运输公司或邮递机构负责的，卖方不负任何责任。

The claims, if any regarding to the quality of the goods, shall be lodged within _____ days after arrival of the goods at the destination, if any regarding to the quantities of the goods, shall be lodged within _____ days after arrival of the goods at the destination. The sellers shall not take any responsibility if any claims concerning the shipping goods is up to the responsibility of insurance company/transportation company/post office.

人力不可抗拒：

Force Majeure：

如因人力不可抗拒的原因造成本合同全部或部分不能履约，卖方概不负责，但卖方应将上述发生的情况及时通知买方。

The sellers shall not hold any responsibility for partial or total non-performance of this contract due to Force Majeure. But the sellers advise the buyers on time of such occurrence.

争议解决方式：

Disputes settlement：

凡因执行本合同而发生的或与本合同有关的争议，双方应协商解决。如果协商不能得到解决，应提交仲裁。仲裁地点在被告方所在国内，或者在双方同意的第三国。仲裁裁决是终局的，对双方都有约束力，仲裁费用由败诉方承担。

All disputes arising out of the contract or concerning the contract, shall be amicably settled through negotiation. In case no amicable settlement can be reached between the two parties, the case under dispute shall be submitted to arbitration, which shall be held in the country where the defendant resides, or in third country agreed by both parties. The award of the arbitration shall be accepted as final and binding upon both parties. The arbitration fees shall be borne by the losing party.

法律适用：

Law application：

本合同之签订地，或发生争议时货物所在地在中华人民共和国境内或被诉人为中国法人的，适用中华人民共和国法律，除此规定外，适用《联合国国际货物销售公约》。

It will be governed by the law of the People's Republic of China under the circumstances that the contract is signed or the goods while the disputes arising are in the People's Republic of China or the defendant is Chinese legal person, otherwise it is governed by Untied Nations Convention on Contract for the International Sale of Goods.

本合同使用的价格术语系根据国际商会《INCOTERMS® 2010》。

The terms in the contract are based on INCOTERMS® 2010 of the International Chamber of Commerce.

文字：

Versions：

本合同中、英两种文字具有同等法律效力，在文字解释上，若有异议，以中文解释为准。

This contract is made out in both Chinese and English of which version is equally effective. Conflicts between these two languages arising therefrom, if any, shall be subject to Chinese version.

本合同共_____份，自双方代表签字（盖章）之日起生效。

This contract is in _____ copies, effective since being signed/sealed by both parties.

Sellers： Buyers：

Sample Sales Confirmation

Sales Confirmation

No.: 344
Date: November 1, 2017
Signed at: Guangzhou

Sellers: China National Chemicals Import & Export Corporation
Buyers: Smith & Sons Co. Ltd.

The undersigned sellers and buyers have agreed to close the following transactions according to the terms and conditions stipulated below:

(1) Commodity, Specifications & Packing: Lithopone Zn, content 28% min., glass-fiber bags, paper-lined
(2) Quantity: 50 MT/s
(3) Unit Price: US＄110 per M/T CIFC3% Singapore
(4) Total Value: US＄5,500 (SAY US DOLLARS FIVE THOUSAND FIVE HUNDRED ONLY) (The Sellers are allowed to load 5% more or less and the price shall be calculated according to the unit price.)
(5) Shipping Mark: At sellers' option
(6) Insurance: To be covered by the sellers for 110% of the invoice value against All Risks & War Risk as per the relevant Ocean Marine Cargo Clauses of the People's Insurance Company of China. If other coverage or an additional amount is required, the buyers must have the consent of the sellers before shipment, and the additional premium is to be borne by the buyers.
(7) Port of Shipment: Guangzhou
(8) Port of Destination: Singapore
(9) Time of Shipment: During December, allowing partial shipments and transshipment.
(10) Terms of Payment: The buyers shall open with a bank acceptable to the sellers an irrevocable, sight letter of credit to reach the sellers 30 days before the month of shipment, valid for negotiation in China until the 15th day after the month of shipment.
(11) Commodity Inspection: It is mutually agreed that certificate of quality and weight issued by the Chinese Import and Export Commodity Inspection Bureau at the port of shipment shall be taken as the basis of delivery.

Remarks: The buyers shall countersign one copy of this contract and return it to the sellers within 10 days after receipt. Contract number and only brief names of commodity are required to be quoted in the covering L/C.

General Terms:

(1) Claims if any, concerning the goods shipped shall be filed within 30 days after arrival at destination supported by an inspection report. It is understood that the sellers shall not be liable for any discrepancy of the goods shipped due to causes for which the insurance company, shipping company, other transport organization or post office are liable.

(2) All disputes arising from the execution of, or in connection with this contract, shall be settled amicably through friendly consultation. In case no settlement can be reached therefrom, the case under dispute shall then be submitted to the China International Economic and Trade Arbitration Commission of the China Council for the Promotion of International Trade (CCPIT), Beijing for arbitration in accordance with its Provisional Rules of Procedure. The arbitral award is final and binding upon both parties.

(3) The Seller shall not be responsible for late delivery or non-delivery of goods in the event of force majeure of any contingencies beyond the Sellers' control.

Sellers: China National Chemicals Import & Export Corporation
Buyers: Smith & Sons Co. Ltd.

Letter 11-1 Sending a contract for countersign

Dear Mr. Shell,

We are very glad to receive your Order No. 186 for our pharmaceutical products. We are sending you, by separate airmail, our signed Sales Contract No. GH-66 in duplicate. Please countersign and return one copy for our file.

You may rest assured that your order will receive our best attention and the quality of our products will prove to be to your entire satisfaction.

As the date of shipment is approaching, please instruct your bank to issue the relative L/C in our favor as soon as possible, which shall reach us before October 30 so as to avoid delay in shipment.

We trust you will let us have your L/C on time as usual. Our close cooperation will surely develop good relations between us.

Yours sincerely,

Letter 11-2　Reply to letter 11-1

Dear Sirs,
　　We have received your Sales Contract No. GH-66 in duplicate, one of which we have countersigned and returned to you for your file.
　　The relative L/C was opened through ABC Bank last week. It must have reached you. Please arrange the shipment soon and inform us of the shipment date and sailing date.
　　　　　　　　　　　　　　　　　　　　　　　　　　　　　Yours faithfully,

Letter 11-3　Request for fulfilling sales contract

Dear Sirs,
　　We refer to the 4,000 dozen shirts under our S/C No. 136. The date of shipment is approaching, but we haven't received the relevant L/C. We'd like to draw your attention to this fact. Please rush the L/C enabling us to ship your order within the stipulated time.
　　In order to avoid subsequent amendments, please see to it that the L/C stipulations should be in full accordance with the terms in the contract.
　　We look forward to your early reply.
　　　　　　　　　　　　　　　　　　　　　　　　　　　　　Yours faithfully,

Notes

1. contract

   n. 合同；契约
   （1）We always honor our contracts and keep our words.
   　　我们一贯重合同，守信用。
   （2）Enclosed is our Sales Contract No. 11 in duplicate, one copy of which please sign and return to us for our file.
   　　随函寄去第 11 号销售合同一式两份，其中一份请签退供我备档。

   v. 订立合同；承包
   （1）You are to make the shipment in October as contracted.
   　　你应按合同所订 10 月装船。
   （2）We have now contracted with you for 1,000 bicycles.
   　　我们现在已与你方签订 1 000 辆自行车的合同。
   （3）They have contracted the project to a building company.
   　　他们已经把工程承包给一家建筑公司。

2. set forth

   阐明；阐述；陈述

(1) The reasons for our claim were set forth in our previous letters.
我方索赔的理由已在前几次去信中阐明。

(2) We have pleasure in advising you that we have completed the shipment of your Order No. 123 in accordance with the stipulations set forth in L/C No. 789.
很高兴通知你方，我们已按照信用证 789 号的规定将你方订单 123 号项下的货物装运完毕。

3. draw

v. 草拟；制定

(1) The contract is being drawn up.
合同正在草拟之中。

(2) We'll draw up the agreement in a day or two.
我们将在一两天内起草协议。

(3) The terms were drawn from the most common practices of international trade.
这些条款是按国际贸易中最常见的惯例拟定的。

(4) Technical committee shall draw up a report of all its sessions.
技术委员会对其每一届会议均起草一份报告。

开出（汇票）

(1) You may draw a clean draft on us for the value of this sample shipment.
你方可向我开出光票，收取这批样货价款。

(2) The balance of US $110 has been drawn at sight on you.
我们已开出即期汇票，向你方索取余额 110 美元。

(3) We will draw on you for the expenses.
我们将开出汇票向你方索取费用。

(4) We will draw D/P against your purchase.
对你方购货，我们将按付款交单方式收款。

4. stipulate

v. 规定

(1) The contract stipulated that the goods should be delivered in September.
合同规定必须在 9 月交货。

(2) The contract stipulates payment by sight L/C.
该合同规定付款方式为即期信用证。

stipulation

n. 规定；条款

(1) All the stipulations in your L/C should be in conformity with that in the contract.
你方信用证的所有条款都必须与合同条款一致。

(2) The transaction is concluded on the stipulation that L/C (should) be opened 30 days before the commencement of shipment.
交易达成基于这样的规定，即信用证应在装运前 30 天开立。

5. breach

n. 违反；违背

a breach of contract 违反合同

a breach of agreement 违反协议

a breach of promise 违背承诺

We are sorry to inform you that you have committed a breach of international practice.

遗憾地告知，你方违反了国际惯例。

vt. 违反；违背

Both parties should not breach the contract without good reasons.

没有充足的理由，双方均不得违约。

6. govern

v. 支配；指导

governing law 适用法律

7. option

n. 选择；选择权；买卖特权

at the buyer's option 由买方选择

at the seller's option 由卖方选择

We request you to keep the option for one week.

我们要求你方将此报盘保留7天。

8. consent

n. 同意

with the consent of 经……同意

（1）The delegation had to obtain the committee's consent.

此项委派必须得到委员会的同意。

（2）The plan will be put into effect with the consent of the board of directors.

此项计划经董事会同意即予执行。

v. 同意

（1）We tried to persuade the buyer, but he refused to consent.

我们试图说服买主，但他拒不同意。

（2）They consented to make some alterations in the draft agreement.

他们同意对协议草案做些修改。

9. countersign

v. 副署；会签

counter signature n. 副署签名；连署签名

（1）When the Sales Contract has been signed by the seller, it will be countersigned by the buyer.

销售合同经卖方签署后，须经买方会签。

（2）Please return the duplicate completed with your counter signature.

请会签后退回一份。

10. for one's file

以便某方存档，也可用 for one's record(s)。

11. assure

v. 向……保证；使确信。主要用于以下四种结构：

assure sb. of sth.

We assure you of the reliability of the information.

我们可以向你方保证此信息的可靠性。

assure sb. that

We assure you that we shall do our best to expedite shipment.

请确信我们将迅速装运。

be(or：rest)assured of sth.(rest 是系动词)

Please(or：You may)be(or：rest)assured of our continued cooperation.

请确信我方仍将继续合作。

be(or：rest)assured that

You may(Please)be(rest)assured that we will contact you as soon as our fresh supply comes in.

请确信一俟我方新供货到来,我方即与你方联系。

12. payment

    n. 支付；付款

    常用搭配：

    in payment of 支付（某笔费用，如 bill，invoice，charges，commission）

    I'm sending you ten pounds in payment of your bill.

    我现寄去 10 英镑以偿付你的账单。

    in payment for 支付（商品、样品、广告等）

    We've remitted the publishing house 160 Yuan in payment for the dictionary they sent us last month.

    我们已给出版社汇去 160 元，以支付上个月他们寄来的字典。

13. deliver

    v. 送交

    (1) The documents have already been delivered to the bank.

    单据已交到银行。

    (2) All notices must be delivered by messengers, registered mail.

    一切通知必须由专人、挂号信送达。

    v. 交货；交付

    (1) We have to deliver the 300 tons wheat in three equal monthly installments.

    我们得分三批按月等量交付这 300 吨小麦。

    (2) The Bill of Lading can indicate that the goods are to be shipped and delivered to designated party.

    提单可注明货物要发运给所指定的人。

    n. 交货

    常用搭配：

    make delivery 交货

    Your delay in delivery will greatly inconvenience us.

    你方延误交货会给我方带来极大不便。

take delivery 提货

They took delivery as soon as the goods were unloaded at the port of destination.

货物在目的港一卸下就被他们提走了。

14. in case

    如果；万一

    (1) In case no settlement can be reached through negotiation, dispute may be submitted to arbitration.

    如果争端无法通过协商解决，可提交仲裁。

    (2) In case Type No. 123 is out of stock, we could take Type No. 789.

    万一123型没有货，我们也可以接受789型。

15. confirm

    v. 确认；批准

    (1) Please write to confirm your reservation.

    预订后请来函确认。

    (2) We confirmed having placed an order with you for 5,000 tons rice.

    我们确认已向你方订购5 000吨大米。

    v. 证实；肯定

    (1) Further to our letter of June 7th, we can now confirm that all the spare parts you requested are available.

    继我方6月7日函后，现确认贵方所要求的所有备件均已备妥。

    (2) Latest developments confirm our prediction in regard to trend of the market.

    最新的事态发展证实了我们对市场趋势的预测。

    v. 保兑

    (1) Please advise the credit to the beneficiary and have it confirmed.

    请将信用证通知受益人并予以保兑。

    (2) Payment is to be made by confirmed, irrevocable sight L/C.

    付款方式是保兑的、不可撤销的即期信用证。

    confirmation

    n. 确认；证实

    (1) Quantity and price stated in the Invoice are subject to our final confirmation.

    发票所列数量和价格以我公司最后确认为准。

    (2) Please e-mail us your confirmation immediately.

    请立即电邮确认书。

16. arbitration

    n. 仲裁；公断

    (1) The award of the arbitration shall be final and binding upon both parties.

    仲裁裁决是终局的，对双方都有约束力。

    (2) Both sides in the dispute have agreed to go to arbitration.

    争议双方已同意提请仲裁。

    (3) We should include an arbitration clause in the contract.

我们应该在合同中加进仲裁条款。

17. articles

    n. 条款

    （1） Should the articles stipulated in this contract be in conflict with the following supplementary condition, the supplementary conditions should be taken as valid and binding.

    本合同其他条款如与本附加条款有冲突，当以本附加条款为准。

    （2） The country appears to be violating several articles of the convention.

    这个国家看起来违反了公约中的好几项条款。

    （3） This document includes many articles.

    这个文件包括许多条款。

18. provision

    n. 规定；条款

    （1） This provision is not intended to change or increase an organization's legal obligations.

    本条款并无意改变或增加组织的法律义务。

    （2） Without prejudice to the provisions of this letter of credit, all matters relating to the procedure of enforcement shall be regulated by the law of the state where enforcement takes place.

    在不违反本信用证规定的条件下，与执行程序有关的所有事项均应遵守执行地法律的规定。

19. procedure

    n. 程序；步骤

    （1） Police insist that Michael did not follow the correct procedure in applying for a visa.

    警方坚持称迈克尔没有按照正确的程序申请签证。

    （2） There is some confusion about what the right procedure should be.

    对正确的程序还不太明确。

Words and Phrases

contract	n. 合同
confirm	v. 确认；证实；保兑
confirmation	n. 确认；确认书
obligation	n. 义务；责任
binding	adj. 有约束力的；应履行的
enforceable	adj. 可实施的
memorandum	n. 备忘录
annex	v. 附加；添加
seal	n. 印鉴；图章
preamble	n. 导言
indicate	v. 标示；表明

determination	n. 确定
standard	n. 标准；规范
discrepancy	n. 差异；不符合（之处）
arbitration	n. 仲裁
breach	n./v. 破坏；违反
miscellaneous	adj. 不同种类的
occurrence	n. 发生；出现
dispute	n. 争执；争端
amicably	adv. 友善地
defendant	n. 被告
reside	v. 居住；定居
govern	v. 统治；支配
convention	n. 协议；协定
conflict	n. 冲突；争论
version	n. 版本；看法
undersign	v. 签名于末尾
Lithopone	n. 锌钡白（用作涂料等）
coverage	n. 保险险别
consent	n./v. 同意；赞成
remark	n. 评论；备注
countersign	v. 副署；会签
quote	v. 引用；报价
execution	n. 执行；实行
consultation	n. 协商
provision	n. 规定；条款
procedure	n. 程序；步骤
award	n. 裁决；判给
contingency	n. 意外事故
approaching	adj. 临近的
rush	v. 催促；（使）急速行进
subsequent	adj. 随后的
terms and conditions	条款和条件
security standard	安全标准
Force majeure	不可抗力
sales proceeds	销售收益
demand draft	即期汇票
inspection authority	检验机构
take any responsibility	承担任何责任
losing party	败诉方
glass-fiber bags	玻璃纤维袋

beyond the seller's control	超出卖方控制
pharmaceutical products	医药产品
sailing date	启航日期

11.3 外贸实战技巧
Techniques in Foreign Trade Practice

签订外贸合同的注意事项

国际贸易涉及的当事人较多，法律关系复杂，合同一经当事人双方签字生效就具有法律效力。若要避免损害公司利益的条款出现，实现订立合同的预期目的，就要在签订合同之初了解合同的含义和性质。总体来说，外贸合同签订应注意以下事项：

（1）在签订合同前，认真核实、确认对方当事人的主体资格和资信情况。合同的主体即合同当事人必须具有签订合同的权利能力和行为能力，合同主体不合格可能导致合同无效、效力待定或合同无法履行。不同交易主体的定位及风险承担能力存在很大的区别。因此，在签订合同前，应全面了解签约主体的基本情况，如注册地、资产、实际管理机构等信息。

（2）合同的形式和程序要合法。合同形式必须以书面形式签订，合同的签订必须符合法定程序。一般来说，合同当事人对合同内容进行充分协商，达成一致意见，并由其法定代表人或者法定代表人授权的委托代理人签字，同时加盖单位公章，即发生法律效力。

（3）合同条款要具体、完备且合法。合同条款包括合同标的、数量、质量、价款、包装方式等，所有条款的规定要具体、明确，不能含混不清，给合同的履行埋下隐患。在签订合同时经常出现的漏洞有：质量约定不明确，履行地点不明确，履行方式不明确，付款方式不明确，付款期限不明确，违约责任不明确，计量方法不明确以及检验标准不明确等，以上漏洞在签订国际商务合同中要多加注意。

（4）合同的格式和文字要规范、确切。作为一种法律文书，合同的格式应具有一定的规范性，以保证合同的完整、清晰、严谨。在起草和审查合同时，应尽量使合同的文字表述符合以下要求：书写工整，书面整洁，字迹清楚。合同使用的文字应清晰、易懂，切忌使用含混不清的语言。对于国际商务合同要注意合同翻译条款的准确性，使译本与正本的内容保持高度一致。

（5）明确合同争议解决方式并约定争议管辖权。合同争议解决部分最为关键的就是解决方式及适用法律。在争议解决的问题上，由于仲裁比诉讼更容易在国外获得承认和执行，国际商务合同中的争议条款应争取多采用仲裁。订立仲裁条款除应明确仲裁地点、机构、程序规则、效力和费用外，应强调仲裁条款要符合一局终局的原则，选择了仲裁就不能向法院起诉。在采用法院诉讼的情况下，应尽量选择由本国本地的法院管辖。鉴于中国法院的判决在国外执行有一定难度，因此，除非国外客户在中国有财产，否则不建议采用法院诉讼的条款。

（6）约定违约条款。违约条款是明确约定违约的责任，为将来可能的争议打下基础，违约责任要量化为违约金或确定违约赔偿金的计算方法。

（7）注意一致性。在国际贸易中，有的交易活动需要通过多种合同关系才能完成，例如，除了交易双方以外，其中一方或双方还要与租船公司签订运输合同，与保险公司签订保险合同，与银行建立资金清算、结算关系等，因此，在签订合同时，应注意合同条款的一致性，防止出现各个条款之间的矛盾，同时也应注意合同内容与谈判中达成的交易条件内容相一致。

11.4 有用的句子
Useful Sentences

1. The buyer will have the option to renegotiate with the seller for a new delivery date.
   买方有权就新的交货日期与卖方磋商。
2. Each party is responsible for obtaining on its own account any other insurance coverage for the goods that he may desire.
   买卖双方为了各自的利益可为货物投保额外险种，但保险费由其自行负担。
3. If shipment is delayed because the buyer fails to furnish such proof timely, the seller will not be deemed to have breached the contract.
   如果延迟装运是由于买方无法及时提供此类证据，则卖方不应被视为违约。
4. The buyer is entitled to inspect, or to have its agent inspect, the goods at the seller's place of business.
   买方有权在卖方的营业地检验或由其代理人检验货物。
5. If either party notifies the other party that it will not or is unable to perform this agreement, the party receiving notice is entitled to cancel the agreement.
   如果任何一方通知另一方不想或不能履行协议，接到通知的一方有权撤销合同。
6. It is agreed that the parties have to consider what would be a reasonable estimate of the damages each would suffer if the other were to breach this agreement.
   双方商定如果一方违约，双方应就违约给各方带来的损失进行合理估计。
7. A party must notify the other party in writing of any change in address within 90 days of the effective date of the change.
   当地址发生变化时，一方必须在变动后 90 天内通知另一方。
8. This contract will be binding on both parties as of the date on which it is signed by the seller.
   本合同自卖方签约之日起对双方具有约束力。
9. No alternation, deletion, or addition to these conditions will have any effect unless the seller accepts the change in writing.
   除卖方以书面形式接受更改外，对这些条款的更改、删除和添加均无效。
10. If the delay in delivery results because of the seller's efforts to comply with particular specifications supplied by the buyer, the buyer will not have a right to cancel the contract.
    延迟交货如果是由于卖方努力提供符合买方要求的特别规格货物所造成的，则买方无权撤销合同。
11. The seller will not consider any claim for damages or loss unless the buyer presents a separate written notice and claim to the carrier concerned.

如果买方没给相关承运人书面通知或提出索赔要求，卖方将不再考虑对货物损坏或损失的赔偿。

12. This contract is made by and between the Buyer and the Seller, whereby the Buyer agrees to buy and the Seller agrees to sell the under-mentioned commodity according to the terms and conditions stipulated below.

    兹经买卖双方同意，由卖方售出、买方购进下列货物，并按下列条款签订本合同。

13. Pursuant to the contract, whether the goods are delivered to the buyer or not, the seller will retain the title to the goods until the buyer has paid the price in full.

    依据本协议无论货物是否移交买方，卖方保留货物所有权直到买方付清全部货款。

14. The parties acknowledge that they intend to establish a mutually beneficial relationship, to this end, they will strive to resolve the disputes through amicable negotiation.

    双方承认他们将建立一个互利互惠的关系，为此他们将努力通过友好磋商的方式解决。

15. The manufacturers agree to manufacture and reserve a quantity of goods sufficient to deliver timely all the goods that the sale representative may sell.

    制造商同意制造和保留足以交付给分销商代表的一定数量的货物。

11.5 补充商务信函
Letters for Further Reading

Letter 11-4

Dear Garros,

We are much honored to receive your repeat Order No. YL-68 for our "Bingshan" Refrigerators. The high quality of our products and the smooth execution of your first order lead to further cooperation between us. We assure you of our full cooperation and trust that you will be satisfied with the high quality of our products.

We are sending you our signed Sales Confirmation No. YR-36 in duplicate via courier. Please sign and return one copy for our file. If there is any problem, please do not hesitate to contact us.

As you need this batch of goods urgently, please instruct your bank to open the relevant L/C as soon as possible so that we can arrange shipment in due time.

We are looking forward to your early response.

Yours sincerely,

Encl.: Contract No. ZH745 in duplicate

Letter 11-5

Dear Sirs,

Contract No. ZH745

 Enclosed we are sending you Contract No. ZH745 in duplicate. Please return to us one of them by airmail, complete with your signature.

 We are glad to inform you that we shall open the covering letter of credit very soon. Please advise us when the goods are ready for shipment, so that we can arrange the shipping space and insurance.

Faithfully yours,

Letter 11-6

Dear Mr. White,

Re: S/C No. SH453

 In reply to your letter dated March 10th, 2017, we are pleased to confirm your order for 5,000 TV sets. Enclosed you will find our S/C No. SH1100 in duplicate, a copy of which is to be signed and returned to us for our records.

 It is understood that the letter of credit covering the above mentioned goods will be established immediately. Please make sure that the stipulations in the relevant L/C conform exactly to the terms stated in our S/C so as to avoid subsequent amendments. Upon receipt of your L/C, we will ship the goods without delay.

 We wish to thank you for your cooperation and hope that this transaction will pave the way for further development of business between us.

Yours sincerely,

Letter 11-7

Gentlemen:

 We are pleased to confirm the above order from you and are sending you our Sales Confirmation No. HZ1034 in duplicate, one copy of which is to be countersigned and returned for our file.

 It is understood that a letter of credit in our favor covering the silk textiles will be established on or about the 25th of the month. The stipulations in the relative credit should strictly conform to the terms stated in our Sales Confirmation in order to avoid the trouble of subsequent amendments.

 We appreciate your cooperation and trust that the first partial shipment which is to be effected in July will turn out to your complete satisfaction.

Truly yours,

Encl.: Sales Confirmation

11.6 练习

Exercises

Ⅰ. Translate the following phrases into Chinese.
1. written contract
2. validity of the contract
3. commercial documents
4. arbitration clause
5. inspection certificate
6. terms of payment
7. governing law
8. port of destination
9. purchase confirmation
10. force majeure

Ⅱ. Choose the best answer.
1. We understand that you have built up _____ wide connections among buyers in the African market.
   A. the
   B. a
   C. some
   D. to
2. If the first shipment proves _____, we shall place a repeat order.
   A. to be satisfactory
   B. be satisfy
   C. satisfied
   D. satisfy
3. It would be _____ your interest to accept our offer because you can hardly obtain similar supplies at our prices elsewhere.
   A. in
   B. of
   C. to
   D. on
4. We await _____ keen interest your trial order.
   A. on
   B. of
   C. at
   D. with
5. We are not _____ in your country now and would very much like to work an arrangement with you. We can provide our references from leading banks.
   A. buying
   B. represented
   C. selling
   D. exporting
6. After careful consideration, we have decided to entrust you _____ the sole agency for our products in the territory of South Asia.
   A. of
   B. for
   C. with
   D. about
7. Both of the parties hope that after the trial period is over, the agreement _____ .
   A. is made
   B. is continued
   C. expands
   D. extends
8. Please send us an indication of the conditions under which we can _____ your company in Brazil.
   A. represent
   B. work as an agent
   C. handle
   D. be on behalf of
9. The general agent has _____ to take care of the advertising and publicity.
   A. entitled
   B. authorized

C. been entitled D. entrusted
10. We would like to know on what terms you are willing to _____ an agency agreement.
    A. come B. conclude
    C. agree D. arrange

Ⅲ. Fill in the blanks.
1. We don't think any of the item is _____ interest _____ our buyers.
2. We can assure you that the good were _____ perfect order when they left here, and the damage must have therefore, occurred _____ the transit.
3. We refer you _____ our letter dated October 13 _____ which we inform you that your price is too high.
4. The best we can do is to make a reduction _____ 1% _____ our price.
5. We hope you will agree _____ our proposal and look forward _____ receiving your early reply.
6. We would like to inform you _____ regret that the L/C _____ S/C No. 34 did not reach us until May 5.
7. It is impossible _____ us to effect shipment _____ the time you stated.
8. Please extend the validity _____ a further period _____ one month.
9. We wish to enter into business relations with you _____ the line of native produces.
10. _____ examination, we find most of the parcels were damaged _____ sea water.

Ⅳ. Translate the following sentences into Chinese.
1. Do you have any comment on this clause?
2. Please check all the terms listed in the contract and see if there is anything not in conformity with the terms we agreed on.
3. We hope to sign the contract by next Monday.
4. We are very pleased to confirm having concluded the following transaction with you.
5. Neither party may assign the agreement without the written consent of the other party.
6. The buyer is responsible for the following costs and charges in the sale and transport of goods.
7. The arbitral award is final and binding upon both parties.
8. The seller understands and agrees that law of China will be applied to interpret the contract.
9. All modifications of this agreement must be in writing and signed by the parties.
10. We are enclosing our Sales Confirmation in duplicate, please countersign and return one copy for our file.

Ⅴ. Translate the following sentences into English.
1. 我已经准备好签署这份协议。
2. 我们对条款没有问题。
3. 如果一方不履行合同，另一方有权取消。
4. 随函附上我方第 NO. HW-116 号售货确认书一式三份，请签退一份供我们存档。
5. 你方应立即开出保兑的、凭即期汇票支付的信用证。
6. 相关信用证中的规定必须与售货确认书中的条款完全一致，以避免随后的修改。
7. 需要强调的是以我方为受益人的相关信用证必须由花旗银行开立。
8. 我们已经及时签署了售货确认书并按要求退回一份供你们备案，同时我们已经开出了相关信用证，它很快会到达你方。
9. 如果这个购买合同的执行令人满意，那么将来会有稳定的订单。
10. 请寄给我们你方签好的一式两份的售货确认书供我们会签，感谢你方合作。

Ⅵ. Writing task.

Fill in the contract form with information gathered from the following correspondences:

(1) Incoming letter

July 28, 2017

Sunny Trading Company Limited,
Guangzhou, China

Dear Sirs,

  One of our clients in Hamburg is in the market for a parcel of 3,000 dozen of Ladies' Blouses. We would therefore ask you to make us an offer based on CIF Hamburg including our commission of 2%.

  We shall appreciate it if you will arrange for shipment to be made as early as possible by direct steamer for Hamburg.

  As usual, our sight irrevocable L/C will be opened in your favor 30 days before the time of shipment.

Yours faithfully,
ABC TRADING CO., LTD.

---

(2) Outgoing letter

ABC Trading Co. Ltd.,
Hamburg, Germany

Dear Sirs,

  Thank you for your letter of July 28 inquiring for 3,000 dozen Ladies' Blouses.

  We take a pleasure in making you an offer as follows, subject to your acceptance reaching here not later than August 18 3,000 dozen of Art. No. 108 Ladies' Blouses in pink, blue and yellow colors, equally assorted, with the size assortment of S/3, M/6, and L/3 per dozen, packed in cartons, at US $26.00 per dozen CIFC2% Hamburg, for shipment from any China's port in October.

  Please note that, since there is no direct steamer available for Hamburg in October, we find it only possible to ship the parcel with transshipment at Tokyo.

  We look forward to your early reply.

Yours faithfully,
SUNNY TRADING COMPANY LIMITED

(3) Incoming letter

August 9, 2017

Sunny Trading Company Limited
Guangzhou, China

Dear Sirs,

Thank you for your letter of August 2 offering us 3,000 dozen of Ladies' Blouses at US$26.00 per dozen CIFC 2% Hamburg.

We are glad to have been able to persuade our client to accept your price, though they found it a bit on the high side. We are now arranging with our bank for the relevant L/C.

When making shipment, kindly see to it that insurance is to be effected against All Risks and War risk for 110% of the invoice value. As to the shipping mark, we will let you know soon.

Yours faithfully,
ABC TRADING CO., LTD.

Sales Contract

No. 01-115

Sellers: _____

Buyers: _____

This contract is made by and between the Buyers and the Sellers, whereby the Buyers agree to buy and the Sellers agree to sell the under mentioned commodity according to the terms and conditions stipulated below:

Commodity: _____
Specifications: _____
Quantity: _____
Unit Price: _____
Total Value: _____
Packing: _____
Shipping Mark: _____
Insurance: _____
Time of Shipment: _____
Port of Shipment: _____
Port of Destination: _____
Terms of Payment: _____

Done and signed in Guangzhou on this 20th day of August, 2017.

Appendix I
附录 I

有用的短语
Useful Expressions

A

a copy of　一份/本/册
a great quantity of　大量的
a full range of samples　全套样品
a full set of documents　全套单据
a parcel of　一批
a variety of　各种各样的
acceptance　承兑
accept an order　接受订单
accept draft　承兑汇票
according to　根据
acknowledge an order　确认订单
acquaint sb. with sth.　使某人熟悉某事
actual total loss　实际全损
additional cost　额外费用
additional risks　附加险
ad valorem　从价税
advise sb. of sth.　通知某人某事
advising/notifying bank　通知行
affiliate　附属公司
after date　出票后（定期付款）
after sight　见票后
agreement price　协议价
airport　航空港；飞机场
airway bill　空运单
airway transport　航空运输

All Risks　一切险
allow sb. a discount　给某人折扣
alteration surcharge　变更卸货港附加费
amend L/C　修改信用证
amendment to an L/C　信用证修改书
anticipatory L/C　预支信用证
applicant　开证申请人
approach sb. for sth.　与某人联系某事
arbitration award　仲裁裁决
arbitration clause　仲裁条款
arrange insurance　投保
arrive at/come to an agreement　达成协议
article number（Art. No.）　货号
as a result of　结果
as a rule　按惯例
as a special accommodation　作为特殊照顾
as agreed　按商定
as an exceptional case　破例
as compared with　和……相比
as follows　如下
as per　根据
as per sample　按照样品
as regards　关于
as required　按要求
as soon as possible　尽快
as stipulated　按规定
as to　就……而言；关于
assure sb. of sth.　向某人保证某事
at a time　同时；一次
at intervals of　每隔……时间
at least　至少
at sight　即期
at one's request　按某人要求
at your end　在你处
attribute...to...　归因于……
avail oneself of　利用

B

back to back L/C　背对背信用证
balance of payments　国际收支

balance of trade 贸易差额
bank draft 银行汇票
banker's letter of guarantee (L/G) 银行保证书
bank note 钞票
barter trade 易货交易
base price 基价
be acceptable to sb. 可以为某人所接受
be accustomed to 习惯于
be acquainted with 对……了解；熟悉
be assured of 请放心
be available for supply 可供货
be desirous of 想要
be engaged in 从事
be familiar with 熟悉；通晓
be firm/good/valid for... 有效期为……
be in a position to do 能够
be interested in 对……感兴趣
be in the market for 欲购买
be on the high/low side 价格偏高/低
be popular 畅销
be ready for shipment 备妥待运
be satisfied with 对……满意
be within the scope of 属于……业务范围
bearer B/L (to bearer) 不记名提单/来人抬头提单
beneficiary 受益人
bid a price 递价
bill for collection 托收票据
bill of exchange 汇票
bill of lading 提单
bills payable 应付票据
bills receivable 应收票据
blank endorsement 空白背书/不记名背书
board of directors 董事会
bona fide holder 善意持票人
book an order with sb. 向某人订货
book shipping space 订舱
book up 订完
bottom price 最低价格
breach/violation of contract 违反合同
bridge over the gap 弥补差价

bring up a claim against 向……提出索赔
building contractor 建筑承包商；营造商
bulk cargo 散装货
bulk delivery 大宗货物的交付
by separate mail 另寄；另邮

C

CAD（cash against document） 凭单付现
call at 停靠；停泊
call/draw one's attention to 请某人注意
cancel orders 撤销订单
captioned goods 标题商品
captioned order 标题所述订单
care of 烦转
cargo forwarding agent/cargo forwarder 货运代理
cargo receipt （承运）货物收据
Carriage and Insurance Paid to（CIP） 运费、保险费付至……
carry out orders 执行订单
cash account 现金账户
cash against delivery 货到付款
cash against document 凭单付款
cash in advance 预付现金
cash on delivery（COD） 交货后付款
cash payment 现金付款
cash with order 订单付款
C/C（Chamber of Commerce） 商会
CCIB（China Commodity Inspection Bureau） 中国商品检验局
CCPIT（China Council for the Promotion of International Trade） 中国国际贸易促进委员会
ceiling price 限价
certificate of origin 原产地证书
CFS（container freight station） 货柜集散场
charter party B/L 租船提单
charter ship 租船
charter transport 租船运输
CIC（China Insurance Clause） 中国保险条款
CIF ex tackle CIF 吊钩交货
CIF landed CIF 卸到岸上
CIF Liner terms CIF 班轮条件
clean B/L 清洁提单
clean credit 光票信用证

clean draft　光票；净票
collecting bank　代收行
close the price gap　弥补差价
coincide with　与……一致；符合
come into effect　生效
come to terms　达成交易
come up to　达到；符合
commercial draft　商业汇票
commercial invoice　商业发票
commercial packing　商业包装
commission agent　佣金代理人
compensation trade　补偿贸易
competitive price　具有竞争力的价格
complain about/of　抱怨
comply with　与……一致；符合
computed tare　约定皮重
conditioned weight　公量
confirm an order　确认订单
confirmed letter of credit　保兑信用证
conform with　与……一致；符合
constructive delivery　推定交货
constructive total loss　推定全损
consular invoice　领事发票
consumer goods　消费品
container B/L　集装箱提单
contracted price　合同所列价格
contractual obligation　合同义务
conventional export packing　传统出口包装
copy B/L　副本提单
correspondent bank　代理行
cost and freight (CFR)　成本加运费
cost, insurance and freight (CIF)　成本加保险费和运费
cost price　成本价
counter bid　还价
counter offer　还盘
counter sample　对等样品
counter sign　会签；副署
cover insurance　投保
cover one's loss　弥补……损失
credit account　贷方账户

credit standing/status　信用状况
crossed check　划线支票
C. T. D.（combined transportation documents）　多式联运单据
current price　现价；时价
customary packing　习惯包装
customary practice　习惯做法
customs broker　报关员，海关经纪人
customs duties　关税
customs formalities　海关手续
customs invoice　海关发票

D

D/A（documents against acceptance）　承兑交单
date of delivery　交货期
date of departure　离港日期
date of expiry　到期日
date of shipment　装运时间
days of grace　宽限日
D/D（remittance by banker's Demand Draft）　票汇
dead freight　空载运费
debit note　借方通知
deck cargo　甲板货
deferred payment　延期付款
delay in　在……耽搁
dangerous cargo mark　危险品标志
delivered duty paid（DDP）　完税后交货
delivered duty unpaid（DDU）　未完税交货
delivery time/date　装运期
demand draft　即期汇票
demurrage　滞期费
deposit　押金
description of goods　品名
direct additional　直航附加费
direct B/L　直达提单
direct streamer　直达船
discrepancy and claim clause　异议、索赔条款
dishonor　拒付
dispatch money　速遣费
do business with　与……交易
D/P（documents against payment）　付款交单

documentary credit　跟单信用证
documentary draft　跟单汇票
do one's best/utmost　尽力；努力
down payment　预付定金
D/P after sight　远期付款交单
D/P at sight　即期付款交单
draw a draft on sb.　开立以……为付款人的汇票
draw up　起草
due date　到期日
due to　由于
due to arrive　预计到达
duplicate sample　复样
durable goods　耐用品

E

effect delivery　交货
EMP (European Main Ports)　欧洲主要港口
end-user　最终用户
enjoy a good reputation　享有盛名
enjoy fast sales　畅销
enjoy popularity　受欢迎；享有盛名
enlarge/expand the market　扩大市场
enter into/establish business relations with　与……建立业务关系
establish L/C　开证
exchange control　外汇管制
exchange settlement　结汇
excise tax　消费税
expedite L/C　催证
export license　出口许可证
ex S/S　由……轮运来
extend L/C　展证
extraneous risks　外来风险
ex works　工厂交货

F

factoring　保理
fail to　没有；未能
fair average quality　良好平均品质
fall in line with　同意；符合
fall within the business scope of　属于……业务范围

favorable price　优惠价格
feasible price　可行的价格
few and far between　（船）稀少
figure up　指出；算出
fill in　填写；填满
financial standing　资金情况
find a market　找到销路
firm offer　实盘
floating policy　流动保险单；统保单
FOB liner terms　FOB 班轮条件
FOB stowed　FOB 包括理仓
FOB trimmed　FOB 包括平仓
FOB under tackle　FOB 吊钩下交货
force majeure　不可抗力
foreign exchange　外汇
for one's account　由某人负担（费用）
for one's file　供某人存档
for one's information/reference　供某人参考
for the purpose of　为……目的
for the sake of　为……起见
forward exchange　远期外汇
forwarding agent　货运代理
forward price　期货价
for your consideration/reference　供你方考虑/参考
foul B/L　不清洁提单
FPA (Free from Particular Average)　平安险
franchise　免赔率
free alongside ship (FAS)　船边交货
free carrier (FCA)　货交承运人
free in　船方管卸不管装
free in and out　船方不管装卸
free in, out, stowed and trimmed　装卸、堆储、平仓船方均不负责
free of charge　免费
free on board (FOB)　装运港船上交货
free on rail　火车上交货
free on steamer　轮船上交货
free on truck　卡车上交货
free out　船方管装不管卸
freight forwarder　货运代理人
freight to collect/freight to be paid　运费到付

freight prepaid/freight paid　运费已付
fresh order　新订单
from stock　供现货
frontier trade　边境贸易
full container load（FCL）　整箱货
full set of bills of lading　全套提单
fundamental breach　根本违反

G

general additional risks　一般附加险
GATT（General Agreement on Tariff and Trade）　关税与贸易总协定
general average　共同海损
general terms and conditions　一般交易条件
give priority to　优先考虑
go halfway　各让一半
good merchantable quality　良好可售品质
gross for net　以毛作净
gross price　毛价；总价
gross shipping weight　装运总重量
gross terms/liner terms/berth terms　船方负担装货费和卸货费
gross weight　毛重

H

half-finished goods　半制成品
half price　半价
handle claims　理赔
hasten L/C　催证
have a confidence in　对……有信心
have extensive connections with　与……有广泛联系
have heavy commitments　订货太多
head office　总公司
high quality　高质量
holder in due course　正当持票人
hold one's responsible for　使某人对……负责
honor one's draft on presentations　见票承兑
Hook Damage　钩损险

I

IBRD（International Bank for Reconstruction and Development）　国际复兴开发银行
ICC（International Chamber of Commerce）　国际商会

illustrated catalogue　带插图的目录
IMF (International Monetary Fund)　国际货币基金组织
import license　进口许可证
in a large quantity　大量地
in a position to　能够
in accordance with　根据；按照；与……一致
in addition to　除……之外
in bad/poor condition　状况不好
in bulk　散装
in case of　假如；万一；如果
in charge of　负责；主管
income tax　所得税
in conformity with　符合；与……一致
in details　详细地
in due course　及时地
in duplicate　一式两份
in excessive of　超过
in good condition　（表面）状况良好
in line with the market　与市价相符
in one's favor　以某人为受益人
in order　整齐；无误
in quadruplicate　一式四份
in receipt of　收到
in regard to　关于
in reply　答复
in short/scare supply　缺货
inspection certificate　检验证书
in stock　有存货
insurance policy　保险单
insured amount　保险金额
in terms of　就……而言
in the amount of　总金额达到
in the line of　经营某商品
in this respect　在这方面
in transit　运输途中
in triplicate　一式三份
in two equal lots　同等数量两批
in view of　鉴于
in your place　在你处
inclusive of　包括，包含

INCOTERMS (International Rules for the Interpretation of Trade Terms) 国际贸易术语解释通则
indicative mark 指示性标志
inferior quality 质量低劣
inferior to 质量次于
inform sb. of sth. 通知某人某事
initial order 首批订单
inland water transportation 内河运输
inner packing 内包装
inquire for 询价
Institute Cargo Clauses 协会货物条款
insurable interest 可保利益原则
insurance agent 保险代理人
insurance broker 保险经纪人
insurance certificate 保险凭证
insurance claim 保险索赔
insurance company 保险公司
insurance coverage 保险范围
insurance policy 保险单
insurer 保险商
intermodal transport/multimodal transport 多式联运
international combined transport 国际联运
invitation to offer 邀请发盘
invite one's attention to 请某人注意
irrevocable L/C 不可撤销信用证
ISO (International Standardization Organization) 国家标准化组织
issue/establish/open L/C 开证
issuing bank 开证行

J

joint efforts 通过共同努力
joint venture 合资企业

K

keep account 记账
keep in touch with 与……联系
keep sb. advised/informed/posted of 随时通知某人

L

land-bridge transport 大陆桥运输
lay time 装卸时间

lead to　导致
legal weight　法定重量
less than container load（LCL）　拼箱货
letter of authority　授权书
letter of credit　信用证
letter of guarantee　担保函
lie within the scope of　属于……业务范围
limited quantity　有限数量
line of business　业务/经营范围
liner's freight tariff　班轮运价表
liner transport　班轮运输
Lloyd's agent　劳埃德保险公司代理
lodge a claim　索赔
look forward to　盼望
look into　调查
lump-sum freight　整船包价运费

M

mail transfer　信汇
make a price reduction　减价
make allowance　折让
make an exception　破例
make an offer　发盘
make compensation for　赔偿
make out a contract　缮制合同
make up the order　备货
market potential　市场潜力
marketing packing　销售包装
marine insurance　海上保险
M/T（mail transfer）　信汇
material breach　重大违约
mate's receipt　大副收据
maximum discount　最大折扣
maximum quantity　最大数量
measurement ton　尺码吨
measure up to　达到；符合
meet each other half way　各让一半
metric ton　公吨
minimum quantity　最小数量
minor breach　轻微违约

mode of payment   付款方式
moderate price   适中的价格
money order   汇款单；汇票
monopoly price   垄断价格
measurement ton   尺码吨
more or less clause   数量溢短装条款

N

name of commodity   品名
negotiating bank   议付行
net price   净价
net weight   净重
neutral packing   中性包装
non-firm offer   虚盘
non-payment   拒付
not later than   不迟于
not less than   不少于
notify party   被通知方
nude cargo   裸装货

O

obtain indemnity   获得赔偿
ocean B/L   海运提单
ocean freight   海运运费
ocean marine cargo insurance   海洋运输货物保险
offer sheet   报盘单
offer without engagement   不具约束力的报盘
official marks   官方标志
on arrival of   到达
on board/shipped B/L   已装船提单
on deck B/L   舱面提单
on the basis of   按……基础
on the high side   （价格）偏高
on the part of   在……方面；就……而言
on the recommendation of   由……推荐
on perusal   仔细阅读之后
on/under…terms   按……方式
open account trade   赊账交易
open an account   开立账户
opening/issuing bank   开证行

open policy　预约保单
open rate　临时议定运价
optional fees　选择港附加费
optional port　选择港
order B/L　指示提单
original B/L　提单正本
outer packing　外包装
owing to　由于

P

packing list　装箱单
parcel post　包裹邮件
parcel receipt　包裹收据
parent company　母公司
partial loss　部分损失
partial shipment　分批装运
particular average　单独海损
pay in advance　预付
pay on delivery　货到付款
paying bank　付款行
payment in advance　预付货款
payment by installments　分期付款
per annum　每年
performance guarantee　履行保证书
PICC (People's Insurance Company of China)　中国人民保险公司
place an order with　向……订货
poor quality　劣质
port congestion surcharge　港口拥堵附加费
port of destination　目的港
port of loading/port of shipment　装运港
port of transshipment　转运港
port surcharge　港口附加费
premium　保险费
presenting bank　提示行
present/prevailing price　现行价格
press for L/C　催证
price adjustment　价格调整
price list　价格表；价目表
price/trade terms　价格/贸易术语
process an order　处理订单；备货

processed goods　加工品
proforma invoice　形式发票
progression/installment payment　分期付款
promissory note　本票
prompt attention　立即办理
prompt shipment　即期装运
purchase contract　购货合同
push the sales of　推销

Q

quality certificate　品质证书
quality tolerance　质量公差
quotation sheet　报价单

R

rail transport　铁路运输
raise a claim　索赔
real estate　不动产
real/actual tare　实际皮重
reasonable price　合理价格
received for shipment B/L　备运提单
receiving/paying bank　汇入行/付款行
reciprocal credit　对开信用证
refer to　参阅
refuse/reject an order　拒受订单
regular customer　老顾客
regular order　定期订单，经常订单
regular purchase　定期购货
relative/relate to　有关的；关于
remitting bank　汇付行
repeat order　续订单
replace A with B　用 B 代替 A
replenish stocks　补充库存；进货
representative sample　代表性样品
restrictive endorsement　限制性背书
result from　产生于
result in　导致
retail price　零售价
revocable L/C　可撤销信用证
revolving L/C　循环信用证

Risk of Clash and Breakage　碰损破碎险
Risk of Leakage　渗漏险
Risk of Odor　串味险
Risk of Rust　锈损险
Risk of Shortage　短量险
road transportation　公路运输
rock-bottom price　最低底价
rough handling　粗鲁搬运
ruling price　现价
running or consecutive days/hours　连续日或时
rush L/C　催证

S

sale by grade　凭等级买卖
sale by sample　凭样品买卖
sale by specification　凭规格买卖
sale by standard　凭标准买卖
sales contract　销售合同
sales literature　促销资料
salvage charges　救助费用
sample cutting　剪样
sample order　凭样品订货
seaworthy packing　适合海运包装
see one's way to do sth.　想办法干某事
see to it　注意做到
sell fast/well　畅销
settle claim　理赔
settlement of claim　理赔
shipping advice　装船通知
shipping documents　装运单据
shipping instruction　装运提示
shipping mark　装运标志；唛头
shipping note　装运通知单
shipping space　仓位
short ton　短吨
sight/demand draft　即期汇票
sight L/C　即期信用证
sign a contract　签订合同
Society for Worldwide Interbank Financial Telecommunication（SWIFT）　环球银行财务电讯协会
S. O. S.　紧急求救信号

special additional risks　特殊附加险
specialize in　专门经营
specific inquiry　具体询价
spot price　现货价
SRCC (Strikes, Riots & Civil Commotions)　罢工、暴动、民变险
stale B/L　过期提单
statement of account　账单
standard quality　标准质量
standby L/C　备用信用证
stencil shipping marks　刷唛头
step up　加速
straight B/L　记名提单
subject goods　标题商品
subject matter insured　保险标的
subject to　以……为条件
subsidiary　子公司
superior quality　优质
supply from the stock　提供现货
survey report　检验报告

T

take delivery　提货
take effect　生效
take out insurance　投保
take sth. into consideration　考虑到
telegraphic transfer　电汇
tender guarantee　投标保证书
the insured　被保险人，投保人
theoretical weight　理论重量
through B/L　联运提单
time charter　定期租船
time of shipment　装运期
time/usance draft　远期汇票
to one's order　凭……指定
to our mutual benefit　对双方互利
top priority　最优先考虑的事
top quality　上等质量
total loss　全损
TPND (Theft, Pilferage & Non-Delivery)　偷窃、提货不着险
trade in/deal in　经营

trade discount 贸易折扣
trademark 商标
trade practice 贸易惯例
trade terms 贸易术语；贸易条件
tramp 不定期租船
transshipment B/L 转船提单
transport packing/outer packing 运输包装
transit trade 转口贸易；过境贸易
traveler check (cheque) 旅行支票
trial order 试销订单
T/T (telegraphic transfer) 电汇
turn out to be 结果是

U

unclean B/L 不洁提单
unconfirmed L/C 非保兑信用证
underwriter 保险商
Uniform Customs and Practices for Documentary Credits (UCP) 跟单信用证统一惯例
unit price 单价
unless otherwise instructed 除非另有通知
unloading charges 卸货费
unloading port 卸货港
up to date 最新的
usance bill 远期汇票
usance L/C 远期信用证

V

volume of exports 出口量
volume of imports 进口量
volume of trade 贸易额；交易量
voluntary offer 主动发盘
voyage/trip charter 定程租船

W

warehouse warrant 仓单
war risk 战争险
warning mark 警告性标志
waterproof packing 防水包装
weather working days 晴天工作日
weight certificate 重量证明书

weight ton　重量吨
wholesale price　批发价
with a view to/with an eye to　为了……；目的在于……
with particular average（WPA）　水渍险
with recourse　有追索权
with the validity of　有效期是……
withdraw an order　取消订单
without engagement　无约束力
working day　工作日
working hour　工作小时
work out　算出；拟订（计划）
world market　世界市场
written agreement　书面协议
written evidence　字据
written permission　书面许可
WTO（World Trade Organization）　世界贸易组织
W/W（Warehouse to Warehouse）clause　仓至仓条款

Appendix II
附录 II

练习答案
Key to Exercises

Chapter 1 Fundamentals of Business Letter Writing

I. Answer the following questions.
1. The principles of writing the business letter are the 7Cs. They are courtesy, consideration, completeness, clarity, conciseness, concreteness, and correctness.
2. There are several styles of business letters, for example, full-block style, indented style, modified block style with indented paragraphs, etc. Among them, full-block style and modified block with indented paragraphs style are the two main patterns in use at present.
3. The body part is composed of opening paragraph, middle paragraph and closing paragraph.
4. P. S. means postscript. When you find something forgotten to be included in the letter body before the envelope is to be sealed up, you may state it in a postscript with a simple signature again.
5. The recipient's name and address should be typed about half way down the envelope.
6. It's usually written in the upper left space of the envelope.

II. Write a letter using the items given below, inserting the necessary capitals and punctuations.

Sandy Han Stationery Co., Ltd.

15 Zhongshan Road, Shanghai, P. R. C.

Tel.: 86-21-64339808

E-mail address: shangtex@sina.com

March 4, 2017

Vermeer Manufacturing Company
675 Maple Street, Lagos, Nigeria

Dear Sirs,

Re: Filing cabinets

  We thank you for your letter of January 5 inquiring for the captioned goods. The enclosed catalog contains details of all our filing cabinets and will enable you to make a suitable selection.

  We look forward to receiving your specific enquiry with keen interest.

Yours faithfully,

Ⅲ. Address an envelope in blocked form using the following names and addresses.

```
Mr. Wang Gang
China National Food Corporation                              (Stamp)
48 Dongsanhuan Road
Beijing, China
                                    Mr. John Smith, Sales Manager
                                    Horizon Food Corporation
                                    58 Lancastor House
                                    Manchester, U.K.
```

Chapter 2 Establishing Business Relations

Ⅰ. Translate the following phrases into Chinese.
1. 供贵方参考
2. 国有企业
3. 另封邮寄
4. 价格表
5. 经济商务参赞处
6. 平等互利
7. 财务状况
8. 轻工业产品
9. 商务伙伴
10. 想要购买

Ⅱ. Choose the best answer.
1~5 DCACC
6~10 BDAAB

Ⅲ. Fill in the blanks.
1. for
2. with
3. to
4. in
5. in; to
6. available
7. please find
8. the courtesy of
9. by; as
10. appreciate
11. with
12. regret
13. in
14. Upon
15. for

Ⅳ. Translate the following sentences into Chinese.
1. 从中国国际贸易促进委员会获悉，你们有意购买电器用品。
2. 我们有幸自荐，以期与你公司建立业务关系。
3. 请提供你公司电冰箱的各种详细规格，并告知付款条件和折扣率。
4. 我们的业务银行是香港汇丰银行，他们可向你方提供有关我方的业务及资金情况。
5. 从你处商会获悉你公司地址，我们高兴地致信你公司，希望能建立兴旺互利的业务关系。
6. 如蒙你方寄给样品和价格将不胜感激。
7. 贵公司若有所需求，我公司定尽力效劳。

8. 这样可以使我方经营者具有很强的竞争力，还可获得最大的利润。
9. 如果你们有意经营我公司的其他产品，请告知你方要求及往来银行的名称和地址。
10. 鉴于我们在亚洲地区业务的迅速发展，有必要在下列地点设立分公司。

V. Translate the following sentences into English.
1. We have learned from the Commercial Counselor's office of our Embassy in your country that you are one of the leading importers of electronic products.
2. We have been handling light industrial products for 15 years.
3. If you find our price reasonable, please contact us.
4. We obtain your name and address from the Internet.
5. We are an exporter specializing in ceramic products.
6. Our company has various kinds of carpets and other textile floor coverings available for export.
7. We avail ourselves of this opportunity to inform you that we wish to expand our business into African market.
8. Samples and quotations at favorable prices will be sent to you upon receipt of your specific enquiry.
9. Enclosed please find our price-list and brochure for our new products.
10. We trade with businessmen in all countries on the basis of equality and mutual benefit.

VI. Writing task.
Dear Sirs,

  With reference to your letter of June 27, we are glad to learn that you wish to enter into trade relations with us, which also meets our interest.

  To give you a general idea of our products, we are sending you by air a catalogue showing various products being handled by this corporation with detailed specification and means of packing. Quotations and sample will be sent upon receipt of your specific enquiries.

  As we have not had the pleasure of doing business with you in the past, we would like to inform you that our goods for export are to be inspected by the Shanghai Commodity Inspection Bureau before shipment, and necessary certificates in regard to the quality and quantity of the shipment will be provided.

  We are looking forward to your early reply.

Yours faithfully,

Chapter 3　Inquiries and Replies

I. Translate the following phrases into Chinese.
1. 附有插图的目录
2. 对等样品
3. 数量折扣
4. 市价；时价
5. 有现货
6. 询价单
7. 具体询盘
8. 最低价格
9. 业务能力
10. 惯常条款

Ⅱ. Choose the best answer.

1~5　BBACA

6~10　ABCAC

Ⅲ. Fill in the blanks.

impressed, displayed/exhibited, supply, both, orders, sight, in, meet/supply, appreciate, prompt

Ⅳ. Translate the following sentences into Chinese.

1. 我公司意欲购买贵方的"米老鼠"牌文具。请报运抵中国大连的 CIF 价格。

2. 我们愿得到有关此事更多的信息。

3. 另函附寄样品、目录和价格表。

4. 我们从事优质优价的高档商品的零售业务。

5. 我们用料讲究，上乘的工艺更能吸引高品位的顾客。

6. 听说贵公司能够大量供货，且价格较低，我公司打算在贵处购买。

7. 目前我方建材市场供过于求。

8. 请告知我们你方对煤的年需求量是多少。

9. 我们从事玩具贸易已经将近 20 年了。

10. 随信附寄一份我方的最新价目表，请查收。

Ⅴ. Translate the following sentences into English.

1. We are very pleased to hear that you are interested in our products.

2. We sell various manufactures of plastics locally.

3. We used to purchase these goods from other sources.

4. We shall be grateful if you kindly send us a copy of your catalogue with details of your prices and payment terms.

5. We have a wide range of leather gloves which you may be interested in.

6. We are confident that we could place regular orders with you provided your prices are competitive.

7. Please quote us your lowest price for the under-mentioned, CIF Shanghai, and the earliest shipment.

8. The goods we require should be durable, colorful and attractive.

9. We will appreciate it if you will let us have your comments on our products after trial use.

10. Another supplier in your market offered us the similar article at a price 3% lower.

Ⅵ. Writing task.

Dear Sirs,

　　We have seen your advertisement in "The Financial Times". We are considering the purchase of tablecloths. Please send us your catalogue, price list and your best delivery date. We may be able to place a large order if your prices are competitive and deliveries prompt. We are looking forward to receiving your early reply.

　　　　　　　　　　　　　　　　　　　　　　　　　　　　Yours faithfully,

Chapter 4　Offers and Counter-offers

Ⅰ. Translate the following phrases into Chinese.
1. 终止发盘
2. 净价
3. 实盘
4. 销售条件
5. 类似产品
6. 虚盘
7. 售后服务
8. 由买方选择
9. 订单最低起订量
10. 货号

Ⅱ. Choose the best answer.

1~5　CBABB

6~10　ABCAC

Ⅲ. Fill in the blanks.
1. are prepared/are able, by, with
2. valid/good/open, subject to
3. indicated
4. entertain/accept
5. for, running out of
6. discount
7. Acceptance
8. exception
9. request
10. quote
11. withdrawn
12. of
13. for
14. make
15. accept
16. with
17. of
18. subjects to
19. To my regret
20. reduce

Ⅳ. Translate the following sentences into Chinese.
1. 我们准备买足够一次装运数量的这种商品。
2. 今年进口大米的数量与去年大致相同。
3. 5 000 平方米的羊毛地毯超过了我们以往的订货。
4. 如果你们的订货量能翻一倍,我们将乐于与你讨论批量订货的折扣问题。
5. 随函寄去我们的报价,此报价有效期仅为两周。
6. 我们愿尽一切所能帮助你方开展新的业务,因此如你能在一个月内付款,我们准备给你方3%特别折扣。
7. 感谢你方 12 月 23 日的来信,要求我方对 2 月运往新加坡的 10 000 公吨标题小麦报盘。
8. 我方价格没有下调的空间。
9. 目前行市坚挺并有上涨趋势,短期内大幅度波动的可能性不大。
10. 很遗憾,我方不能接受你方的还盘。

Ⅴ. Translate the following sentences into English.
1. The rates of export drawback will be reduced by 4% in our country after Jan 1, 2009, and our prices will also be increased accordingly, so we hope you will accept our re-counter offer as soon as possible.
2. As the market price is falling, we recommend your immediate acceptance.
3. To be candid with you, we regret that your price seems to be on the high side, so may we

suggest you allow a discount on your price?
4. Unfortunately, we cannot accept your offer because suppliers in your market offered us similar article at a price 3% lower than yours.
5. It is view of your long-standing business relationship with us that we make you such an offer.
6. Our products are superior to similar products on the market and are very popular in recent years for its unique design, fashionable style, and reasonable prices.
7. Our offer is kept open until the end of this week.
8. In reply to your letter of quotation, we regret very much to say that our customers here find your price rather on the high side and out of line with the prevailing market level.
9. It is hoped that you will consider our counter offer carefully and inform us of your acceptance at your earliest convenience.
10. If you cannot accept our quotation, please make best possible counter-offer.

Ⅵ. Writing task.

Dear Sirs,

Thank you for your letter of June 15 enquiring for our tablecloths.

We offer you firm on CIF Vancouver basis, September shipment, payment by irrevocable L/C to reach us one month before the time of shipment. This offer is subject to your reply reaching us before July 30.

Enclosed is our price list. We allow a discount of 5% if your order exceeds USD 5,000. We have quoted our best prices and are unable to entertain any counter offer.

There has been a heavy demand for our tablecloths because of the fine quality, attractive designs and reasonable prices. We are sure you will find a ready market for our products.

We are looking forward to receiving your order soon.

Yours faithfully,

Chapter 5 Orders and Acknowledgements

Ⅰ. Translate the following phrases into Chinese.
1. 首次订购
2. 履行合同
3. 价格差距
4. 购货确认书
5. 额外订购
6. 销售合同
7. 续订单
8. 一式两份
9. 定价方法
10. 会签

Ⅱ. Choose the best answer.
1~5   BCDCD
6~10 AABAC

Ⅲ. Fill in the blanks.
1. thanks
2. to
3. at
4. trial
9. in, of
10. in, in
11. to, from
12. of

5. file
6. of, for
7. by, upon, of
8. out, of

13. to, between
14. before
15. of

Ⅳ. Translate the following sentences into Chinese.
1. 你公司2016年9月20日来函内附1 000台缝纫机订单已收到。兹附寄第346号销售确认书一式两份，请签回一份以便存档。
2. 明年如果能增加供应，我们一定考虑你方的要求。
3. 如果你方要购买该产品，我们可以供应你方所需数量。
4. 如果你能说服你方用户接受这种产品，我们可以多供应一些。
5. 兹订购下列各项产品，望能按所订价格供应现货。
6. 我们希望此批餐桌用布可畅销市场，并希望今后向贵公司下更多的订单。
7. 谢谢你方的合作，盼望收到你方更多的订单。
8. 由于国内行情有变化，我们打算取消此货物的订单。
9. 你方订单正在及时处理，你可信赖我方会在规定时间内发运。
10. 对贵方可能向我方订购的任何货物，我们都将万分感激，并深信必将如期完成，并使贵方满意。

Ⅴ. Translate the following sentences into English.
1. If the price is reasonable and the quality is satisfactory, we will place large orders.
2. Thank you for your letter together with Order No. 123 of March 6.
3. We are very pleased to confirm having concluded the following transaction with you.
4. Please note that the stipulations in the relative credit should fully conform to the terms in our Sales Contract in order to avoid subsequent amendments.
5. Enclosed please find our trial order. If the quality measures up to our requirements, we will place large orders before long.
6. Your prompt attention to this order will be appreciated.
7. Please see to it that the goods should reach us by the end of this month.
8. We can reduce our price by 2% if your order is more than 3,000 cases.
9. The specification of the commodity you offered doesn't conform to that we inquired.
10. Owing to heavy commitments, we are not in a position to accept new orders.

Ⅵ. Writing task.
Dear Sirs,

　　We thank you for your letter of May 17 with order for the delivery of 100 sewing machines, but very much regret that we cannot accept the order. The price we quoted in our letter dated May 14 leave us with only the smallest margins, they are in fact lower than those of our competitors for goods of similar quality.

　　We hope it will not prevent you from approaching us on some other occasion. We shall always be very happy to hear from you and will carefully consider any proposals likely to lead to business between us.

Yours faithfully,

Chapter 6　Terms of Payment

Ⅰ. Translate the following phrases into Chinese.
1. 信汇
2. 电汇
3. 票汇
4. 托收行
5. 代收行
6. 付款交单
7. 承兑交单
8. 信用证
9. 开证银行
10. 展期通知
11. 国际商务惯例
12. 习惯做法；惯例
13. 占压资金
14. 宽松的付款条件
15. 付款条件
16. 有利的回复
17. 销售合同
18. 互惠合作
19. 装船时间
20. 装运港

Ⅱ. Choose the best answer.
1~5　AADDC
6~10　CADCA
11~15　BACBD

Ⅲ. Fill in the blanks.
1. by
2. against
3. in, on
4. on
5. in, for
6. by
7. within
8. in, to
9. on
10. to, at, on/upon, to

Ⅳ. Translate the following sentences into Chinese.
1. 我们根据 GF805 号合同开立以贵方为受益人、见票后 60 天付款的跟单信用证。
2. 根据第 2035 号销售确认书的规定，贵方必须在 4 月 20 日前开立有关信用证。
3. 我们已经安排中国银行开立以贵方为受益人的信用证。
4. 贵方必须从速开证，否则，我们就不能在本月底以前装船。
5. 关于第 705 号信用证，我方已指示开证行将装船期和有效期分别延至 5 月 15 日和 5 月 30 日。
6. 根据我方收到的信用证，应在见票后 60 天付款，但是合同规定见票即付，因此，请按以上意见修改信用证
7. 对你方要求以承兑交单方式付款一事，我方歉难考虑。
8. 对我们这样的小公司来说，开信用证花费大，对资金周转影响很大。最好还是采用付款交单或承兑交单付款方式。
9. 对你方这批试订购的货物，我们准备接受付款交单方式付款。
10. 鉴于我们长期的合作关系，我们破例接受 30 天的远期信用证。

Ⅴ. Translate the following sentences into English.
1. With regard to the contract No. 135, we agree to T/T payment terms.
2. The shipment date is drawing near, please expedite the opening of the relative L/C thus

enabling us to effect shipment within the stipulated time.
3. As a special accommodation, we will accept time L/C at 30 days.
4. As direct sailings to your port are few and far between, we have to require that transshipment be allowed.
5. The remittance is in payment of all commissions due to you up to date.
6. Our accommodation in this respect should not set a precedent for future transactions.
7. Please confirm that we can draw on you at 30 days after sight for US $48,000 against your order No. 325 through the Bank of China.
8. In future transactions, D/P will only be acceptable if the amount involved for each transaction is less than EUR 1,000 or the equivalent in RMB at the conversion rate then prevailing.
9. We enclose an application form for documentary credit and shall be glad if you will arrange to open for our account an L/C for US $40,000 in favor of ABC Company, the credit to be valid until July 15.
10. Please see to it that the L/C stipulations must conform strictly to the terms of the contract so as to avoid subsequent amendments.

VI. Situational writing.
1. Writing a letter according to the main points.

Dear Sirs,

We are pleased to inform you that your L/C No. H-15 issued by the Bank of China has just been received. However, upon/on examining the clauses contained therein, we regretfully find that certain points are not in conformity with the terms stipulated in the contract (there are some discrepancies with the stipulations of contract). Please amend your L/C No. H-15 as follows:

(1) Delete the word "long" and insert the word "metric" before "ton"/amend the word "long ton" to read "metric ton".

(2) Decrease the quantity to 120 cases instead of 1,200 cases.

(3) Delete insurance clause of Item 7 and replace it by those stipulated in the contract.

(4) Extend the shipment date and validity of your L/C to the end of October and November 15 respectively and allow partial shipment and transshipment.

On receipt of your amendment advice to the L/C, we will arrange shipment without any delay.

Yours faithfully,

2. Writing a letter in English asking for amendments to the following letter of credit by checking it with the given contract.

Dear Sirs,

Thank you very much for your L/C No. F-12345. However, upon checking, we have found some discrepancies and would request you to make the following amendments:

(1) The place of expiry should be "in China" instead of "in Melbourne".

(2) The amount both in figures and in words should respectively be "USD 150,000" and

"Say US Dollars One Hundred and Fifty Thousand Only".

(3) Transshipment should be allowed.

(4) Delete insurance clause.

(5) The specifications should be tins of "450 grams" instead of "500 grams ".

Please make amendments as soon as possible so as to enable us to arrange shipment.

Yours faithfully,
Guangdong YiYuan Trading Company Limited

Chapter 7　Packing

Ⅰ. Translate the following phrases into Chinese.

1. 包装
2. 瓦楞纸箱
3. 销售包装
4. 指示性标志
5. 毛重
6. 净重
7. 皮重
8. 木箱
9. 集装箱
10. 细致检查
11. 检验报告
12. 粗鲁搬运
13. 运输公司
14. 装船通知
15. 提单
16. 保险凭证
17. 即期汇票
18. 警示性标志
19. 内包装
20. 外包装

Ⅱ. Choose the best answer.

1~5　ABABC

6~10　CCBCD

Ⅲ. Fill in the blanks.

1. to
2. clear
3. for
4. on
5. in
6. With
7. beyond
8. for
9. to
10. On

Ⅳ. Translate the following sentences into Chinese.

1. 请贵方告知能否满足这些要求。
2. 由于玻璃制品极易破碎，因而货物必须包装在塑料袋里，然后装入标准出口木箱里，箱内四周填充泡沫材料，以能经受住运输途中的野蛮装运。
3. 非常感谢你方 8 月 31 日的传真。
4. 盼早日回复。
5. 钢笔 12 支装一盒，200 盒装一木箱。
6. 请采取必要的预防措施使包装能防止货物受潮或雨淋。
7. 兹提及我方 123 号订单中的 200 箱玻璃制品，我方请你们注意以下事项。
8. 希望你方能按我方要求办理。
9. 仪器的损坏主要是由不良包装造成的。它们在木箱内装得太松，又未做填充。

10. 今歉告，我方难以满足你方的包装要求。

V. Translate the following sentences into English.
1. The surveyor maintains that the damage was due to insecure packing and not to any unduly rough handling.
2. On inspection, we found that 50 bags had burst due to the use of substandard bags and that the contents, estimated at 2,500kg, had been irretrievably lost.
3. In reply to your letter of September 2 enquiring about the packing of our Color TV Sets, we wish to state as follows.
4. We agree with your packing instructions.
5. We state the above for your information and shall fulfill your order accordingly if we do not hear from you to the contrary before the end of this month.
6. We hope everything will turn out (to be) satisfactory in the end.
7. The suppliers should be held responsible for short weight resulting from improper packing.
8. In view of the fragile nature of the goods, you need special packing precaution against breakage.
9. Our investigation shows damage was caused by improper packing. Therefore we have to refer this matter to you.
10. As a kind of packing container, cartons have been extensively used in international trade.

VI. Writing task.
Dear Sirs,

　　We feel it necessary to stress the importance of trustworthy packing for your future deliveries to us. As machine parts are susceptible to shock, they must be wrapped in soft materials and firmly packed in seaworthy cases in such a manner that movements inside the cases is impossible.

　　Please make sure to confirm all other packing information before you ship the goods. You would be responsible for any charges or penalty from the customer if there were any mistakes or delay due to your mishandling.

　　We trust that you can meet the above requirements and thank you in advance for your cooperation.

Yours faithfully,

Chapter 8　Shipment

I. Translate the following phrases into Chinese.
1. 装箱单
2. 野蛮装运
3. 卸货港
4. 装运港
5. 分批装运
6. 运费预付
7. 班轮条件
11. 试订单
12. 续订单
13. 运价表
14. 运费
15. 运费率
16. 发送国
17. 代运业务

8. 提单
9. 舱位
10. 运输公司
18. 安全、完好
19. 巴拿马运河
20. 纺纱机

Ⅱ. Choose the best answer.
1~5　BCBAD
6~10　ADAAD

Ⅲ. Fill in the blanks.
1. to/on/of/from/to
2. to/of/to/from
3. on/to
4. into/with
5. of/at
6. in
7. to/be/in
8. for/allow
9. within
10. at

Ⅳ. Translate the following sentences into Chinese.
1. 贵公司订购的货物我方均有现货，可保证在11月将货物装上第一条便船。
2. 特此通知这批货物昨天已装运，空运单号为123。
3. 万一你方没有在12月23日或之前收到货物，请告知我方。
4. 出口到东南亚的货物的装运条件已大大改善了。
5. 有时因为在生产国找不到合适的装运港口，我们不得不转船。
6. 据我所知，在香港转船期间有货物被盗或损坏的风险。
7. 假如要预订货舱，请将需要填写的订舱表寄给我们。
8. 我们认为联运这批货物十分必要。
9. 假如货物在整个运输途中需要转换运输工具，即称为"联合运输"。
10. 货装上船后，你可以得到由船长签字的提单。

Ⅴ. Translate the following sentences into English.
1. The shipment is to be made in three equal lots beginning from June with transshipment at Copenhagen.
2. Since the deal is made on the basis of FOB, you are to ship the goods from our port.
3. Since there is no direct steamer to your port from Shanghai, the goods have to be shipped via Hong Kong.
4. We have booked shipping space on S. S. "Fengqing", which is scheduled to arrive at Hamburg on or about March 20.
5. This is to advise/inform/notify you that 500 Sets bicycles under Order No. 2008 were shipped per S. S. "Prince" on 20 of this month and are expected to reach your port early next month.
6. Owing to the delay in opening the relative L/C, shipment cannot be made in May as contracted and should be postponed until June.
7. As the purchase is made under FOB terms, you should ship the goods from Liverpool on a steamer to be designated by us.
8. The goods are ready for shipment for a long time. Please inform us of the name, the voyage number and the ETA of the vessel to enable us to effect shipment in time.

9. It is regretful that we cannot see our way clear to advance time of shipment to July, because our factory has been heavily committed.

10. We believe the goods under your Order No. 306 will arrive at your end in good and perfect condition.

Ⅵ. Situational writing.

Dear Sirs,

　　We have a consignment of color TV sets now waiting to be shipped to Messrs Clements Co. of Kuala Lumpur. Will you please arrange for the consignment to be collected from the above address and arrange shipment to Kuala Lumpur by the first possible sailing?

　　The TV sets are packed in three cases and the enclosed copy of the invoice shows quantities and total value of $1,800.

　　When the goods are shipped, please send the original bill of lading and one copy to us, together with the insurance policy and any other necessary documents.

Yours faithfully,

Chapter 9　Insurance

Ⅰ. Translate the following phrases into Chinese.

1. 基本险
2. 一般附加险
3. 发票金额
4. 装运通知
5. 保险金额
6. 保险范围/险别
7. 保险费
8. 保险费率
9. 投保货物
10. 保险代理
11. 保险经纪人
12. 保险单
13. 保险凭证
14. 预约保单
15. 平安险
16. 水渍险
17. 一切险
18. 保险费回扣
19. 保险费率表
20. 额外保险费

Ⅱ. Choose the best answer.

1~5　CDACA

6~10　DCBCB

Ⅲ. Fill in the blanks.

1. against, in, of, from
2. on, by, for, of, for, by
3. for, for, of, on, for, on, about
4. to, in, of
5. in, by, for, above, against, in
6. comply/meet, insurance
7. coverage/covered
8. supported
9. coverage
10. buyer's

Ⅳ. Translate the following sentences into Chinese.

1. 保险费是根据投保险别的保险费率计算的。
2. 我们不能投保此项险别，因为海洋货物运输保险条款中没有包括这一险别。
3. 我们采用国际保险中常用的"仓至仓"的责任条款。

4. 按照国际惯例，我们不投保这些险别，除非买主提出要求投保。
5. 只要是在保险责任范围内，保险公司就应负责赔偿。
6. 请问根据你们常用的 CIF 价格条件，投保的险别有哪些？
7. 阅读保险单上的"细则"对你是十分重要的，这样就能知道你购买的保险的承保范围。
8. 我们所报的保险费率是很适中的，当然，保险费随保险范围的不同而有所不同。
9. 你不仅要研究保险协议为你带来的利益，还要研究貌似能够满足你的需求的保险协议的条款及限制。
10. 按照我们的惯例，只保基本险，按发票金额 110% 投保。如果要加保其他险别，例如破碎险、渗漏险、偷窃提货不着险、钩损和污染险等，额外保险费由买方负担。

Ⅴ. Translate the following sentences into English.
1. We shall cover insurance for 110% of the invoice value in accordance with your request.
2. Since the premium varies with the extent of insurance, extra premium is for the buyer's account, should additional risks be covered.
3. As these goods are to be purchased on CIF basis, we would like to be informed whether you can accept the insurance for them against All Risks.
4. If you wish to secure protection against TPND, it can be easily done upon the payment of the additional premium.
5. As the contract stipulates that insurance should cover 110% of the invoice value. If you desire to cover insurance for 130% instead, the extra premium should be for your account.
6. We regularly get a considerable premium rebate from the insurance underwriter.
7. In case you have no definite instructions, we will insure WPA and against War Risk as usual.
8. As to 300 sets Sewing Machines under No. 345, we would cover insurance on our own account.
9. The premium rate for Breakage is 1.2%. If you would like to insure against Breakage, we will effect it for your account.
10. We regret that we cannot accept this claim as you didn't cover on Breakage terms.

Ⅵ. Situational writing.

Dear Sirs,

　　We are pleased to inform you that regarding your S/C No. 777 for 500 cases of black tea, we have opened letter of credit No. 999 for EUR 2,000 with the Bank of China, London, valid till July 15.

　　Please see to it that the above mentioned goods are shipped before July 15 and that the shipment is to be covered for 130% of the invoice value against All Risks. We know that according to your usual practice, you insure the goods only for 10% above the invoice value, therefore the extra premium will be for our account.

　　We trust you will arrange accordingly and look forward to receiving your shipping advice soon.

　　　　　　　　　　　　　　　　　　　　　　　　　　　　　　　Yours faithfully,

Chapter 10　Claims

Ⅰ. Translate the following phrases into Chinese.
1. 有效措施
2. 经济赔偿
3. 开拓市场
4. 索赔
5. 国际商务交易
6. 数量不符
7. 唛头不清
8. 货物损失
9. 错发货物
10. 有缺陷的包装
11. 不安全的包装
12. 卸货港
13. 清偿债务
14. 短交；缺交
15. 短装；装载不足
16. 理赔；解决索赔
17. 结汇
18. 装货港
19. 不幸事件
20. 满足某人的订单

Ⅱ. Choose the best answer.
1~5　BADCD
6~10　CAABB

Ⅲ. Fill in the blanks.
1. on/by/for
2. find
3. at/of/ex（by）/in/with
4. prompt（immediate）/let
5. to/shipment
6. covered/against
7. no/but
8. up/to
9. against/for
10. with/for/for

Ⅳ. Translate the following sentences into Chinese.
1. 恐怕贵公司要赔偿我方合同全部金额的5%。
2. 恐怕我们对你方遭受的损失深表歉意，同时向你们赔偿500美元。
3. 请调查此事，并尽快将货物发给我们以弥补数量的不足。
4. 由于你方未能及时交货，我方将向你方提出由此而遭受的全部损失的索赔。
5. 看来情况已十分清楚，我们希望你能设法尽快解决问题。
6. 我方检验证明，货物受损是由于包装不当造成的。因此，我们不得不将此事提交你处解决。
7. 由于这些产品质量低劣，所以我方把20箱全部退回，并务必请贵方更换这些商品。
8. 我们希望这一不幸事件将不会影响到我们双方之间的关系。
9. 内附有鉴定人对这破损的三箱货物的鉴定报告。
10. 延期索赔是对卖方没有按时装运货物而提出的索赔。

Ⅴ. Translate the following sentences into English.
1. We regret to tell you that your claim can't be entertained as it is raised far beyond the time limit stipulated in the contract.
2. As regards inferior quality of your goods, we claim a compensation of $10,000.
3. We shall lodge a claim for all the losses incurred as a consequence of your failure to ship our order in time.
4. Any complaint about the quality of the products should be lodged within 15 days after their

arrival.

5. We regret that your claim on shortage cannot be accepted.
6. It would be not fair if the loss be totally imposed on us, as the liability rests with both parties. We are ready to pay 50% of the loss only.
7. The wrong pieces may be returned per next available steamer, but it is preferable if you dispose of them in your market.
8. The shortage you alleged might have occurred in the course of transit, and that is a matter over which we can exercise no control.
9. With mutual cooperation, this case has been settled amicably and we shall remit to you an amount of $3,546 in compensation for the loss arising therefore.
10. Without sufficient evidence to support, your claim is untenable, and we can see no point in pursuing it further.

Ⅵ. Translate the following passage into English.

Dear Sirs,

We enclose Survey Report No. SH(89)135 issued by the Shanghai Commodity Inspection Bureau certifying that the quality of the above goods is much inferior to that of the sample sent previously. As this consignment is entirely useless to us, you are requested, therefore, to return us the invoice value and the inspection charges involved, totaling US $25,000.

We trust you will settle this claim promptly. As soon as it is settled, we shall have the consignment returned to you with all expenses for your account.

Yours faithfully,

Chapter 11 International Business contract

Ⅰ. Translate the following phrases into Chinese.
1. 书面合同
2. 合同有效期
3. 商业单据
4. 仲裁条款
5. 检验报告
6. 支付条款
7. 适用法律
8. 目的港口
9. 购货确认书
10. 不可抗力

Ⅱ. Choose the best answer.
1~5   BACDB
6~10 CDACB

Ⅲ. Fill in the blanks.
1. of, to
2. in, in
3. to, in
4. of, in
5. to, to
6. with, under
7. for, within
8. for, of
9. in
10. Upon/On, by

Ⅳ. Translate the following sentences into Chinese.
1. 贵方对此条款有意见吗?

2. 请检查合同中列出的所有条款是否与我们商定的条款相符。
3. 我们希望下周一前签订合同。
4. 我们很高兴确认与你方达成以下交易。
5. 任何一方不可不经另一方书面同意转让本合同。
6. 买方应承担下列货物销售和运输的成本和费用。
7. 仲裁的裁决是终局的,对双方都有约束力。
8. 双方理解并同意此合同适用于中国法律。
9. 对本协议的任何修改都应以书面形式做出,并由双方签署。
10. 现寄去我们的销货确认书一式二份,请签退其中一份以供我方存档。

Ⅴ. Translate the following sentences into English.
1. I am ready to sign the agreement.
2. We have no questions about the terms.
3. If one party fails to honor the contract, the other party is entitled to rescind it.
4. Enclosed please find our Sales Confirmation NO. HW-116 in triplicate. Please sign and return one copy to us for our file.
5. A confirmed, irrevocable L/C payable by draft at sight shall be established immediately.
6. The stipulations in the covering L/C shall be in exact accordance with the terms in the S/C so as to avoid subsequent amendments.
7. Emphasis is to be laid on the point that the relevant L/C must be opened in our favor through the Citibank.
8. We have duly signed our S/C and return one copy to you for your file as requested. Meanwhile, we have opened the relevant L/C and it will reach you very soon.
9. If your execution of this Purchase Contract proves to be satisfactory, regular orders will be placed in the future.
10. Please let us have your signed S/C in duplicate for our counter-signing and thank you for your cooperation.

Ⅵ. Writing task.

Sales Contract

No. 01-115

Sellers: <u>SUNNY TRADING COMPANY LIMITED</u>
Buyers: <u>ABC TRADING CO., LTD.</u>

This contract is made by and between the Buyers and the Sellers, whereby the Buyers agree to buy and the Sellers agree to sell the under mentioned commodity according to the terms and conditions stipulated below:

Commodity: <u>Art. No. 108 Ladies' Blouses</u>

Specifications: <u>equally assorted in pink, blue and yellow with the size assortment of S/3, M/6, and L/3</u>

Quantity: <u>3,000 dozen</u>

Unit Price: <u>at US＄26.00 per dozen CIFC2% Hamburg</u>

Total Value: <u>US＄78,000</u>

Packing: in cartons

Shipping Mark: at the buyer's option

Insurance: to be effected by seller against All Risks and War Risk for 110% of the invoice value

Time of Shipment: in October

Port of Shipment: any China's port

Port of Destination: Hamburg

Terms of Payment: sight irrevocable L/C to be opened 30 days before the time of shipment

Done and signed in Guangzhou on this 20th day of August, 2017.

参 考 文 献
References

1. 胡鉴明．商务英语函电［M］．北京：中国商务出版社，2004．
2. 兰天．外贸英语函电［M］．大连：东北财经大学出版社，2004．
3. 郑敏．商务英语函电与合同［M］．北京：清华大学出版社，北京交通大学出版社，2005．
4. 葛萍．外贸英语函电［M］．上海：上海财经大学出版社，2004．
5. 尹小莹．外贸英语函电［M］．西安：西安交通大学出版社，2004．
6. 李爽．国际商务函电［M］．北京：清华大学出版社，2008．
7. 凌芳．商务英语函电模板手册［M］．北京：机械工业出版社，2008．
8. 王美玲．商务英语函电［M］．北京：中国商务出版社，2007．
9. 仲鑫．外贸函电［M］．北京：机械工业出版社，2006．
10. 蔡惠伟．外经贸函电教程［M］．上海：华东理工大学出版社，2007．
11. 李卓文．国际贸易函电及实务［M］．北京：中国商务出版社，2007．
12. 易露霞，王娜娜，陈原．外贸英语函电［M］．北京：清华大学出版社，2008．
13. 冼燕华．国际商务英语函电［M］．广州：暨南大学出版社，2007．
14. 冼燕华．国际商务英语函电练习册及参考答案［M］．广州：暨南大学出版社，2005．
15. 郭继荣．商务英语函电与沟通［M］．西安：西安交通大学出版社，2008．
16. 束光辉．新编商务英语函电［M］．北京：清华大学出版社，北京交通大学出版社，2007．
17. 陆墨珠．国际商务函电［M］．北京：中国商务出版社，2006．
18. 田运银．国际贸易单证精讲［M］．北京：中国海关出版社，2010．
19. 王研，刘亚卓．外贸函电［M］．北京：北京大学出版社，2013．
20. 吴百福，徐小薇．进出口贸易实务教程［M］．上海：上海人民出版社，2011．
21. 金泽虎，王桂平．国际商务函电［M］．北京：北京大学出版社，2013．
22. 王秉乾．国际商事合同［M］．北京：对外经济贸易大学出版社，2013．
23. 王立非．国际商务合同实践教程［M］．上海：上海外语教育出版社，2012．
24. 隋思忠，向容．外贸英语函电［M］．大连：东北财经大学出版社，2016．
25. 乔焕然．英语合同阅读指南—英语合同的结构、条款、句型与词汇分析［M］．北京：中国法制出版社，2015．
26. 段婕．国际商务函电写作［M］．西安：西北工业大学出版社，2016．
27. 刘宏．外贸英语函电［M］．大连：东北财经大学出版社，2015．
28. 葛群．外贸英语函电［M］．大连：东北财经大学出版社，2016．
29. 杨静．国际商务合同双语教程［M］．大连：东北财经大学出版社，2016．
30. 董金玲，郝景亚，郑凌霄，孙洁．国际商务函电双语教程［M］．北京：机械工业出版社，2016．
31. 余敏，邹勇．国际商务英语实务［M］．成都：西南财经大学出版社，2015．